THE OUTER CITY

John Herington

Harper & Row, Publishers
London

Cambridge
Hagerstown
Philadelphia
New York

San Francisco
Mexico City
Sao Paulo
Sydney

First published 1984
Harper & Row Ltd
28 Tavistock Street
London WC2E 7PN

British Library Cataloguing in Publication Data

Herington, John
  The outer city.
  1. Cities and towns — Growth — Government policy — Great Britain
  I. Title
  307'.14   HT169.G7
  ISBN 0-06-318237-8

Typeset by Burns and Smith, Derby
Printed and bound by Butler & Tanner Ltd, Frome and London

To Anna and Michael

Contents

List of figures   *viii*

Preface   *ix*

List of abbreviations   *xi*

Part One: The Dispersal Phenomenon

Chapter 1   The city beyond the city   *page*   1

Chapter 2   The dispersal process   12

Chapter 3   The problems of growth management   36

Part Two: The Strategies

Chapter 4   The role of central government   61

Chapter 5   The regional dimension   82

Chapter 6   The role of the counties   96

Chapter 7   County-district relations   117

Chapter 8   The role of the housebuilders   133

Chapter 9   The anit-growth lobby   147

Chapter 10   Lessons for the future   163

Glossary   183

Select bibliography

Index

Figures

1. Stages of growth of the outer city   *page* 8

2. Population of towns 1971-1981   15

3. Percentage change in population, 1961-1971,
   district authorities   16

4. Percentage change in population, 1971-1981,
   district authorities   17

5. Science and high-technology parks   39

6. Environment impact of the M25   41

7. Green Belts, New and Expanded Towns in England   65

8. Structure plan provision for location of housing
   growth to the end of the 1980s outside London   88

9. Growth and restraint: the stategic plan for the
   South East   90

10. Cheshire county structure plan: proposed alterations   107

The possible location of London's new 'villages'   143

Preface

For too long academic contributions to public policy have focussed on the plight of declining inner cities and remoter rural areas, giving little attention to the areas under pressure for urban growth. This book therefore addresses itself to the problems facing government authorities and professional planners in coping with the massive redistribution of population and the associated relocation of industry in the outer-metropolitan areas of Britain. The policies created in the 1940s for tackling urban growth and urban sprawl are being reinterpreted in the 1980s in the context of national economic recession. As industrial expansion is seen to be necessary and desirable, further restrictions on the urbanization of the countryside are becoming difficult to justify. At the same time regeneration of the inner city requires that the outer areas forsake a certain share of new enterprise and investment. Continued dispersal raises an issue central to the future direction of urban policy in Britain. Should containment be abandoned in favour of economic development, or should the planning system be strengthened and recast to achieve the redirection of resources into the inner cities?

With this issue in mind this book has been written for a wide audience. It is not a detailed account of geographical research or of the operation of the planning system. Such accounts are available elsewhere. Rather it seeks to relate our knowledge of geographical change in the outer zones of cities to the different strategies operating to regulate it. Outward dispersal and growth are not the inevitable processes they sometimes appear to be. They are intimately related to the role of planning system and the state. The book therefore seeks to answer three questions. What are the underlying socio-economic and political reasons for the continued growth of 'outer cities'? What problems face government authorities in the areas affected by dispersal? How effectively is the planning system containing dispersed urban growth in the 1980s?

Part One examines some of the causes and consequences of outer-metropolitan growth and change. Part Two evaluates the role played by three agents of urban change: central and local government; the housing developers; and the conservation lobbies. It examines their goals and their priorities, the way their strategies operate in practice, and the impact of their policies on the 'outer cities'. The final chapter considers the implications for future urban policy.

The book is intended to appeal to students of town planning, geography and administration, as well as to politicians, professional planners and private interests such as developers and industrialists. The treatment is deliberately comprehensive and includes wherever possible examples of 'outer city' problems in provincial Britain in order to avoid the familiar preoccupation of academics with London and the surrounding counties. This aim cannot be entirely achieved since the documentation of other metropolitan regions is often poor and empirical evidence is therefore scanty. Although there were some studies of suburban growth and urban containment in the 1960s, there are no up-to-date reviews of research-based studies or of the changing policy context. Considerable use has therefore been made of contemporary planning sources — much of it previously unevaluated — to demonstrate how recent changes in political philosophy are affecting 'outer cities'.

The idea for a book on this theme was sparked off by my research for the Social Science Research Council on the processes of household movement and settlement planning policy in outer commuter settlements near Leicester. This showed the considerable direct effect which local controls were having on the spatial redistribution of residential development and its indirect social consequences. It was written before the major changes in planning legislation that followed the arrival in power of a new Conservative regime in 1979. Since then the influence of local planning authorities over the location of development has been somewhat diminished and the impact on the 'outer cities' is less predictable. It is important therefore to examine the nature of current planning thinking against the background of urban containment policies in Britain since the war. What makes the present period fascinating is the question of whether we are witnessing a fundamental U-turn in national urban policy or whether the relaxation in favour of unhampered growth is merely temporary.

Many friends and colleagues have commented on the initial ideas and on the drafts of the book. It is not possible to acknowledge them all, but I would like to thank in particular the following: Professor Gordon Cherry, (University of Birmingham), Peter Hall and John Short (University of Reading), Mark Blacksell (University of Exeter), Jean Forbes (University of Glasgow), and Patsy Healey (Oxford Polytechnic). A special word of thanks is due to Ron Blake (Trent Polytechnic) for the thankless and painstaking work he did on the text. Among professional policy makers, I am greatly indebted to: Anthony Long (Council for Protection of Rural England), Steven Campbell (Association of County Councils), Keith Storey (Association of District Councils), Elyot Turner (Standing Conference for London and South East Regional Planning), John Holmes and Jonathan Hales (Charnwood Borough Council), Philip Durban (Leicestershire County Council), Jim Parke (Strathclyde Regional Council), Ray Green (Exeter City Council), Jamie Mackie (Consultant Planner), and Mervyn Dobson (House-Builders Federation). To my friends in the Department of Geography at Loughborough a special word of thanks: especially to Professor Robin Butlin, for his encouragement and support throughout, to Colin Read and David Evans for invaluable comment on the drafts, to Ruth Austin and Jenny Jarvis for typing the draft copy, Anne Tarver for the cartography, and Joanne and Clay Oliver for helping prepare the bibliography. A special word of thanks is due to Gwyneth Barnwell for typing the final version of the text so speedily. The final result is of course my own responsibility.

John Herington
Loughborough
April 1984

Abbreviations

ACC	Association of County Councils
ADC	Association of District Councils
AES	Alternative Economic Strategy
AMA	Association of Metropolitan Authorities
AONB	Area of Outstanding Natural Beauty
CLA	County Landowners' Association
COSIRA	Council for Small Industries in Rural Areas
CPOS	County Planning Officers' Society
CPRE	Council for the Protection of Rural England
DEA	Department of Economic Affairs
DEPRA	Directorate of Environmental Protection & Rural Affairs
DoE	Department of Employment
DoI	Department of Industry
DoT	Department of Transport
EPC	Economic Planning Council
HBF	House-Builders Federation
IER	Investment in Existing Roads
JLRC	Joint Lands Requirement Committee
LDC	Land Decade Council
MAFF	Ministry of Agriculture, Fisheries, Forestry & Food
NFU	National Farmers Union
RTPI	Royal Town Planning Institute
SCSERP	Standing Conference on London & South East Regional Planning
SMLA	Standard Metropolitan Labour Area
TCPA	Town & Country Planning Association

PART ONE

THE DISPERSAL PHENOMENON

1   The City Beyond the City

> The country will take upon itself many of the qualities of the city.
> (H.G. Wells. 1902)

It might seem perverse to write a book about Britain's outer cities at a time when governments have effectively abandoned their commitment to planned decentralization and turned their attention to the problems of inner city decline. Apart from the difficulty of defining the term, there is no consensus about the nature of the 'outer city problem'. It was, after all, the movement of people *into* cities, and not out of them, which brought about the urban growth and urban sprawl we associate with conurbations like London or Glasgow. It was the disadvantages of big-city living that prompted the need for public management of urban change. The strategies and plans for dispersing people and jobs out from the cities were seen as a solution to urban growth. But have they proved to be good solutions? We now recognize the association between accelerated dispersal and inner-city decline — although we cannot blame the latter solely on the New and Expanded Towns. But very little thought has been given to the consequences, intentional and unintentional, that outward dispersal and growth have had for the communities at the receiving end.

The causes for concern

At first sight it may seem that the problems of outer-city areas have become irrelevant · since the 1950s and 1960s, when the pressure for urban expansion reached a peak in Britain and the problems of finding land for development were most acute.[1] The onset of recession in mid-1970 heralded a greatly reduced scale of economic growth. Housebuilding programmes were cut back. The slum clearance programme, associated with the overspill of population into the rural hinterlands, came to an end. A much more pressing national concern was persistent industrial decline and rising unemployment. However, it is now clear that there is a marked regional and intra-regional dimension to the current recession.[2] More to the point, recession has not actually reduced the pressure for demographic, economic or spatial change. The latest research confirms that the outer zones of our cities are the most rapidly growing and dynamic areas of Britain, and that the contrasts between their performance and that of the inner cities has become more stark.

    The 1981 *Census* reveals a key demographic trend: between 1971 and 1981 every metropolitan county lost population but all non-metropolitan counties gained population.[3] This reflects trends in Britain since World War II. The decline of the conurbations and inner-city areas has been associated with massive dispersal of population, and later employment, into small settlements in the outer-metropolitan zone.[4] The process is less advanced in this country than in America, but more advanced than in any other country of Europe.[5] There has been a continuing outward population increase associated with net outflows from the cities and the redistribution and growth of population within the outer zones. Admittedly, not all places have experienced increase, or similar rates of increase, but the overall trend is clear —

a continuing outward dispersal into rural areas which no longer include just the immediate hinterlands of cities. Less densely settled and remote regions that have for long suffered depopulation are now gaining population. It is remarkable that despite economic recession and the national stabilization in population growth rates, the decentralization process has continued so strongly into the 1970s and 1980s.[6]

The dispersal and growth of population has been matched by a later but no less pervasive shift of employment from cities to small independent centres.[7] This so-called 'urban-rural shift' has been a marked feature in Britain since the early 1960s, and it is not unique to this country. Conurbations have lost employment, especially manufacturing jobs, while the country towns have gained, especially in the service sector. We must be careful to note that this gain is due as much to new enterprises as to an actual movement of enterprises. (There is an interesting parallel with population gain, which is due more to growth *within* the outer areas than to in-migration.) Despite the increasing intensity of employment decline, some outer-metropolitan zones, particularly those surrounding London, have experienced a growth of employment. In part this reflects the geography of recent economic activity in Britain. In the context of growing international competition the most attractive places for new manufacturing industry are those where skilled labour and social infrastructure are already available or cheap to provide in the short run. Those are generally speaking the outer areas. Furthermore, although the onset of recession has resulted in job losses, it has also had the effect of stimulating the formation of new jobs. The restructuring of industry, combined with growing redundancy and unemployment, has ironically triggered the birth of new plants and new jobs in the more favoured sub-regions outside the conurbations.[8] National economic recovery will not bring a net increase in jobs, but growth industries will continue to create some employment in less densely populated and accessible rural environments.[9]

The shift in population and employment has been socially selective. Generally the wealthy, the enterprising, and skilled occupational groups have moved out and stayed in the outer areas. This might now seem a healthy trend, since, as Lloyd and Dicken's work shows, it is precisely these groups which seem to be innovators and create new firms. But there is another perspective. As outward decentralization continues, the geographical and social separation between rich and poor grows wider due to the disproportionate increase in the prosperity of rural communities over the past three decades.[10] In-migration is selective by house type and tenure, with higher-income groups buying private houses, both new and existing — although the New and Expanded towns are exceptions to the rule. Further more, these groups do not suffer from unemployment to the same degree as the unskilled. The net impact on the social characteristics of the outer settlements has been considerable: these now contain the majority of owner-occupier households, the best housing conditions, and the least overcrowding; they also benefit from greater opportunities for female employment especially in service industries.[11] These interpretations are probably too rosy, but they convey the point — that in contrast to the inner cities the outer areas are relatively affluent and prosperous.

We must be careful not to argue that demographic, social, and economic growth, *necessarily* constitute a problem. Some will claim that continued dispersal is an inevitable and desirable trend and one which offers the best opportunity for national economic recovery in the long term. Urban prosperity does not seem to be such a problem for society as urban deprivation. Why then should dispersal cause concern?

First, there is *the historical momentum of planned dispersal.* The outward decentralization trend has been observable through much of the twentieth century in Britain. But it quickened in the post-war period. Between 1945 and 1975 it was actively encouraged by the state or was implicit in strong public planning. The settlements which were at the frontier of the first wave of dispersal have now begun to create their own pressures for expansion. The New Towns illustrate this well. Further growth in housing and jobs has had to take place in neighbouring settlements outside the original boundaries of the towns. As they grow they are having an increasing impact on the outer regions.[12] The same point might be made about the Expanded Towns, where the initial build-up of population has led to a cumulative growth of jobs and further inward migration. What this means is that the geographical focus of urban growth and the problem of finding land for expansion has shifted outwards from the conurbations and suburbs to the smaller villages, country towns, and planned settlements beyond the Green Belts.

Second, there is evidence that *the physical pressures for urban development in the countryside are growing more intense.* The evidence is plain to see along any one of our national motorways, but particularly the M1, M4, M5 and M6 in England and Wales and the M8 and M74 in Scotland. New warehousing, out-of-town shopping stores, 'science parks' and speculative housing are very apparent. The proposed M25, which would run for almost its entire length through the London Green Belt, and the M40, which will carry traffic from Oxford to Birmingham, create enormous potential pressures for growth in central and southern England.[13] Nor should it be forgotten that major residential expansion in the outer areas still occurs.[14] New kinds of capital intensive, high-technology industry find these environments particularly attractive.[15] Nowhere is the attraction of greenfield sites for industry, housing and commercial development, better illustrated than in the corridor of land astride the M4 motorway between London and Bristol,[16] sometimes termed the 'sun-belt' (see Glossary). Economic recession has not reduced pressure for urban change in outer-metropolitan Britain.

Third, the *environmental conflicts* associated with the pressure for urban development are most acute in the outer areas. Since 1945 governments have been committed to the principle of urban containment.[17] Containment was based on the argument that a small island like Britain could not afford to squander its agricultural and landscape resources. Hence the market in land should not be permitted to operate in a free and unfettered manner. There should be a land-use planning system, the fundamental purpose of which should be to control urban growth and protect the countryside. Containment implied, or seemed to imply, the existence of a national consensus in favour of protecting the countryside. Such a consensus no longer exists.[18] Recession has made the public more receptive toward industrial change in the countryside. But some groups see industrial dispersal as a threat to rural environments. The battles between developers and conservationists become more intense, and the latter are beginning to lose out.[19]

Fourth, *the ability of the planning system to contain urban change is diminishing.* Governments have traditionally taken a harsh attitude to manufacturing industry in villages and in the countryside. But the purpose of controlling environmental change is now being questioned. Some people claim that planning has been too negative and has inhibited the potential for economic development. Hence the progressive recasting of the system of development control and the modification of some planning powers introduced by the Local Government Planning and Land Act 1980. The transfer of power from county to district councils further weakens strategic planning. There is now a real fear that containment is breaking down under the combined impact of legislative change and the way in which new legislation is being interpreted.[20] The amount of protection in non-Green Belt areas — precisely those under the greatest pressure — has been noticeably reduced, although the government still appears committed to Green Belts in general. The coordinated and planned dispersal of jobs and population has now been abandoned. New Towns will grow in the future only by private investment.[21] In 1982 regional policy for the location of industry was substantially modified and the strict control of industrial and office development was virtually abandoned.[22] Finally, and most significantly, planning for urban change at regional and sub-regional level has been effectively dismantled, making it very difficult to coordinate the location, timing and release of public and private investment in growth points, or to provide consistent countryside policy.

Fifth, there is *the effect of outer city growth on inner city decline* (the 'beggar-my-neighbour' argument). The social and economic changes associated with the redistribution of population and the relocation of industry raise enormous problems for society as a whole, especially at a time when the financial resources to overcome them are severely strained. Continued dispersal works against the inner city. It requires increasing amounts of investment in new roads, water supply, sewerage, education, health and welfare — all of which could be spent in inner area locations.[23] Furthermore, government attempts to regenerate the inner cities by attracting private capital, either to industry or to housing or to both, are hampered by the dispersal of this capital to outer areas. One solution is a more restrictive attitude to the private market in the outer areas. Stronger urban containment policies could simultaneously reduce the pressures on the environment, reverse the fortunes of the cities, and reduce the geographical expression of polarization between the rich and the poor.[24]

The outer regions surrounding Britain's cities play a crucial, even dominant role in national recovery. They are currently the most dynamic areas of demographic, economic, and social change. At a time of recession, governments naturally seek to promote their economic development. At the same time, growth raises ill-charted problems for urban governance. New political tensions emerge as the pursuit of wealth clashes with the traditional goals of urban containment, especially protection of the environment. Any policy aimed at the redistribution of wealth is brought into disrepute by capital formation in the outer cities. We are left wondering how society can best meet the challenge of economic change. At issue is a fundamental political choice: should urban containment be abandoned?

Planning and the management of urban change

There is growing awareness that the causes of contemporary urban change are political and that to understand them we must focus on the role of state planning.[25] The state contains urban growth by controlling the use of land. The land-use plan-making system interacts with the formal and informal planning strategies produced by various other public and private agencies including commercial, industrial and housing developers and individual pressure groups. About the latter process we still have little knowledge.[26] There is a close association between planning viewed as a political process and the other socio-economic processes behind outer city change. It would clearly be wrong to ignore the many reasons why people and jobs are pushed into the rural hinterlands, but it is equally important to take into account opportunities for movement created by the public planning system. In Chapter 2 we discuss the ways in which planning has affected demographic shifts. But the planning system is now breaking down under the influence of changing philosophies. New conflicts and tensions are created by the dispersal of population into the outer areas and these are examined in Chapter 3. The decentralization process and the associated problems may be traced back to the different strategies for regulating urban change (examined in Chapters 4–10).

The strategies which affect our cities are twofold: those which channel urban change in the direction of greater physical and economic expansion (growth and development) and those which seek the reverse (restraint and conservation). This is of course a crude over-simplification, since some agencies are ambivalent towards growth and restraint. All state strategies are formally committed to urban containment, but they are not equally committed to the principles of restraint implied by containment. Many are changing in style. The general balance is shifting from restraint in favour of growth — sometimes unconsciously, sometimes openly. But it would be misleading to argue that containment has been jettisoned. It still provides an accurate description of the direction to which strategies — particularly those of the public planning agencies and conservation lobbies — are ostensibly aimed. In addition, containment is a very confusing term; while it implies overall restraint on urban development in the outer cities, it never precluded the redistribution of growth into selected towns and villages. Indeed the spatial concentration of housing, industry and services into 'growth points' provided a strong underlying rationale for containment philosphy. The planned overspill schemes for New and Expanded Towns, for example, were part and parcel of containment, although now officially abandoned.

Many of the spatial, social, and economic consequences of these strategies lie some time in the future, and about these we must perforce speculate. The outcome of some decisions, however, is soon obvious on the ground. We have also given particular weight to those strategies which have a bearing on residential development. Housing is by far the most significant element in urban spatial change, as Robin Best's studies illustrate well.[27] It is not only subject to more effective and consistent planning control than industry, but the socio-demographic conditions that result from changes in the housing stock have a powerful contributory effect on associated employment changes and the problems of conflict discussed in Chapter 3.

We shall study urban strategy at several levels of the planning process. Central government has been a key agent in promoting the dispersal and growth of population and employment in the outer areas. At regional level, are the plans produced jointly by teams of professional central and local government planning officers. These reflect the tensions between the growth aspirations of central government, most notably the Department of Trade and Industry, and the restraint strategies of the county councils. On balance the interests of central government have prevailed. County councils have traditionally been the most restrictive agencies in their attitude to new residential and industrial development, but there is a shift in favour of growth oriented strategies in response both to central government initiatives and economic recession. The balance given to growth or restraint still varies considerably between one authority and another. The counties' ability to restrain growth in the outer cities has in any case been heavily constrained by the operational weaknesses of land planning legislation and local government reorganisation. Districts councils have a duty to implement the structure plans produced by the counties, but in practice have become much more active in the pursuit of growth and development. This has brought them into conflict with the counties and led to delay in the decision-making process. In the private domain are the housebuilders, seeking a greater release of housing land in the outer cities. Although partly successful in lobbying central government, the developers still have restraint forced upon them by local government and the actions of the pressure groups. Finally, there is the conservation lobby. It has been most vociferous in its opposition to urban development in the outer cities and protested against the growth policies of central and local government and the housebuilding industry. In one sense it is the most significant of all the agents discussed because it expresses public attitudes to change in the outer cities. The amenity lobby finds some allies among planners who believe in urban containment and a strong planning system which works for restraint rather than growth.

Chapter 10 attempts to evaluate these various approaches to growth and restraint before considering the questions they raise for the future direction of urban policy in Britain. Our critique examines three key assumptions that underlie contemporary strategies for urban change in the outer cities — that planning can do little to control the demographic, social, and economic pressures building up in the outer cities; that a shift from restraint to growth is desirable because it will provide jobs (the evidence is that it will not); and that containment should take the form of urban concentration rather than planned dispersal.

The outer city: defining our terms

The book is arranged around the theme of the 'outer city'. A word of caution is needed about this term. The changes visible in the rural hinterlands of cities are in part the outcome of processes that affect the spatial organization of the entire urban system. The effects of national planning, for example, will be felt on both inner and outer areas of cities. Are we right therefore to treat outer and inner cities as discrete spatial entities? There is a case for not doing so,[28] but this book takes a less dogmatic position. It cannot be claimed that outer city growth is simply the reverse side of the coin to inner city decline. The processes which cause decline are not the same as those which induce growth. While the influence of economic factors is paramount in the case of the inner cities, it is clear that political factors are relatively more important in the case of the outer cities. Public planning policies have, for instance, had a direct impact on the spatial evolution of outer areas, whereas the inner cities were the product of an era when planning barely existed. Moreover, earlier conceptions of rural hinterlands as relatively homogeneous middle-class residential communities relying upon the cities for work and leisure are now simplistic because these places have themselves been urbanized. Functional dependence between inner and outer parts of the urban system is breaking down, although clearly the stage reached by urbanization varies between different metropolitan regions. We still have too little knowledge about the structural organization and external relationships between inner and outer cities in Britain. The American experience warns us that we must not fall into the trap of assuming intimate ties — 'differentiation between central cities and their suburbs is more complex than generally assumed, and it is regionally based'.[29]

We do know that the economic linkages have become more complex, a point noted in the earlier literature on suburban growth.[30] Jobs have moved into and grown within the outer cities, so that more people are tending to live and work in the same areas. Commuting patterns have changed, with an increase in local journeys and reverse commuting (travel to work journeys from central locations to suburban areas).[31] The growth of local labour markets has reached its most advanced stage in the London region. Some of the fastest employment growth in both absolute and percentage terms has been in Berkshire, Buckinghamshire, Hampshire and west Sussex. In the outer South East long distance commuting by rail to central London declined during the 1970s in association with a loss of 18,000 jobs in 'business and professional services' between 1971 and 1976 and a marked growth of local journeys to work.[32] A decentralization of jobs has been taking place around other British cities, with similar effects on the pattern of commuting. Indeed, localized journeys to work within the outer-metropolitan rings are growing in importance. Although some villages are termed 'commuter settlements', implying few jobs relative to resident population, recent research shows this to be a gross oversimplification. At Ringmer, a 'commuter settlement' in Sussex[33] nearly a third of all heads of household worked in the village, 86 percent worked within 11 miles, and very few commuted to London — the journey patterns appear to have become noticeably more localized over time. In the commuting settlements around Leicester 85 percent of new in-migrants found jobs within a radius of 10 miles, 37 percent between 2 and 6 miles and 23 percent within 2 miles.[34]

There is also evidence of increasingly localized patterns of social interaction. At Ringmer 'all the more commonly carried out activities, with the exception of car outings, tend to occur in the village or, less frequently, in Lewes. The more formal pursuits usually entail a trip into Brighton. Recreational trips to London are extremely rare. In all, the pattern of social activities is much more localised than might have been expected'.[35] Studies of commuter villages in outer Bristol showed that visits to the cities were irregular — a more dominant pattern was the intense network of social interaction within and between neighbouring villages.[36] In the New and Expanded Towns localism is more obviously at work since many more households own no car and must rely on public transport; surveys have shown, moreover, that migrants give access to London low priority in comparison with the local advantages of living in these new communities.[37]

These changes in the linkages between the centres of cities and their outer regions are associated with the specialization of industrial activity. Manufacturing and service employment has grown in the outer areas, encouraging the expansion of local housing markets, despite the existence of planning controls. We see emerging a new form of settlement organization called the 'regional city', the outer parts of which contain dispersed settlement patterns which most approximate to the notion of the 'outer city'(Figure 1). Defining the spatial attributes of this 'outer city' is fraught with difficulty because terms like 'urban-rural fringe' and 'exurbia' refer to distinct but overlapping areas.[38] Nonetheless, Figure 1 provides some conceptual framework for examining the patterns and problems of dispersed urban growth.

Some observers regard the outward spread of settlement and land-use change as an orderly, progressive, shift.[39] But this is to over-simplify.[40] A variety of planning, landownership and other factors affect settlement change in the outer areas. Here, settlement is heterogeneous — with commuter villages, New and Expanded Towns, industrial and retail centres, isolated dwellings, individual farms and second homes all set within a varied landscape of farmland and woodland. The underlying forces vary by region. Where dispersal is relatively limited, the physical spread of urban areas takes the form merely of an extension to the suburbs. But where it is advanced, large settlements are intermingled with smaller ones some distance from the central city in a form of 'exurban' development.[41] If we attempt to define the internal boundaries of the outer city in terms of social process rather than urban forms we run into trouble, as Dennis and Clout point out.[42] There are a large number of influences at work: in-migration, commuting, retirement, second homes and so on. We lack the data to adequately measure the locational parameters of each influence or to group them in combination. Population change is the simplest surrogate we can use to show regional and sub-regional variations in the spatial extent of Britain's outer cities (Figure 2).

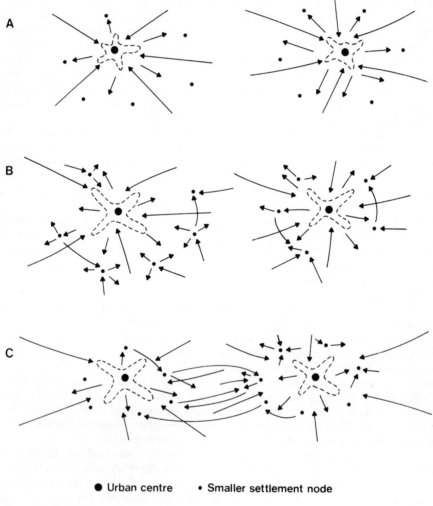

A

B

C

● Urban centre   • Smaller settlement node

Figure 1.   Stages of growth of the outer city

To sum up. There are two kinds of 'outer city' in Britain: first, those whose social and economic life is still oriented to the city in whose region they are located (*a* and *b* in Figure 1); second, those which have grown to develop strong internal functional linkages and rely much less on the dominant city (*c* and *d* in Figure 1). Both represent stages in the evolution of the 'regional city'. The precise boundaries are of academic interest, although some attempt to depict them is made in Figure 2. Which part of Britain falls into which category depends on the scale and rate of population or employment shift or both. We must now examine these patterns and the complex, yet interrelated, processes that underpin them.

Notes

1.   A classic account of the pressures and problems of outer-metropolitan growth in the 1950s is in PETER SELF, *Cities in Flood: the problems of urban growth* (Faber and Faber, 1961). The history of planning for city-regions is discussed by PETER HALL in *Urban and Regional Planning* (Penguin 1974).

2.   See for instance R. L. MARTIN, 'Job loss and the regional incidence of redundancies in the current recession', *Cambridge Journal of Economics*, vol. 6, 1982, and C. HAMNETT, 'The conditions in England's inner cities on the eve of the 1981 riots', *Area*, vol. 15, no. 1, 1983.

3.   Office of Population Censuses and Surveys (1981), *Census 1981, Preliminary Report, England and Wales* (London, HMSO).

4.   Department of Environment, *'British Cities; Urban population and employment trends 1951-71'* (Urban change in Britain 1951-71. Final Report, Part 1), Research Report 10, 1976.

5.   Contrast, for instance, B. J. L. BERRY, 'The counter-urbanization process: urban America since 1970', in B. J. L. BERRY. (ed.) *Urbanization and Counter-Urbanization:* Urban Affairs Annual Review, vol. 11 (Beverley Hills: Sage Publications, 1976); and P. HALL and D. HEY, *Growth Centres in the European Urban Systems* (London, Heinemann, 1980).

6.   These points are well made in C. HAMNETT and W. RANDOLPH, 'The changing population distribution of England and Wales, 1961-1981: clean break or consistent progression?', *Built Environment*, vol. 8, no. 4, 1983.

7.   S. FOTHERGILL AND G. GUDGIN, *Unequal Growth: Urban and Regional Employment Change in the U.K.* (Heinemann, 1982).

8.   See recent research by P. LLOYD and P. DICKEN, 'Industrial change: local manufacturing firms in Manchester and Merseyside', *DoE Inner City Programme Number 6*, 1982; and C. MASON, 'New Manufacturing Firms in South Hampshire: Survey Results', University of Southampton, Department of Geography, Paper 13, 1982.

9.   D. KEEBLE, 'De-industrialisation means unequal growth', *Geographical Magazine*, vol. LIII, no. 7, April 1981.

10.   C. G. BENTHAM, 'The changing distribution of low income households in the British urban system', *Area*, vol. 15, no. 1, 1983.

11.   D. DONNISON and P. SOTO, *The Good City: A Study of Urban Development and Policy in Great Britain* (Heinemann, 1980).

12.   A. G. CHAMPION, K. CLEGG and R. L. DAVIES, *Facts about the New Towns: a socio-economic digest* (Retailing and Planning Associates, 1977).

13. See for instance Standing Conference on London and South East Regional Planning, *The Impact of the M25* (SCLSERP, January 1982); the problems of the M40 are discussed by T. LONG, 'The missing link', *Town and Country Planning*, vol. 52, no. 6, June 1983.

14. M. SPRING, 'What recession? A private new town for 12,000 people is being built near Swindon', *Building*, vol. 239, no. 7153 (34), 22 August 1980.

15. J. F. D. WILLIAMS, *A Review of Science Parks and High Technology Developments* (Drivas Jones, Chartered Surveyors and Planning Consultants, August 1982).

16. See for instance 'Western Corridor: a special report', *The Times*, 30 June 1983; 'Britain's sunrise strip'. *The Economist*, 30 January 1983.

17. P. HALL *et al, The Containment of Urban England* (George Allen and Unwin, 1973).

18. An evaluation of post-1970 shifts in national attitudes and policy is given by D. H. McKAY (ed.), *Planning and Politics in Western Europe* (Croom Helm, 1982).

19. P. HALL, 'Dark prospect', *Town and Country Planning*, vol. 49, no. 1, 1980.

20. A very useful summary of recent changes in approach to the planning system is given by T. LONG in Section III of the discussion paper published by the Council for the Protection of Rural England, *'Planning — friend or foes?'* (CPRE, 1981).

21. Report in *Planning*, vol. 45, 13 February 1981.

22. A. R. TOWNSEND, 'Unemployment geography and the new government's regional aid', *Area*, vol. 12, no. 1, 1980.

23. P. HALL, 'Planning for no growth', *New Society*, vol. 43, no. 808, 1978. The issue is also discussed by M. DOWER, 'The bleeding of the Cities', *Town and Country Planning*, vol. 51, no. 2, February 1982.

24. D. EVERSLEY, 'Can planners keep up if the flight from the cities continues to accelerate?', Royal Town Planning Institute Annual Conference, 1982.

25. See for instance R.J. JOHNSTON, *Geography and the State: an essay in political geography* (Macmillan, 1982); D. H. McKAY and A.W. COX, *The Politics of Urban Change* (Croom Helm, 1979).

26. The manner by which these kinds of organization exercise power over urban change has been termed 'imperfect pluralism' by J. SIMMIE, *Power, Property and Corporatism: the Political Sociology of Planning* (Macmillan, 1981).

27. R. BEST, *Land Use and Living Space* (Methuen, 1981).

28. The argument is fully discussed by P. HALL (ed.), *The Inner City in Context*, the final report of the Social Science Research Council Inner Cities Working Party (Heinemann, 1981).

29. P. GOBER, 'Central Cities and Suburbs as distinct place types: myth or fact?' *Economic Geography*, vol. 58, pt. 4, October 1982.

30. P. WOOD, 'Urban manufacturing: a view from the fringe' in J. H. JOHNSON (ed.), *Suburban Growth* (Wiley, 1974).

31. Useful review by K. O'CONNOR, 'The analysis of journey to work patterns in human geography', *Progress in Human Geography*, vol. 4 (4), 1980.

32. Standing Conference on London and South East Regional Planning, *The Commuting Study*, SCLSERP, July 1981.

33. P. AMBROSE, *The Quiet Revolution: Social change in a Sussex village, 1871-1971* (Chatto and Windus, 1974).

34.   J. HERINGTON and D. EVANS, 'The social characteristics of household movement in 'key' and 'non-key' settlements', Research Paper no. 4, Department of Geography, Loughborough University, 1980.

35.   P. AMBROSE, op. cit. p. 77.

36.   M. MACGREGOR, 'The rural culture', *New Society*, 9 March 1972.

37.   N. DEAKIN and C. UNGERSON, *Leaving London: planned mobility and the inner city* (Heinemann, 1977).

38.   A full explanation of the regional city is given in C. R. BRYANT, L. H. RUSSWURM, and A. G. McLELLAN, *The City's Countryside* (Longman, 1982).

39.   See, for instance, A. COLEMAN, 'The Countryside Endangered', *Country Life*, 2 July 1981.

40.   M. ELSON, 'The Urban Fringe: Open land policies and programmes in the metropolitan counties', Countryside Commission, 1977.

41.   Useful summary of spatial trends is given by D. MILLS, 'Suburban and exurban growth' in *Social Sciences: a Second Level course*, Urban Development Unit 24 (Open University Press, 1973).

42.   R. DENNIS and H. CLOUT, *A Social Geography of England and Wales* (Pergamon Press, 1980).

2   The Dispersal Process

> One of the most powerful influences in the development of post-1945 new residential
> areas has been not economic growth...but the deliberate policy of governments both as to
> the need for such residential areas and also as to their siting and subsequent economic
> development.
> (D.C. Thorns, 1972)

Post-war Britain has witnessed a fundamental and progressive redirection of
population away from the cities after the urban growth of the nineteenth century.
There has been both a localised movement of population to adjacent hinterlands and a
related movement to more distant rural areas traditionally affected by depopulation.
This process, sometimes known as 'counter-urbanization', has meant that population
and employment growth are now taking place in rural areas on the margins of the
metropolitan regions and beyond. Repopulation has become a national phenomenon,
while depopulation, which still occurs in certain localities, is now a much less
significant trend.

   We still know rather little about the reasons for population dispersal to the outer
cities. Clearly there are several interrelated processes at work and these are reflected in
the decisions of individual households, commercial and industrial developers, and
government planners. Dispersal occurs, for instance, as a result of new environmental
values held by households able to exercise choice in residential location. These are the
values of a post-industrial society, whose members, enjoying increased mobility and
leisure, set great store on having a 'rural' lifestyle, pleasant surroundings and open
space. Dispersal is also encouraged by productive investment in the outer regions. The
building of new housing has a critical effect on the volume and character of migration
in the outer city, and the shift in employment opportunities, while not the root cause of
population shift, has been strongly associated with the subsequent growth of the outer
cities. Slum clearance, planned overspill, transport provision, regional development,
land use and rural settlement, have also tended to push people out of the cities. Indeed,
planning has played a major role in the dispersal process. In this chapter we shall try to
untangle the complexity of these social, economic and political processes and to
evaluate their relative effect on population decentralization.

The demographic context

A commonly used framework for defining population dispersal in Britain is the
Metropolitan Economic Labour Area (MELA) or 'functional urban region'. The
centre of this region is a core of employment (20,000 or more jobs) surrounded by an
inner and an outer ring from which resident workers commute to the core. The core
plus the inner ring comprise the Standard Metropolitan Labour Area (SMLA) which
has a total population of 50,000; at least 15 percent of resident workers commute from
the inner ring to the core. The outer metropolitan ring, which lies outside the SMLA,
extends further to include those residents who commute to the core in preference to
any other core. The SMLA plus the outer ring is called the Metropolitan Economic
Labour Area (MELA) and has a total population of 60,000.

Undoubtedly the most comprehensive portrait of population decentralization in England and Wales comes from the comparative analysis of SMLAs and MELAs carried out by Peter Hall, followed by the studies of urban change directed by Drewett, Goddard and Spence for the Department of Environment.[1] This research provides valuable knowledge about aggregate population trends for individual urban regions of England and Wales over the period between 1951 and 1974. During this time the dispersal of population from the cities was marked by a number of distinct phases. In the 1950s the inner metropolitan rings were gaining faster than the urban cores. The London ring of New Towns grew especially fast. In the 1960s and 1970s the rings continued to grow but the cores suffered decline. In the later 1970s, partly in response to a national decline in the birth rate, poor economic performance, and a slow-down in the rate of planned decentralization, it appears that although the inner rings grew much more in absolute terms than either the city cores or the outer rings, the rate of dispersal outwards may have diminished, at least among cities of more than one million inhabitants.[2]

Analysis of metropolitan population trends reveals great differences in the scale and rate of core-ring shift between individual SMLAs. SMLAs closest to the largest cities and affected most by the first wave of outward movement in the 1950s grew more slowly in the 1960s when the inner rings surrounding freestanding cities such as Southampton, Bristol and Leicester were affected by accelerated growth.[3] There is also something of a regional effect at work. The prosperous central and southern regions of Britain experienced more widely diffused population movement and growth at an earlier stage than the regions of industrial decline in Scotland, the North of England, Yorkshire–Humberside and Wales. The scale of dispersal has been greatest in what has been termed the 'North London Fringe', defined as a zone of contiguous SMLAs, which recorded a 50 percent population increase between 1950 and 1970 at a time when the national growth rate was only 10.6 percent; this has been (and probably still is) one of the fastest megapolitan growth zones in Europe.[4]

One limitation of the MELA framework is that it can lead to misconceptions about population trends. Although there may be an overall concentric pattern to outward population shift, empirical studies reveal considerable variety in the volume, distance and direction of migration. Around Glasgow, for example, there has been a massive volume of relatively short distance transfer *within* the core and to the immediately adjacent suburban areas, while only recently has population begun to increase in smaller settlements beyond the Green Belt around the city.[5] Around Bristol, on the other hand, in-movement of people from other regions of England (for employment and retirement) has been a more potent phenomenon than the core-ring shift; and around Leicester, most population movement has its origin and destination *within* the metropolitan ring and is characterised by a great deal of short distance exchange between and within commuter settlements.[6] Hence the variety in the demographic experience of outer cities may be concealed by aggregate analysis of trends.

Nor can MELA framework be used so easily for the period since the reorganisation of local government in 1974, because the smaller administrative units used in the definition of core and ring areas were substantially reduced in number, thus making delimitation of 'functional urban regions' very difficult. The available evidence suggests, however, that urban cores continued to lose population more slowly than in the 1960s; that there was a progressive outward shift of population into remoter areas which had previously experienced decline; and that a new wave of net in-migration took place in a belt from the South West to the West Midlands (excluding Coventry), and in East Anglia, Cheshire, and North Wales. All of these trends seem like a continuation of the pattern already described in which population moves further out but retains its links with metropolitan centres through commuting.[7] Some commentators argue that the population growth of remoter areas well beyond the immediate commuting hinterlands represents a 'clean break' with previous patterns of movement.[8] The main question, however, is whether net migration gains are continuing due to metropolitan spillover into the more distant rural areas and migration from the inner to outer metropolitan rings.[9]

Sadly, the preliminary results of the 1981 Census do not enable us to examine these trends in migration or to investigate whether they represent an extension of commuter hinterlands. What we know is that the pattern of population gain is still changing at the regional and sub-regional scale in a way that strongly suggests widening dispersal beyond the conventionally drawn boundaries of metropolitan Britain, notwithstanding still substantial absolute gains in areas of planned growth in the inner and outermetropolitan rings (Figures 2 & 4).

Comparison of percentage population change for 1961–71 and 1971–81 by local authority district also reveals a number of interesting features[10] (Figures 3 & 4). In the 1970s many districts experienced a declining rate of growth as a consequence of the reduction in national rates of change (from 5.7 percent in 1961–71 to 0.54 percent in 1971–81). Yet large absolute and percentage gains occurred in many settlements between 1971 and 1981, with the fastest growth being recorded in New and Expanded Towns. Some districts that grew in the 1960s lost population in the 1970s — freestanding urban areas, which were at the receiving end of earlier decentralization, began to lose population to adjacent districts, for example around Brighton, Southampton, Reading, and Ipswich. A broken ring of authorities surrounding Greater London, and, to a lesser extent, adjacent to Liverpool, Manchester and Birmingham, all lost population, revealing a zone of inner city decline behind the outward shift. Finally, several districts experienced either accelerated growth in the 1970s or moved from a position of loss to one of gain between the 1960s and 1970s. These districts included areas close to major metropolitan centres — for example, parts of Gloucestershire and south Herefordshire, as well as remoter areas peripheral to urban England, such as Wales, Cumbria and Northumberland.

The interpretation of these regional and local changes is a source of much academic speculation. Some commentators interpret the growth of remoter rural areas, for example, as a 'rush to the country' or 'flight from the cities'. We may question whether there is a 'rush' but it certainly does seem the case that metropolitan overflow occurs over a much wider area than it did in the past. Significantly, the upturn in population of some remoter areas has been modest compared to the large absolute gains in areas of planned growth closer to metropolitan centres.[11] The 1981 Census shows little evidence of depopulation at the county or district level. Study of parish population trends reveals a more complex pattern of redistribution, with some remoter areas suffering contraction, although local government reorganization masks the true extent of local depopulation and repopulation. Growth in remoter areas may be due to reduced out-migration as much as to growing in-migration.

Population trends in the 1970s, therefore, do not represent a distinct break with earlier periods of outward shift. The spillover effect continues, though in a different form and on a larger scale than in the 1950s and 1960s. Adminstrative boundaries and statistical definitions of metropolitan and non-metropolitan Britain, of 'conurban' and 'rural regions',[12] have been rendered meaningless by a national phenomenon of repopulation which is virtually ubiquitous outside the old industrial cores. The concept of an outer city embracing both the more accessible and some of the more remote rural areas appears to be increasingly relevant.

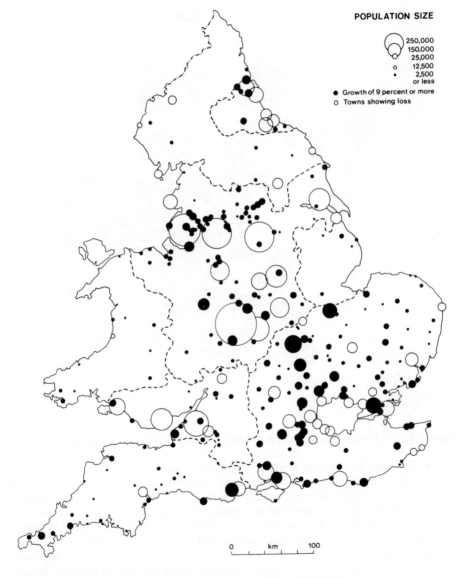

Figure 2.   Population of towns in Britain's outer cities 1971-1981

Population growth
>15 per cent

0   km   100

Figure 3.   Percentage change in population, 1961–1971, district authorities

In this outer city several kinds of migration process are at work, each having a distinct spatial dimension. Localised dispersal is linked to the extension of commuter belts into the countryside surrounding cities and smaller towns. Commuting is associated chiefly with professional and managerial workers who move further and further away from their work into the outer metropolitan regions and beyond,[13] though commuting also involves some lower-income and younger middle-class households.[14] Another significant process is the acquisition of second homes, which for some migrants may represent the first step towards a permanent rural residence. Second homes have grown in number especially since the mid 1950s, and were increasing at a rate of 11,000–12,000 per annum by the late 1970s. The principal second home destinations lie beyond the main commuter zones, especially on the coasts of west Wales, Lincolnshire, north Norfolk and south west England, although there are some second homes nearer the conurbations. The ownership of second homes is associated with high income households. Despite the level of private car ownership among second home owners, owners of second homes seldom travel far from their first home, an average of 100 miles being common. Seventy-five percent of second homes in Shropshire for instance, were found to be owned by households living only 50 miles away. This evidence makes clear that 'second homes should not be regarded as isolated rural phenomena . . . but elements in the economy of the city region which have substantial spatial and temporal variations'.[15]

Finally, retirement migration undoubtedly accounted for a proportion of population gain in areas distant from the cities, above all on the coastal fringes.[16] Londoners have traditionally moved to the south coast, Midlanders to the east coast, and the coastal plain of north west Lancashire has attracted retirees from Manchester and Liverpool. Smaller towns and villages closer to the cities also contain significant retirement populations, for example in Hampshire and Wiltshire. Some of the fastest growth since 1971 has taken place in Norfolk, Suffolk and Cambridgeshire.[17]

Commuting, second homing and retirement are thus part of the complex dispersal process taking place in the outer areas of Britain's cities. In each case the pattern of gross migration flow varies somewhat. The net in-migration of commuters may be

Figure 4.   Percentage change in population, 1971–1981, district authorities

related to an out-migration of agricultural workers; retirees may move in while young or middle aged wage earners move out. But these readjustments take place within the context of an overall net population gain in the rural areas. It is to the explanation of these gains that we now turn.

Environmental values

One of the principal reasons why people move out of cities is the desire for more spacious and attractive living environments. This is usually the prerogative of those who can afford to exercise choice in residential selection. The desire for countryside living is of course not new, as suburban history testifies; the scenic attraction of settlements around cities, the historic country house tradition, and the desire to escape the crowded city, have traditionally drawn people further out.[18] But as higher incomes became more widely diffused in the twentieth century, the desire for a place in the country has become generalized. Improvements in road and rail transport have enabled more and more people to live some distance from the cities. Car ownership continues to rise in all regions.[19] One significant factor has been the increased financial assistance offered by employers towards the cost of owning and running a car. There is evidence to show that households owning company cars will consider living in a much wider area than other types of car-owning family and are moving outwards from the conurbations. Two-car households, of which there are a growing number, are even more mobile and less dependent upon having close access to services, thus making further out migration possible.[20] Improvements in public transport notably rail, also enlarge the commuter's range.[21] Improvements in communication such as telephone and television have likewise enhanced the potential for dispersal.

All these factors have permitted the expression of environmental preferences, first in the immediate suburban fringes of cities and, later, further out in the countryside. But most commentators agree that the growing desire to live in the outer cities is an expression of more fundamental economic and social changes. The importance which some groups now attach to country landscapes may reflect the emergence of a 'post-industrial economy', whose essential characteristic is a reduction in the importance of the primary and manufacturing sectors in relation to the service sector and the new quaternary industries such as financial and banking services. White-collar work is carried out by a predominately skilled, non-manual labour force which enjoys rising levels of per capita income, car and home ownership and increased leisure time. It is these social parameters which determine environmental values and hence the pattern of geographical mobility.[22] Moreover, there appears to be a spatial dimension to the post-industrial economy itself. The decline in primary and manufacturing employment has been heaviest in remote rural areas and old industrial centres, while service employment has grown in many of the rural counties.[23] New forms of capital intensive and research-based industry have developed in more accessible and attractive environments outside the conurbations. The studies by Donnison and Soto strongly suggest that the 'post-industrial economy' is most advanced in central and southern Britain, although there are important differences between the outer Birmingham area, which is still dominated by manufacturing industry, and the outer South East. Southern England, and above all the area between Bristol and Bath, has been dubbed the 'U.K. sun-belt'.[24] Affluence and social status are highest in smaller towns, residential and industrial suburbs, New Towns and seaside resorts which depend on service industries and non-manual workers.[25]

The present economic recession in Britain may suggest that the availability of jobs might offer a more plausible explanation of population migration than environmental values. Yet it has to be remembered that the economies of the outer areas have generally withstood recession better than those of the inner cities and the industrial heartlands. High levels of upward social and geographical mobility have long been found in such areas, as numerous studies of residential mobility in the 1960s demonstrated.[26] It would thus appear that environmental preferences as measured by the scale of geographical dispersal show their greatest expression where real Gross Domestic Product and employment have been running at a high level.[27]

The countryside around large cities has become a potent symbol of affluence, one well captured in the 1960s' image of the 'London cocktail belt'. Advertisements for lawn mowers, building societies and bottles of gin appear side by side with desirable 'conservation' villages.[28] Whole tracts of countryside, especially in southern Britain — the 'Sussex Downs', 'edge of the Cotswolds', the 'Malverns', 'Charnwood Forest' — are not simply beautiful areas but symbols of a rural idyll. Land use planning and countryside conservation have ensured that some of the most appealing landscapes of the past have been preserved — and these are associated with the nobility and upper classes. The notion of a 'U.K. sun-belt' stretching across southern England from Somerset towards East Anglia conveys the reality of this historical landscape and settlement pattern. The 'sun-belt' is also an environment that attracts 'post-industrial' enterprises and it is surprising that one classic if rather audacious model of environmental preferences named this area as the ultimately desirable location for ambitious working class and upper class people.[29]

The desire for upward social mobility and status has long been associated with living in the countryside. A cumulative historical process has operated in which the wealthier households who once moved into residential suburbs immediately on the fringe of the conurbations have since made a second move to high class commuter villages further out.[30] But a simple status-seeking model of this kind provides a rather limited explanation for the core-ring shift, both to the inner and to the outer rings. Population decentralization has involved working-class, lower-middle and middle-class groups too. For people seeking a job in New and Expanded Towns, environmental preferences *decrease* in importance with distance from London. Their opinions about where they would like to live are only one factor in the final selection of residence — others include the type of employment available, the conditions of pay and finance, and the nature of the housing provided in the outer regions.[31]

Social groups value low-density housing environments in different ways, and this gives us a clue to the enlarged geographical scale of dispersal. Lower-middle-class groups, such as clerical workers or insurance and sales personnel, as well as skilled groups like foremen and supervisors, seem to value the suburban areas more highly than other members of the middle class who live in the suburbs. This is possibly due to the greater importance they attach to home and family, to the children's education, to access to facilities, and to the opportunities for material advancement which the suburbs present.[32] In contrast, upper-middle-class groups in professional and managerial occupations appear to value exurban areas and spacious housing environments because these offer the prospect of a more relaxed working environment and a rural life-style. Admittedly, differences in income affect the expression of environmental values, but income may be less influential than differences in behaviour and life-style. Commuters, second homers and retirees, are motivated by some of these environmental concerns, as are the increasing number who work from home, and those who have deliberately given up their urban jobs to 'drop-out' of society.[33] Hence neither suburbanites nor people who wish to move further afield are merely status seekers: they are also seeking a rather easier, less stressful way of life.[34]

Environmental preferences do not of course provide a complete explanation for the spatial patterns of migration found in Britain's outer cities. It is difficult to discern their influence at work in regions of economic decline or traditionally low social mobility, although the core-ring shift has been strong in such areas as Mid-Glamorgan,[35] in the area between Liverpool and Manchester,[36] and even in Greater Glasgow, a region affected by severe economic recession.[37] Furthermore, environmental values are not independent influences upon population dispersal. They are shaped by many constraints, including the availability of housing and the management of environmental change through public policy; indeed, environmental perceptions themselves are increasingly manipulated in the interests of commercial and industrial developers and of local authorities.[38] The spatial patterns that people value so highly would not exist in their present form were it not for the restraints upon suburban growth applied by the town and country planning authorities.[39] Local concern for the environment is another important check on plans to extend the outer city: longstanding reaction to urbanization and urban ways of life is very strong, especially among those who have moved out and 'shut the gate' behind them.

Housing availability

Another principal reason why people have moved out of cities in large numbers has been the desire for new and cheaper housing. We know this from studies of the reasons for housing and labour migration in Britain carried out over recent years.[40] Residential mobility in the private sector has been especially associated with the supply of new owner-occupied housing on the inner suburban fringes of cities and further out in small villages and country towns.[41] When households in the public sector have been encouraged to move out — for instance under the planned programmes of overspill to New and Expanded Towns — migration also appears to be overwhelmingly motivated by the desire for a better house and an improved residential environment.[42]

Housing is only one of several considerations prompting households to move; others include divorce and family fission, employment changes and environmental preferences. But the availability of housing has a crucial effect on where households move to. Changes in the amount of housing available in an area will influence the scale of core-ring shift and the internal redistribution of population within the outer areas. The age, tenure and type of housing will tend to decide what sort of households move in[43] and what sort stay behind.[44] Considerable regional and local variations in the supply of different kinds of housing tenure in Britain are correlated with a wide range of socio-demographic characteristics, including occupation, social class, age, sex, and household size. The most obvious example is the way in which commuters congregate around the big cities in a belt running north-south through central and southern England, and retirees in peripheral areas west and east.[45]

The trend of rising home-ownership creates great pressure for housing in the outer cities. The rising price of housing throughout the 1970s, the relative increase (allowing for inflation) in tax relief on building society mortgages, and high capital appreciation on house property, have all encouraged home ownership as an investment, with the result that house purchase has been an attractive hedge against inflation.[46] Owner-occupation now dominates the pattern of housing supply in England where, in 1980, 55 percent of households in rural districts owned their own houses. The position is different in Scotland where only 33 percent owned their own home. The rate of change in owner-occupation in England has a spatial dimension. Some outer-metropolitan areas in north-west England, especially Lancashire, have seen rapid increases in privately owned housing; this is also true of many areas in the outer South-East. In part this reflects the long tradition of owner occupation in outer areas, in contrast to the cities, where the housing stock is dominated by the public sector. The proportion of housing stock owned by local authorities in non-metropolitan counties varies greatly. In 1981 it was only 16.6 percent in Lancashire, 17.0 percent in Surrey and 16.9 percent in Sussex. But in Hertfordshire it was 32.3 percent, higher than the figure of 30.9 percent for Greater London; and in Staffordshire it was 26.8 percent.[47]

Most commentators agree that three important factors affect access to owner-occupied housing in the outer cities: the availability of mortgage finance; the price of housing; and (related to price) the scale of house building activity, especially the number of *new* houses being built.

There is plenty of evidence to show that patterns of building society lending have generally encouraged dispersal,[48] because mortgages are easier to obtain on new (or more recent) properties and where purchasers can afford to meet the down-payment and the repayments. Both these conditions exist in commuter areas, where higher income households are proportionately well represented. The argument is qualified by the evidence of a more flexible attitude by building societies to mortgage allocation in areas of older housing.[49] However, this 'alternative' approach to traditional funding procedures has almost certainly come too late to have more than a marginal impact on dispersal. The support given by building societies to 'starter homes' at the lower end of the house market is more significant, because it could assist the migration of younger households on lower incomes, unless of course such homes were built in larger numbers within the cities — a prospect which seems utopian given the current craze by volumebuilders for erecting new houses on greenfield sites in open countryside.[50]

The second major factor in the level of home ownership has been the price of housing. Household formation, rising incomes, and rising social aspirations have all added to the pressure on house prices. Pressure moderated during the later 1970s when unemployment rose (especially in the cities) and the poor economic situation depressed the level of housing demand. During 1982 and 1983, however, although unemployment remained high, interest rates fell, the value of real income rose, and the demand for housing picked up again. Once more, prices are rising and the level of housebuilding activity increasing. There can be little doubt that we are about to witness renewed pressure for private housing, and that this will fall upon the shire counties in the outer cities since the metropolitan authorities can only make up a limited proportion of the land required for future housing.

In the past the price differential between inner and outer cities has given us one explanation for the core-ring shift in population. The high price of city houses has, generally speaking, put housing out of reach of even highly-paid employees as well as lower-grade, middle, and skilled managers. First-time buyers have suffered more than households who already own a house, because their initial deposits, which reflect the sale price of their present properties, are much higher. This allows existing householders to acquire larger, newer and more expensive properties at the upper end of the market in the countryside. There are still house price differentials between inner and outer areas, although there are regional variations in prices which conceal the true picture, as for example between Greater London and *all* other parts of the U.K., and between the south and north of England.[51]

Rather more interesting, in view of the migration shifts taking place *within* the outer cities, are the price differentials found at a sub-regional and local scale as between large towns and smaller villages. Our knowledge of these is fragmentary and largely anecdotal, but some generalisations can be made. The overall picture is one of high average prices in the areas most attractive to commuters, especially in those subject to severe development restrictions. This is not a recent trend. Hertfordshire, for instance, saw price rises of 4.5 percent per annum in the 1950s, well above the then national average of 2.3 percent per annum, and prices continued to rise disproportionately fast at 21 percent per annum between 1971 and 1976. Relatively low prices persist in larger settlements and/or where new housing has been built on any scale. In 1980, average house prices in Chester District were significantly higher than in the neighbouring town of Chester, but they ranged from £38,200 in settlements of 1500 persons to £45,000 in settlements smaller than 1000 persons. Similar evidence from Wiltshire and Leicestershire shows average prices to be higher in smaller settlements.[52]

Third, price differentials in the outer city are associated with the way in which housing developers have approached the task of acquiring land and building houses.[53] Developers building for a 'volume' market find land costs low and assembly easiest on greenfield sites. They have been able to build low-cost housing by constructing smaller houses of standard design at medium densities, often in large estates. Small building companies have had to make do with 'infill' sites; unable to achieve economies of scale, they have specialised in high density 'exclusive' housing, often made more expensive by planning authorities as a result of design restrictions. New housing at reasonable prices has been available only in the large settlements or new villages like Bar Hill, Cambridgeshire, or New Ash Green, Kent. In small villages very high prices are associated with a population limited in turnover and highly selective by occupation and social class, a situation favouring the better-off commuters, employees of large companies, and so on.[54]

What these various studies demonstrate is that the scale and location of new housebuilding has an important effect on the price paid by different income groups for housing. The quantity of house-building is also an indicator of the extent of building land with planning permission. There are great regional variations in the amount of land close enough to services to make it suitable for building on and for which permission for site development has been given, as recent surveys by county planning authorities and housebuilders demonstrate.[55] Although there is much vacant inner city land, some of which is available for housing, the greatest supply continues to be provided on the fringe of the conurbations, at least where not restricted by Green Belt policies, or further out in 'growth points'. This is partly because local planning authorities have allocated land for housing in those places. Contrasts between the metropolitan areas and their surrounding regions show that as a result, percentage increase in the total stock of dwellings between 1976 and 1981 was always higher outside the metropolis.

Although the market in land is a very important factor in the dispersal process, the intervention of the public planning system closely affects the operation of the market. The extent of land available for residential development is determined by strategic and local planning policy operating under the ever-watchful eye of central government.[56] Housing availability cannot be treated independently of public policy for land use and settlement change. In general, the planning system appears to have encouraged a greater increase in the supply of residential land in small settlements than in large settlements. Hence, ironically, the attempt to steer urban growth away from the edge of cities may have inflated the total area of residential land developed, and may have indirectly promoted the urban-rural population shift.[57] Of course, this does not explain why or how more land has become available in smaller settlements through the planning system. To find this out we must examine the thinking behind housing land strategy and the influence it has had on the housebuilding industry. This is discussed more fully in Part Two.

Public housing has played a limited, though at times important, role in population dispersal. Publicly rented housing has been declining in the post-war period relative to the rise in owner-occupation, although the spatial pattern varies between cities and outer areas, with somewhat higher proportions of public housing in the North West, and even greater proportions in Scotland. Public housing provision in the outer cities is of course intertwined with the long history of urban-regional planning, in which the twin policies of slum clearance and overspill to new communities provided the cornerstone. By and large, the public provision of housing under this dispersal programme accounts for only a limited proportion of out-migration from the cities. Between 1966 and 1971, the twenty-eight New Towns in Britain received from the seven official conurbations a net inflow which amounted to only one-eighth of the net migration loss from those conurbations. Only 8 percent of all those leaving conurbations during this period went to the New Towns, whether in the same region or further away. Central Clydeside and Merseyside were the most affected, with New Towns taking 25 and 12 percent respectively of their out-migrants.[58] These figures relate to the total flow of migrants regardless of whether they moved into public or private housing — hence public sector flows will be smaller still.

Nevertheless, public housing provision has had an impact on the scale and distribution of the core-ring population shift. The Scottish experience is particularly instructive. Around Glasgow, Development Corporation housing contributed to the massive scale of localized dispersal which took place during the period 1966-76. The decision to build East Kilbride and Cumbernauld close to the conurbation and strong government commitment to shun clearance and overspill were related influences. By contrast, the more recently designated New Towns in the outer South-East have played a much more limited role in encouraging decentralization from London. Public housing represents only 50 percent of less of their total housing stock. Distance from the conurbation and weakening government commitment to overspill policy have not helped.

The pattern of housing tenure in the New Towns is not dominated by public housing. Indeed, the level of owner-occupation has been steadily climbing in many

New Towns; in Central Lancashire and Warrington it has always been relatively high. The combination of declining public sector housing and rising private ownership has meant that planned towns have come to play a more important role in redistributing than in dispersing the population. The proportion of migrants moving into planned towns from the cities has declined in relation to more local household movements. Warrington and Central Lancashire draw most households from the outer areas surrounding Merseyside and Manchester, and Cwmbran receives as much inmigration from small towns in Gwent and mid-Glamorgan as from Cardiff. Furthermore, we cannot ignore the fact that around several of the larger 'free-standing cities', Leicester and Bristol for example, public housing has had a minimal aggregate impact on the volume of migration from the cities. Either it hasn't existed, or else the scale of provision has been limited to 'mini-overspill' schemes or growth centres that have not acquired the status of New Towns. Such public housing may of course represent a relatively high proportion of total stock in the 'free-standing' cities and thus have an important influence on the character of *local* population redistribution, particularly in providing the opportunity for lower income households to stay in the commuting areas rather than move to the cities for a house.

Finally, all discussion of housing availability as an explanation for decentralization must be related back to the activities of private and public housing agencies, on which government planning policy has had a critical bearing. It is commonly thought that one of the central features of the dispersal proces is its 'voluntary' nature, with individual households making free choices about whether and where to move. But the effect of planning on dispersal is profound. It is not confined to the New and Expanded Towns programme operated by central government. The location, scale and price of private housing in the outer cities is strongly conditioned by the less formal local planning system, which determines expansion, 'infill' or the creation of new villages. As we find out more about the role of settlement planning in the dispersal process, it seems less valid to sustain the long held distinction between 'voluntary' and 'planned' migration.

Employment opportunity

At a time of economic recession and rising unemployment, it may seem somewhat perverse to talk of jobs as a factor in population dispersal. Employment loss is a national phenomenon, but the rate of loss experienced by the outer cities has in general been much less than in the conurbations, with the consequence that throughout the 1970s unemployment levels remained at half the level found in the inner cities.[59] In the early 1980s the recession grew worse, but the economies of the outer cities remained relatively buoyant in contrast to the profoundly depressing conditions in some inner cities.

Admittedly, it is dangerous to oversimplify: the closure of firms has become much more widespread, and even the more advanced technological industries, which find favour with outer city locations, are shedding labour. Mismatch between the demand for and the supply of labour is known to occur especially in the older industrial estates and housing estates found in Scotland, Wales and the North of England. Kirkby, built to absorb Liverpool's overspill, experienced an unemployment rate of 40 percent in mid-1982.[60] In the outer Glasgow area, unemployment rose dramatically between 1971 and 1978, reaching levels of 25 percent in the New Towns as well as in the city and the older industrial towns — only the suburbs performed rather better.[61]

Despite the varied economic experience of settlements in the outer city, the general impression is one of economic optimism. Many smaller towns still attract new manufacturing and service enterprises, and although this trend is more noticeable in southern England, there is plenty of evidence for such expansion around the cities in the North West and South Wales. One explanation is that the outer cities enjoy certain underlying structural advantages over the inner cities: a greater number of skilled and geographically mobile occupational groups; a potentially large economically active workforce; and, most important, increasing participation among females in local employment. Such conditions are strongly associated with population growth and the socially selective character of in-migration. The growth and geographical dispersal of industrial activity has been fundamentally related to these basic socio-demographic variables. We can go further: population decentralization and the spatial characteristics of labour supply in the outer cities have probably been a stronger influence on industrial movement and expansion than has been the influence of job availability on residential mobility, at least until very recent times.

There are good grounds for supporting this line of reasoning. The relationship between employment change and population dispersal is a complex one because jobs, like people, have shifted out from the cities for related but different reasons and at different times. We know that employment decentralization *followed* population decentralization, and did so in a number of sequential stages. The broader trends are well documented for the twenty-year period between 1950 and 1970.[62] The most rapid shift in employment did not take place until the 1960s, by which time population dispersal was well advanced. Between 1961 and 1971 the inner metropolitan rings increased their employment by 15 percent, or 707,000 jobs, with the result that their share of total UK working population rose from 35 to 38 percent (with a corresponding fall from 62 to 59 percent in the urban cores). The important point is that at this stage the outer MELA rings played a very important role in job dispersal — indeed their share of total UK employment actually fell slightly from 2.9 percent in 1950 to 2.7 percent in 1970.[63]

Much of the employment shift in this twenty-year period involved the actual movement of firms out from cities, and can thus be seen as a direct response to massive population shifts which increased the supply of labour in the inner-metropolitan rings. The sequence in which this occurs is not very clear, but it appears that the relocation of population builds up its own demand for local service industry and thus employment. Since household costs are passed on to the employer in the form of a higher wages bill, the costs of commuting to jobs in the cities forces employers either to pay high wages and contract, or else decentralize their activities to the metropolitan rings. The constantly rising cost of commuting encourages further dispersal of service and manufacturing, as does the constantly rising cost of housing in outer areas. Over time the balance between population dispersal and jobs dispersal will improve.[64]

All this assumes that a kind of 'natural' process of adjustment between labour supply and demand is operating. But this is not so. Technological changes in British industry have helped to make the outer cities attractive locations for productive investment.[65] Separation of production within multi-plant concerns,[66] greater corporate control of large over small firms,[67] and a host of other complex economic processes, are involved in locational decision-making. The availability of land has also played a fundamental role in determining how much industrial development could take place and where — it helps to explain, for example, why major employment dispersal has not generally gone beyond the inner metropolitan rings. Land availability patterns are in turn governed by local land-use planning controls, urban-regional planning, and regional planning policy. The evidence we have shows that local land 'restraint' policies have had an important though variable spatial effect on employment change particularly around London; that the New and Expanded Towns have played a significant independent role in channelling industrial movement, again mainly in the outer South-East; and that regional policy has steered employment away from the West Midlands more effectively than from Greater London.[68] It seems that employment decentralization in the industrial heartlands themselves is the result of the long-distance transfer of jobs resulting from regional policy rather than the out-movement of local firms.[69]

The 'in situ' closure and birth of factories helps to explain employment change better than actual movement.[70] Indeed, Fothergill and Gudgeon point out that the contribution of enterprise movement to total employment change between 1959 and 1975 accounted for only one-third of the total urban-rural shift in employment, although admittedly moves were rather higher in remote areas. The expansion of existing firms and the formation of new enterprises account for the relatively fast rate of increase in manufacturing employment between 1959 and 1975 in rural sub-regions.[71] But these changes need to be viewed in context: what we now recognise as 'in situ' growth may be the direct consequence of previous industrial movement. The transfer of firms into New and Expanded Towns appears to have promoted the expansion of existing firms and new firm formation.[72] Similarly, the expansion of research and development employment has continued in areas with an existing legacy of research establishments.[73] Nor must we underestimate the continued part played by industrial movement — especially in the service sector of the economy. Service employment continues to move to free-standing cities and industrial towns in the metropolitan rings at a rapid rate. Between 1979 and 1982, 82 firms took 13,000 office jobs with them — although this was less than half the rate for 1964–1978.[74]

In recent years the relationship between employment opportunity and population dispersal appears to have changed somewhat with the onset of economic recession. At a time of high unemployment it is expected that industrial relocation will become a more critical influence on population mobility. The principal effect will be a net migration gain in those more prosperous urban regions which are experiencing employment growth in their outer areas. Throughout the decade 1970–80 net out-migration from the South East, including Greater London, fell from $-28,000$ in 1976 to $-6,000$ in 1978, with a small net gain of $+1000$ recorded in 1980. Between mid-1981 and mid-1982 the South East *outside* London experienced a net gain of $+41,000$, much higher than for any other region and followed only by East Anglia ($+13,000$).[75] It might also be the case that some of the population growth which took place in remoter rural areas between 1971 and 1981 was a reflection of 'in situ' employment growth, though we still know little about the processes involved. The main point seems to be that the relatively good employment performance of smaller towns in the 'sun-belt' will encourage increased inter-regional movement — not because there are many job vacancies but because the chances of getting a new job are likely to be higher here than in any other region.[76]

Although jobs are clearly becoming a more important motive for migration, the fundamental relationship between population and employment shifts has not altered. The formation of new firms in smaller county towns and rural areas is in part connected with the legacy of the very first phases of population movement when the wealthy and more industrious moved out, hence creating a social climate favourable to future entrepreneurship. The combined presence of skilled labour, risk capital, and managerial expertise, helps to explain the employment experience of new and existing plants in the more favoured and prosperous outer cities in the south of England.[77] Population shifts still take place primarily for reasons having little to do with shifts in employment. Changes in employment opportunity may affect inter-regional migration, but they have little real bearing on the vast bulk of local short-distance dispersal and population redistribution, which is overwhelmingly associated with environmental and housing factors (see Table 1).[78] Nor do they directly influence the growing scale of retirement and second home migration.

Table 1: *Net migration rates for economically active males 1966–1971 by migrant stream (rate/1000)*

	Environment-related stream	Housing stream	Employment stream
Inner London	−56	−84	−2
Outer London	−45	+34	−25
Outer Metropolitan Area	+25	+14	+7
London Metropolitan Region	−21	−3	−7

British Road Federation, 1980, p. 18.

Public policy — a synthesis

A number of reasons have been advanced in this chapter for the enlarged scale of population dispersal. Environmental values have become more widely diffused under conditions of rising personal mobility. The search for better housing outside the cities has prompted the mass exodus of both high-income and low-income groups; and the prospect of finding a job in the outer city has become a greater reality as economic activity has dispersed outwards and new enterprises have sprung up in smaller towns and villages. Dispersal does not appear, however, to be an inevitable product of the new preferences for dispersed living. Public policy has governed, directly and indirectly, the scale and form of migration into and within the outer areas and modified the 'natural' processes of urban change.

In Britain public policy has been an important factor in population decentralization since 1945. Before that time, suburban population growth occurred in response to improved transportation and the activities of speculative housebuilders.[79] It was the damaging social impact of such building strategies, particularly the steady encroachment of cities onto productive farmland (an important concern at the beginning of World War II), and the loss of familiar and cherished countryside landscapes, which prompted the emergence of a public planning system committed to the containment of suburban growth. Under the Town and Country Planning Act 1947, local planning authorities were given power to withhold or approve permission for changes in the use of land. The primary object of planning was to keep the public costs of sporadic building to a minimum (especially expenditure on public utilities like water, gas and sewerage), to protect farmland, and to maintain environmental quality in the countryside. But several other objectives emerged during the post-war years, the most important of which was to contain the scale and rate of growth of the large conurbations.[80]

Protection of countryside environments provided the rationale for Green Belts or 'collars', which were imposed around the continuously built-up areas. Green Belts effectively sterilize agricultural land and permit a limited amount of recreation close to the cities. Green Belts were introduced at different times: in the mid-1940s around Greater London and Greater Glasgow, in the mid-1960s around Birmingham, and, later still, in West Yorkshire and Tyne and Wear. Many commentators acknowledge the major impact of Green Belts in deflecting localized population dispersal and upon the migration of middle class and high-income social groups.[81] Green Belts restricted the availability of housing and hence preserved desirable areas for those groups who could afford to live in them. However, some large provincial cities have failed to adopt Green Belts (Cardiff, Leicester and Hull for instance) and others have come to it very late in the day. Moreover, Green Belts are not the only public policies for countryside protection in the outer-metropolitan areas: the so-called 'Areas of Outstanding Natural Beauty' (AONB) and areas of 'Great Landscape Value' have modified the scale and pattern of migration beyond the Green Belts (Figure 7).

However policies for population redistribution have also been a major feature of post-war planning.[82] A programme of large scale overspill of population from the conurbations was instituted under the New Towns Act 1946 and the Town Development Act 1952. Many settlements close to the big cities and, later, well beyond the Green Belts, received overspill population. The actual number of migrants was always quite small in relation to total out-migration — and was much less than the protagonists of new communities hoped for — but the New Towns have grown rapidly as a result of subsequent natural increase among 'second generation' households. The increased rate of decentralization is evident from the 1981 Census, which shows that, almost without exception, the fastest growing towns in Britain between 1971 and 1981 were the New and Expanded Towns (Table 2). Policies for the redistribution of population have also been implemented by the concentration of housing, industry and services in many smaller rural settlements within the commuter hinterlands. Although not accorded the status of New Towns, their role has been somewhat similar: to absorb overspill from neighbouring large towns and cities. The main difference between these settlements and the 'New' Towns, is the absence of a coherently planned housing provision for low-income households and the attempt to systematically link housing and jobs — as under the Industrial Selection Scheme operating in the New Towns. Notwithstanding these limitations, by creating opportunities for private house-building and public housing provision, the 'key' settlements defined by local authorities in the 1960s and 1970s have had a major impact on settlement change and consequent migration patterns in the outer city.[83]

Table 2: *Largest relative population changes 1971–1981: towns with 1981 population of 10,000 or more. Population present on census night 1971 and 1981.*

Largest increases			
Town and county	*Status	1971–1981 population increase– percentage	1981 population present
Washington (Tyne and Wear)	NT	102.6	53,783
Milton Keynes (Buckinghamshire)	NT	102.0	106,974
Runcorn (Cheshire)	NT	78.1	64,117
St Ives (Cambridgeshire)		71.8	12,278
Redditch (Hereford and Worcester)	NT	63.1	66,854
Tamworth (Staffordshire	ET	59.6	64,315
Leighton Linslade (Bedfordshire)		46.3	29,772
Witham (Essex)	ET	46.0	25,373
Seaton Valley (Northumberland)	ET	44.1	46,141
Bracknell (Berkshire)	NT	43.1	48,752
Guisborough (Cleveland)	ET	42.8	19,903
Thetford (Norfolk)	ET	42.7	19,591
Royston (Hertfordshire)		42.7	11,799
Skelmersdale and Holland (Lancs)	NT	42.1	43,464
Droitwich (Hereford and Worcester)	ET	41.8	18,073
St Neots (Cambridgeshire)	ET	39.3	21,185
Minehead (Somerset)		38.7	11,176
Ashby-de-la-Zouch (Leicestershire)		38.6	11,518
Haverhill (Suffolk)	ET	38.0	17,146
Daventry (Northamptonshire)	ET	36.9	16,178

*NT = New Town, ET = Expanded Town,

A second public policy impinging on the outer cities has been the attempt to redistribute employment opportunity. This was to be done through measures designed to encourage relocation of industry away from the 'prosperous' southern regions of the South-East and West Midlands to the 'less prosperous' regions of Scotland, Wales and the North of England. Control over industrial development was brought about in 1947 through the normal planning machinery, and also through the requirement which obliged manufacturing industry to obtain Industrial Development Certificates; in 1965, offices were required to obtain an office development permit. The Assisted Areas nominally took precedence in the award of these permits, but many permits were granted to enterprises moving into New and Expanded Towns, enabling these to become established centres of decentralized employment. Only in 1977 and 1978 were these rules governing manufacturing and office jobs changed in favour of the inner cities.

The effect of public policy on the dispersal process has been neither direct nor immediate. While official post-war planning orthodoxy favoured planned decentralization and urban containment, in broad terms the policies for controlling suburban growth and redistributing population and employment operated within an outmoded organizational framework which patently failed to adjust to the changing geography of social and economic activity around the cities and, moreover, divided planning functions between different levels of government. Furthermore, the implementation of dispersal policy has had to contend with the local political process and constantly shifting national economic and political priorities.

Local government units created in 1888 were the framework for planning control between 1947 and 1974. These units, the old county boroughs and the surrounding counties, were too small to allow the proper co-ordination of overspill policy, hence encouraging a variety of different kinds of sub-regional planning study. Attempts to devise larger local government units covering cities and their hinterlands were the basis of the Royal Commission on Local Government in England (the Redcliffe-Maud report) published in 1969. In 1974, the government reduced the 1210 existing authorities to about 400 shire and metropolitan counties and districts, the boundaries of which were tightly drawn along the built-up edge of the cities, so retaining the difficulty of planning overspill on a comprehensive basis. The functions of these authorities were changed, thus adding to the complicated pattern of administration. The shire counties were responsible for broad structure plans (under the Town and Country Planning Acts 1968 and 1980) and the local districts were to produce and implement more detailed plans. This division of planning functions has been the source of much political conflict, similar to the battles which took place between the old county boroughs and rural counties before reorganization. Some counties contributed to dispersal by encouraging a share of private sector overspill in order to boost their income, but strongly opposed public overspill, arguing with the cities about the scale and location of suburban housing[84] and the necessity for New Towns. Districts have also failed to operate tight land use control in the Green Belts, encouraging a greater degree of dispersed residential development and migration than intended.[85] All these conflicts have been exacerbated by the increasing tendency among post-war governments to decentralize power to local authorities and hence to relinquish firm national control over official dispersal policy. Thus land use and settlement planning has in practice been highly variable in the outer commuting zones, even in areas with similar or overlapping problems. Moreover, this diversity of local response appears to work in favour of current central government thinking, which is towards greater economic development wherever it can be found. The outcome has been more population and employment decentralization at a time when national control of dispersal has come to an end.

We should therefore not be surprised at the spatial development of the outer city or at the social and economic changes occurring there. For at least thirty years, governments have encouraged and laid down the conditions for dispersal through a combination of interlocking strategic plans and sector programmes.[86] Public dispersal policies have had a much longer and, to date, more successful pedigree than recent and still embryonic attempts to bring life back to the cities. Their development spans the entire history of post-war urban and regional planning in Britain, and they played a powerful formative role in the growing scale of dispersal. The causes of dispersal are hence firmly rooted in the goals and strategies that have permeated the post-war anti-urban tradition in Britain.

Notes

1. For a discussion see R. DREWETT, J. GODDARD and N. SPENCE, 'Urban Britain: beyond containment' in B. L. BERRY (ed.), *Urbanization and Counter-urbanization* (Sage, 1976).

2. J. B. GODDARD, 'British cities in transition', *Geographical Magazine*, vol. 53(8), 1981.

3. D. EVERSLEY and A. EVANS (eds), *The Inner City: Employment and Industry* (Heinemann, 1980).

4. P. HALL and D. HAY, *Growth Centres in the European Urban System* (Heinemann, 1980).

5. See for instance J. FORBES and I. ROBERTSON, 'Patterns of Residential Movement in Greater Glasgow', *Scottish Geographical Magazine*, vol. 97, no. 2, 1981; and K. J. LEA, 'Greater Glasgow', *Scottish Geographical Magazine*, vol. 96(1), 1980.

6. J. HERINGTON and D. EVANS, 'The spatial pattern of household movements in outer Leicester', Department of Geography, Loughborough University, Research Paper Series no. 3, 1980.

7. S. KENNETT and N. SPENCE, 'British population trends in the 1970s', *Town and Country Planning*, vol. 48(7), 1979.

8. D. VINING and T. KONTULY, 'Population dispersal from major metropolitan regions: an international comparison', *International Regional Science Review*, vol. 3(1), 1978.

9. A. G. CHAMPION, 'Counter-urbanisation and rural rejuvenation in Britain: an evaluation of population trends since 1971', Department of Geography Seminar Paper no. 38, University of Newcastle-upon-Tyne, 1981.

10. This discussion is based partly on the summary given in C. HAMNETT and W. RANDOLPH, 'The changing population distribution of England and Wales, 1961–81: clean break or consistent progression?' *Built Environment*, vol. 8, no. 4, 1983. See also W. RANDOLPH and S. ROBERT, 'Population redistribution in Great Britain 1971–1981', *Town and Country Planning*, vol. 50(9), September 1981.

11. See the preliminary results of the 1981 Census for England and Wales, *Population Trends*, vol. 25, Autumn 1981.

12. R. J. GREEN, *Country Planning: The Future of the Rural Regions* (Manchester University Press, 1971).

13. M. WAUGH, 'The changing distribution of professional and managerial manpower of England and Wales 1961–1966', *Regional Studies*, vol. 3, 1969.

14. R. E. PAHL described these people as 'reluctant commuters' forced to live in the countryside because they cannot get a house in the city; see *Whose City?* (Penguin 1975).

15. A. W. ROGERS, 'Second Homes in England and Wales: A Spatial View' in J. T. COPPOCK (ed.), *Second Homes: Curse or Blessing?* (Pergamon, 1977).

16. C. M. LAW and A. M. WARNES, 'Retirement migration', *Town and Country Planning*, vol. 50(2), 1981.

17. M. MOSELEY, *Power, Planning and People in Rural East Anglia* (Centre for East Anglian Studies, University of East Anglia, 1982).

18. P. BALMER, 'Aspects of migration in some Surrey villages, 1841–71', Unpub. Cambridge Ph.D. 1982.

19. K. J. BUTTON, 'The geographical distribution of car ownership in Great Britain — some recent trends', *Annals of Regional Science*, vol. 14, pt. 2, 1980.

20. M. C. DIX AND H. R. T. POLLARD, 'Company-financed motoring and its effects on household car use', *Traffic Engineering and Control*, vol. 21(11), November 1980.

21. P. ACTON, 'Electrification boosts public transport in Hertfordshire', *Transport*, vol. 1(3), July/August 1980.

22. R. DENNIS and H. CLOUT, *A Social Geography of England and Wales* (Pergamon, 1980).

23. D. DEEBLE, 'De-industrialisation means unemployment', *Geographical Magazine*, vol. LIII, no. 7, April 1981.

24. See for instance 'Britain's sunrise strip', *The Economist*, 30 January, 1982.

25. D. DONNISON and P. SOTO, *The Good City: A Study of Urban Development and Policy in Great Britain* (Heinemann, 1980).

26. See for instance R. E. PAHL, 'Commuting and social change in rural areas', *Official Architecture and Planning*, July/August 1966.

27. D. EVERSLEY and A. EVANS (eds.), *The Inner City: Employment and Industry* (Heinemann, 1980).

28. D. WHITE, 'Villages of the mind — incoming townspeople reversing depopulation', *New Society*, vol. 53, no. 924, 31 July 1980.

29. C. N. PARKINSON, 'Two nations', *The Economist*, vol. 222, 25 March, 1967.

30. R. I. WOODS, 'Migration and social segregation in Birmingham and the West Midlands region', in P. WHITE AND R. WOODS (eds.), *The Geographical Impact of Migration* (Longman, 1980).

31. F. A. GEE, *Homes and Jobs for Londoners in New and Expanding Towns*, Office of Population Censuses and Surveys Social Survey Division, (HMSO, 1972).

32. D. C. THORNS, 'Suburban values and the urban system', *International Journal of Comparative Sociology*, vol. 16, pt. 1-2, 1975.

33. For a discussion of this issue see G. LEWIS, 'Rural Communities' in M. PACIONE (ed.) *Progress in Rural Geography* (Croom Helm, 1983).

34. N. DEAKIN, and C. UNGERSON, *Leaving London: Planned mobility and the inner city* (Heinemann, 1977).

35. D. T. HERBERT, 'Population mobility and social change in South Wales', *Town Planning Review*, vol. 43, no. 4, 1972.

36. S. KENNETT and N. SPENCE, op. cit.

37. J. K. LEE, op. cit.

38. J. A. BURGESS, 'Selling places: environmental images for the executive', *Regional Studies*, vol. 16(1), 1982.

39. A. D. KING, 'Historical patterns of reaction to urbanism in the case of Britain, 1880-1939', *International Journal of Urban and Regional Research*, vol. 4, no. 1, 1980.

40 .See for instance J. SALT and R. FLOWERDEW, 'Labour migration from London', *London Journal*, vol. 6(1), Summer 1980.

41. J. HERINGTON, 'The reasons for household movement to rural settlements in outer Leicester', Department of Geography, Loughborough University Research Paper No. 5, 1980.

42. N. DEAKIN and C. UNGERSON, op. cit.

43. See for instance S. HARPER, 'Migration of commuter populations into rural areas', Unpub. M. Litt. thesis, University of Oxford, 1983; M. PACIONE, 'Differential quality of life in a metropolitan village', *Transactions of Institute of British Geographers*, vol. 5(2), 1980.

44. C. JONES, 'Population decline and home ownership in Glasgow', University of Glasgow, Department of Economic and Social Research, Urban and Regional Studies Discussion Paper, vol. 26, 1978.

45. M. DUNN, M. RAWSON, AND A. ROGERS, *Rural Housing: Competition and Choice* (Allen and Unwin, 1981).

46. See for instance C. HAMNETT, 'Owner-occupation in the 1970s: ownership or investment?', *Estates Gazette*, 262, 1982; A. MURIE and R. FOREST, 'Wealth, inheritance and housing policy', *Policy and Politics*, vol. 8, 1980; C. WHITEHEAD, 'Why owner-occupation?', *CES Review*, vol. 6, 1979.

47. Central Statistical Office, *Regional Trends*, 1982 edition, (HMSO).

48. See for instance K. A. BASSETT and J. R. SHORT, 'Patterns of building society and local authority mortgage lending in the 1970s', *Environment and Planning A*, vol. 12, 1980.

49. T. MELVILLE-ROSS, 'Down market lending by building societies', *Housing Review*, 30, 1981.

50. See for instance 'Builders get hooks into the Green Belt', *Planning*, vol. 529, 29 July, 1983.

51. C. HAMNETT, 'Regional variations in house prices and house price inflation, 1969–1981, *Area*, vol. 15, no. 2, 1983.

52. Department of Environment, *Review of Rural Setlement Policies 1945-1980*, (Martin and Voorhees Associates, October 1980).

53. For a full explanation see E. CRAVEN, 'Private residential expansion in Kent' in R. E. Pahl, *Whose City?* (Longman, 1970); also N. BATHER, 'The speculative residential developer and urban growth', Department of Geography, University of Reading Geographical Papers, No. 47, 1976.

54. J. HERINGTON and D. EVANS, 'The social characteristics of household movement in key and non-key settlements', Department of Geography, Loughborough University, Research Paper No. 4, 1980.

55. House-Builders Federation, 'Housing allocations in structure plans and residential land supply' (HBF, February 1982).

56. See for instance Department of Environment, *Land for private house-building*, Circular 9/80 (HMSO 1980).

57. This argument is partially developed by M. BLACKSELL and A. GILG, *The Countryside: Planning and Change* (Allen and Unwin, 1981).

58. For a full account of these trends see A. G. CHAMPION, K. CLEGG and R. .L. DAVIES, *Facts about New Towns: a Socio-Economic Digest* (Retailing and Planning Associates, 1977).

59. S. KENNETT and P. HALL, 'The inner city in spatial perspective' in P. HALL (ed.), *The Inner City in Context* (Heinemann, 1981).

60. N. GARNETT, 'Kirkby outer city problems', *Planning*, vol. 26, 23 July, 1982.

61. J. FORBES, 'The influence of planning policy on residential patterns in the outer areas of Greater Glasgow', Unpub. paper, Department of Town and Regional Planning, University of Glasgow, May 1983.

62. See for instance Department of Environment, *British Cities: Urban Population and Employment Trends 1951-71* (Urban change in Britain 1951–71. Final Report, Part 1), Research report 10, 1976; A. M . WARNES, 'A long term view of employment decentralisation from the larger English cities' in D. EVERSLEY and A. EVANS (ed.) op. cit.

63. P. HALL and D. HAY, op. cit.

64. Standing Conference on London and South East Regional Planning, *The Commuting Study* SCLSERP, July 1981.

65. D. MASSEY, *The Anatomy of Job Loss* (Methuen, 1982).

66. F. E. .I. HAMILTON, 'Aspects of industrial mobility in the British economy', *Regional Studies*, vol. 12, no. 2, 1978.

67. J. B. GODDARD and I. J. SMITH, 'Changes in corporate control in the British urban system, 1972–77', *Environment and Planning A*, vol. 10, 1978.

68. For a full explanation of these influences see D. KEEBLE, *Industrial location and planning in the United Kingdom* (Methuen, 1976).

69. A. R . TOWNSEND, 'Comparative views from the north east and other northern regions of Britain', in D. EVERSLEY and A. EVANS, op. cit.

70. See for instance R. DENNIS, 'The decline of manufacturing employment in Greater London, 1966–74 in D. EVERSLEY and A. EVANS, op. cit.

71. S. FOTHERGILL and G. GUDGEON, *Unequal Growth: Urban and Regional Employment Change in the U.K.* (Heinemann, 1982).

72. Reported in 'Going beyond the problem areas of Strathclyde region', *Planning*, no. 413, 10 April, 1981.

73. D. WATTS, 'Planning: a key to innovation in industry?', *The Planner*, 63(6), 1977.

74. Reported in *Planning*, vol. 525, 1 July 1983.

75. Office of Population Censuses and Surveys, 'Recorded internal population movements in Great Britain, mid-1981 to mid-1982', January 1983.

76. W. LEVER, 'Employment change in urban and regional systems; the U.K. case', Department of Ecology and Social Research, University of Glasgow Urban and Regional Discussion Paper 28, 1978.

77. See for instance C. MASON, 'New Manufacturing firms in South Hampshire: Survey results', Department of Geography, University of Southampton Paper 13, 1982.

78. British Road Federation, *Impact of the M25: Summary of Conference Papers and Discussion*, October 1980.

79. See for instance J. PATTEN, 'Villages in Suburban London', *Geographical Magazine*, vol. 48(12), 1976; also G. CHERRY, 'Homes for heroes — semis for by-passes: how housing for the masses developed between the two wars', *New Society*, vol. 47, no. 852, 1 February, 1979.

80. P. HALL, *et al.*, *The Containment of Urban England Vols. I and II* (Allen and Unwin, 1973).

81. D. G. GREGORY, 'Green Belt policy and the conurbation', in F. E. JOYCE (ed.), *Metropolitan Development and Change: The West Midlands — A Policy Review* (London, 1973).

82. A full account is given by J. H. JOHNSON and J. SALT, 'Population redistribution policies in Great Britain', in J. W. WEBB, A. NAUKKARINEN, and L. A. KOSINSKI (eds.), *Policies of Population Redistribution* Geographical Society of Northern Finland for the IGU Commission on Population Geography, Oulu, 1981.

83. See for instance P. J. CLOKE, *Introduction to Rural Settlement Planning* (Methuen, 1983); B. J. WOODRUFFE, *Rural Settlement Policies and Plans* (Oxford University Press, 1976).

84. K. YOUNG and J. KRAMER, *Strategy and Conflict in Metropolitan Housing* (Heinemann, 1978).

85. P. HEALEY, 'The implementation of selective restraint policies', Working Paper 45, Oxford Polytechnic Department of Town Planning, 1980.

86. P. HALL *et al.*, 'Policy alternatives — past and future', in P. HALL *et al.*, *The Containment of Urban England*, op. cit.

3   The Problems of Growth Management

> I am certain that one of the most crucial problems during the last quarter of the twentieth century will involve the unprecedented demand for an urban range of choice in a rural setting.
> (R.E. Pahl, 1966).

This chapter moves away from a general discussion of the dispersal process and its causes to examine the specific problems which arise in those areas experiencing dispersed urban growth. Three principal problems face the managers of growth in the outer city: social conflicts arising from the loss of farmland and cherished landscapes; social polarization arising from selective and limited allocation of private and public housing; and, finally, the political tensions created by the provision of land for future developments and the rising public-sector expenditure they entail.

Environmental conflicts

The debate about whether there exists a land shortage in Britain is central to the question of how far urban development should be allowed to encroach upon farmland. Unfortunately there has been considerable disagreement among academics and government officials about the rate of agricultural–urban land transfer and about the implications that the figures have for urban planning policy.[1] Some commentators argue that the extent of land-loss has been exaggerated and, moreover, that planning control has been effective in controlling the rate of change.[2] Others claim the reverse, advocating much stronger containment within a closely defined national strategy for protecting food supplies.[3] Projection of present requirements for all types of urban and rural land into the future, based upon a variety of different assumptions, suggests that there may be a risk of land scarcity in the future, although the greater threat to farmland may come from afforestation.[4] But these claims must be balanced against the possibility that increasing agricultural yields will produce a growing surplus of food in the future.

Although concern over the question of land-loss appeared to diminish somewhat in the late 1970s when economic recession hit the construction industry, it would be short-sighted to imagine that the issue has gone away in the 1980s. The present government's desire for economic recovery (virtually) wherever it can be encouraged, combined with its more relaxed attitude towards urban development in the Green Belts,[5] undoubtedly add a new dimension to the issue of land resources. Fears have already been voiced about the relatively high proportion of new building taking place on farmland outside the main urban areas, as well as about the increased number of urban developments affecting farmland not strictly earmarked for growth in public authority plans. Evidence that the latter claim is justified comes from the record of consultations made between planning authorities and the Ministry of Agriculture, Forestry, Fisheries and Food (MAFF) whenever larger tracts of land or significant 'departures' from approved plans are involved. In 1978, the Ministry cleared plans for 9,162 ha* and opposed 2,519 ha of land. In 1981, they cleared 13,808 ha and opposed 4,934 ha. The ratio of refusals to approvals thus improved from 1:3.6 in 1978 to 1:2.8 in 1981, suggesting that the MAFF was becoming rather firmer in its policy. However,

* ha: hectare(s). 1 hectare = 2.471 acres.

total referrals rose by 7,062 ha between 1978 and 1981, an increase of 60.4 percent, while the amount of land approved rose by 4,646 ha, an increase of 50.7 percent.[6] A further source of disquiet is the possible increase in building on greenfield sites which could result if and when the recession comes to an end, resulting both from more farmland having been allocated for development and more planning applications having been granted on appeal.[7]

A conventional counter-argument to the more alarmist views pronounced on rural land-loss is the historical one which compares the much higher rate of conversion of agricultural land in the 1930s (25,000 ha per annum) with the much more limited change in the 1970s (8,000 ha per annum in 1978) — a trend which suggest that possibly only 14 percent of England and Wales will be developed by the year 2001.[8] However, some doubt about these estimates is raised by the latest available data which shows that for England alone, the average *total* loss of farmland to other uses, excluding forests, over the period 1975–80 was 18,534 ha per annum.[9] Furthermore, recent arguments about agricultural land shortage have been conducted in very general national terms without reference to intra-regional and local variations in development pressures and rates of land-use change. Although we still do not have comprehensive information for the period 1970–80, there is evidence to suggest a continuing and significant increase in the spread of agricultural land conversion well beyond the Green Belts into some rural counties hitherto largely unaffected by urban growth.

This does not imply that environmental conflict has necessarily diminished in the areas closer to the big cities. The encroachment of industrial activity of all kinds has brought with it a loss of farmland, a fragmentation of farms, and a steady deterioration in the quality of the landscape in urban fringes,[10] athough the transfer of agricultural land to urban use has been less important in the Green Belts, where planning restrictions have limited the scale of urban growth. In the urban areas changes in agricultural land use and management practices are pressing issues[11] as is the growing scale of vacant, damaged, or derelict land left behind as developers seek new sites further out.[12] While these conflicts raise important issues for land management and planning policy, they must be viewed against the great pressures for urban development which arise in lowland countryside areas well beyond the Green Belts. The increased demand for urban land in these outer metropolitan zones is partly associated with the population growth and redistribution discussed in the previous chapter, but it is also determined by the changes taking place in national economic policy which are creating new kinds of development pressure in the more attractive and accessible locations.

Robin Best's analysis of a quarter of a century of agricultural displacement helps us to see these problems in historical perspective.[13] Throughout the period 1945–70 the areas mainly affected by loss of farmland have been those closest to the big cities in a central belt of England running north-west to south-east. The rural counties in the periphery of this belt experienced only limited urban growth. Higher than average rates of farmland loss took place between 1950 and 1960 in the London region, close to the conurbation — a reflection of the earlier phase of post-war decentralization associated with suburban expansion and the building of New Towns in Hertfordshire. By the period 1962–67, however, farmland was being lost more rapidly in the outer-metropolitan counties of Hampshire, Berkshire, Northamptonshire, Essex and Kent, counties which contained the new centres of urban growth. The outer areas of Liverpool and Manchester, notably Lancashire and Cheshire, experienced rapid farmland loss in the early 1960s, mainly the result of extensive housing development on greenfield sites, as have other counties affected by population decentralization: Durham on the edge of Tyneside and Teesside, Glamorgan and Monmouthshire in South Wales, and Dumbarton, West Lothian and Midlothian in Central Scotland.

Housing is everywhere the greatest threat to agricultural land. In 1961 housing accounted for 79 percent of the land area in small towns and villages under 10,000 population and 46 percent in the majority of large and medium towns ranging in size from 20,000–500,000; transport was the second largest user of land; and land under manufacturing ranged from no more than 4–9 percent of total urban area in these settlements.[14] The types of industrial and commercial enterprise developed more recently, however, have greater space requirements. Indeed, the fastest rates of change in industrial and commercial floorspace have invariably been in the outer metropolitan districts,[15] which have attracted certain kinds of high technology industry, and where locally available labour, cheap land and motorways encourage the building of new factories and warehouses in countryside where industry had always been a small element in farmland loss. Planning authorities are also relaxing their control on the development of shopping centres. Only offices appear to prefer town centres to greenfield sites, although this depends on whether they are part of a manufacturing, retailing, or warehousing activity. The motorway networks act as a strong catalyst for new urban-industrial development, and where this is approved by the planning authorities motorways assist the dispersal process. Moreover, motorways themselves pose a major threat to the rural environment.

Local authorities are now offering extensive greenfield sites to high-technology companies seeking attractive environments and new locations for expansion,[16] (Figure 5). The aim is to develop 'science parks' on the American model, specializing in micro-electronics, robotics, computer and other forms of information technology.[17] The land-take requirements are considerable. In the North West, Merseyside's proposed Upton Science Park involves taking 20.2 ha of good quality farmland in the Green Belt. The Birchwood Science Park in Warrington New Town, opened in 1973, occupies 34.0 ha near the M6 and M62 (the built-up area itself covers only 20 percent of the site. The Aztec West industrial park adjacent to the M4/M5 interchange north of Bristol covers 67 ha of Grade 2 agricultural land and involved the purchase of 17 separate farms at a cost of £33,000 per acre. Hewlett-Packard are currently building a new factory of 125,000 sq ft. close to the M4. A 12 ha site outside Swindon has just been acquired by Thamesdown Borough Council and the Taylor-Woodrow Property Company for 34,373 square metres of high-technology research and business.[18] Many of these developments affect the corridor astride the M4 motorway between London and Bristol.[19]

There is little data to show that 'science parks' provide much employment, yet planning authorities are sometimes accused of being too restrictive towards such technological developments. Rather nearer the truth is the view that the 'science parks' have become the latest symbol of municipal *machismo*. 'Every local authority that wants to show that it is taking its unemployment problems seriously is pinning its hopes on high technology and talking of creating a science park . . . but space age factories in leafy glades may not provide the universal answer to overcoming unemployment and the recession'.[20]

New warehousing is another major consumer of land. Warehousing invariably gravitates to motorways and the most accessible locations near airports and container

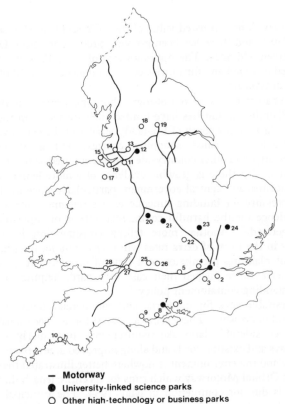

Figure 5. Science and high-technology parks

1 Brunnel University
2 Riddlesdown Quarry, Croydon
3 Woking Business Park
4 Stockley Park, West Drayton
5 Winnersh/Worton Grange, Reading
6 Whiteley Business Park
7 Chilworth (Southampton University
8 Hurn Airport
9 Holton Heath, Poole
10 Charles Cross Court, Plymouth (English Industrial Estates)
11 Birchwood, Warrington
12 U.M.I.S.T.
13 Stowell Technical Park, Salford EZ
14 Haydock Park, St. Helens
15 Upton Science Park, Wirral
16 Ashfield Hall Farm, Ellesmere Port
17 Chester Business Park
18 Lister Hills Science Park, Bradford (EIE)
19 Springhill House, Leeds (EIE)
20 Aston Science Park, Birmingham
21 Warwick University Science Park
22 Linford Wood, Milton Keynes
23 Cranfield Institute of Technology
24 Cambridge Science Park
25 Dorcan, Swindon
26 Windmill Hill, Swindon
27 Aztec West
28 Inmos

facilities. The greatest pressures again come from dynamic growth industries just beyond the Green Belt. In central Berkshire there were found to be a 100 ha of industrial and warehousing land allocated or with planning permission in 1982.[21] Indeed, warehousing floorspace has generally increased at a faster rate than manufacturing floorspace. Between 1967 and 1976 warehousing accounted for half of the additional floorspace in Avon, and the percentage change of warehouse floorspace was much higher than or manufacturing in all the outer districts of Avon.[22] One of the factors in the expansion of warehousing has been the changing nature of the distributive industry. The estimated value of the DIY retail-warehouse sector will be £1.8 billion by 1984, and there has been growing pressure to locate DIY and garden superstores on greenfield sites. The optimum size of the DIY store is considerable, especially if linked to a food and furniture store — a range between 30,000 and 100,000 sq. ft. being not untypical.[23]

The recent characteristics of out-of-town shopping centres in Britain are well documented.[24] Planning authorities have limited their dispersal on the edge of cities and towns, particularly in the south of England, because of the need to safeguard open countryside, protect established shopping centres, and avoid creating traffic congestion. Green Belt and other countryside policies are used as the main grounds for refusing permission. But there is growing evidence of a more lenient attitude on the part of local authorities and central government particularly since the late 1970s, at a time when the pressure for building superstores has remained intense.[25] One factor may be that evidence for the harmful commercial effects of superstores has proved somewhat exaggerated.[26] Another more telling consideration is that substantial financial benefits in the form of extra rates will accrue to a local authority, an added incentive to grant planning permission at a time of economic recession. Moreover, developers themselves have pushed their case very hard, helping to bring about a reversal of long-standing containment policy.[27]

The most desirable sites for industrial and commercial developments are often near new roads and motorways. These act as a catalyst for new locational pressures and themselves have considerable land-take requirements, particularly at the junctions between motorways and existing roads and along improved access roads.[28] The conflict between industry and the environment is nowhere better illustrated than in the case of the M25 London Orbital Motorway which runs for its entire length through London's Green Belt and is due for completion in May 1984. The principal industrial and commercial developments which could be attracted by the M25 are likely to be warehousing, serving national and regional markets, high-technology growth industries, especially in towns just beyond the Green Belt, offices not requiring a central London location, and hypermarkets, superstores and discount shopping stores.[29] The area around the south-western and western sections of the M25 is likely to come under greatest pressure (Figure 6) and it may be difficult, because of the fragmented nature of the Green Belt, to resist development there. In contrast, the area around the section between the A2 and the A3 may better withstand the intense pressure for offices, hotels and warehousing because of the strong restraints consistently applied to local authorities in this area.

The example of the M25 emphasizes that conflict over the environment is a result of the changing balance between economic development pressures and the long-standing commitment to containment in the form of Green Belt and agricultural land protection policies. Building the motorway in the Green Belt was perhaps inevitable given the need to avoid the destruction of properties in inner London and to catch most of the traffic circulating reasonably close to London. There may even be advantages for residents far enough away from the M25 not to be affected by noise or fumes. Moreover, it is surely misguided to take a Canute-like attitude to the M25 since it has enormous economic potential. Some land might be released from the Green Belt without it being too detrimental, and there could be 'green' uses in the Green Belt that would arguably help upgrade already damaged areas.[30] But this is unlikely in the absence of any integrated regional planning for transport and land, and in view of the pressures on local authorities to release land for substantial housing development in the Green Belts.

Conflicts over the environment cannot be viewed in isolation from the history of planning in the urban region. Strong post-war containment policies limited the physical urbanization of the countryside, diminished the aggregate scale of farmland loss, and channelled new development to selected areas. Green Belts and Areas of Outstanding Natural Beauty have seen only limited new building. But the most worrying development in the outer city is that local planning has become a less secure framework for managing urban change.[31] Present policies are clearly not providing the defence against the physical urbanization of the countryside which Peter Hall showed they did so convincingly during the 1950s and 1960s when prevailing economic conditions were much better.[32] Some would argue that today the main aim of planning should be to facilitate economic growth rather than protect the environment. Containment is no longer a relevant response to economic and technological change. If planners limit the growth of economically successful areas, the prosperity of those areas may simply wither away.

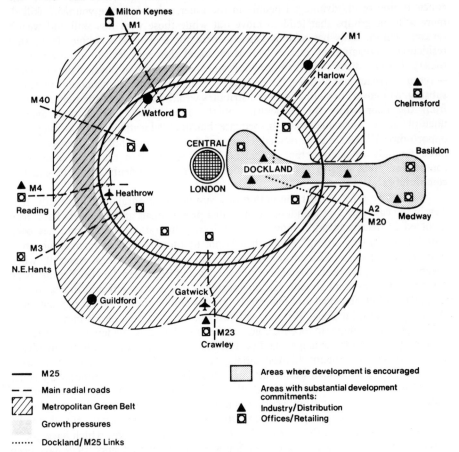

Figure 6.   Environmental impact of the M25

Of course, too much control may wreck the chances for economic recovery, but too little could have serious environmental consequences — a return to rapid urban sprawl, a further loss of agricultural land, and permanent damage to cherished landscapes, indeed all the things that prompted the need for a town and country planning system in the first place. Parallels with the 1930s are appropriate. In 1931 the government sought to balance the budget and hold down interest rates, causing a surge in house building that 'set loose a building boom, the semi-detached results of which ring the towns of southern England'.[33] It is not accidental that the housebuilders, acutely aware of the present government's interest in securing an end to recession, are putting intense pressure on the Secretary of State to review Green Belt policy, and that the fear of a new wave of suburban conflict in the Green Belts should now become an issue of paramount political significance.

Social polarization

Potentially the most serious consequence of decentralization has been the concentration of disadvantaged people in the inner cities. It is the younger, skilled, more affluent groups that tend to move out while those with less skill and wealth remain behind. This has serious consequences for society as a whole. Increasing residential segregation by race as well as by social class may lead to a more divided society. Because dispersed urban growth is an expensive form of physical development — requiring roads and utilities, for example — it requires increasing amounts of public subsidy. Moreover, this effectively redistributes wealth in favour of the rich and away from the poor while the difficulties of the inner cities (higher than average unemployment associated with inadequate housing, educational and employment opportunities)[34] remain to be tackled. However, this catalogue of urban ills may lead us quite wrongly to assume that the dispersal of wealth into the inner and outer commuting areas creates few social problems for the residents living in exurban communities.

Firstly, we must correct the notion of a simple urban-rural shift in wealth. It is clearly the case that a preponderance of skilled professionals and managers have been involved in decentralization movements. Selective migration of this kind has been found around many cities,[35] although it is not ubiquitous. Skilled manual, and to a much lesser extent, unskilled workers have also moved from the cities, especially when cheaper housing has been available as in the New and Expanded Towns. Yet the social composition of migrant streams has obviously had the general effect of increasing the proportion of professional and managerial groups among the employed population in the outer commuting areas. But over emphasis on migrant households may lead us to forget *in situ* changes in occupational structure. There is evidence of increasing unemployment among managers and professionals, although admittedly the incidence of unemployment remains highest among the unskilled. Furthermore, a growing number of working women who traditionally found jobs in the outer commuting zones are finding employment more difficult there. The impact of economic recession also makes it difficult to draw simple contrasts in prosperity between inner cities and outer areas. Although many groups living in outer areas remain prosperous, this is due by and large to the fact that they are employed in service occupations, which have grown disproportionally fast in some counties; job losses in the period since 1979 have been concentrated in manufacturing counties and conurbations. When trends are examined at a sub-regional or county scale, the urban-rural differential appears to be marginal — suggesting a greater range of variation in prosperity within the outer cities than either between inner and outer areas or the South East and Scotland.[36] On the other hand, there is still little evidence to suggest that the position of the outer areas has worsened in aggregate terms relative to inner city areas. On the contrary, comparison of changes in the distribution of low-income households — those falling into the lower quartile of the national income distribution — shows that over the period 1953–80 the position of all rural districts improved steadily. In the 1950s the highest concentrations of low-income households were found in rural districts. Even in the mid-1960s Greater London had a lower proportion of low-income households than did the surrounding parts of the region; after this the position was reversed. Over time it seems that the population living outside the conurbations has shown increasing prosperity.[37]

Secondly, the outer city is more heterogeneous in social structure and suffers from a greater degree of social polarization and social segregation than is commonly supposed. While it has generally been true that the poorer groups have been barred from access to the private housing market, considerable public-sector housing provision in overspill schemes and New Towns, and the existence of an admittedly small and declining rented sector, have 'opened up' some parts of the outer city.[38] The socio-economic characteristics of the population vary in different areas depending in part on the scale, rate and social composition of in-migrants. In Cheshire, employers, managers and professional groups accounted for only 14.5 percent of the population in 1971, whereas skilled manual and unskilled groups represented 35.3 percent. Variations within the county are great, with much higher proportions of semi-skilled and unskilled groups being attracted to cheap housing in the New Towns of Warrington and Runcorn and the expansion schemes at Widnes, Winsford and Ellesmere Port. In contrast, 23.8 percent of the population of Macclesfield District were professional workers, attracted from Greater Manchester by the availability of good quality private housing.[39] Broader patterns of social segregation can conceal more detailed changes within the outer city. Great social contrasts may be found in the same locality and may take the form of a physical separation between areas of new housing lived in by new higher-status groups and council housing inhabited by 'local' working-class groups, although it may be less easy to see these where little or no recent housebuilding has occurred.[40] Household segregation varies by house-type and car ownership between those groups who have capital and can afford to buy a house of 'character' or acquire large old houses in the countryside, those who can afford a three-bedroomed semi-detached house and run a car, and those in a similar situation but with no car.[41] Segregation by housing tenure is the common pattern within villages where some public housing exists alongside private housing.[42]

Furthermore, it is difficult to see a common pattern of social polarization in outer-metropolitan areas experiencing different histories of population and employment decentralization. It may make sense in the leafy exurban villages of the outer South East to define segregation by the increasing dominance of professional and managerial groups, but clearly it is less appropriate to do so where the social structure is weighted towards the skilled-manual working-class groups, as in several industrial counties like Leicestershire, Staffordshire, Glamorgan or Durham and more locally, where the decentralization of manufacturing and services jobs has occurred. Many empirical studies of social polarization have ignored these situations, dwelling almost exclusively on the South of Britain, forgetting the variety of social conditions surrounding the cities of Wales, the Midlands and North West of England (where the pattern of commuting has been spreading outwards beyond the Green Belts into Lancashire and Cheshire).

Thirdly, it is undoubtedly true that limited-growth settlements in certain parts of the outer-metropolitan areas have in recent years shown signs of increasing prosperity associated in general with upward housing mobility. Studies of household mobility carried out between 1975 and 1980 in thirty villages near Leicester, a non-Green Belt Area which had experienced a growth of population of just under 5000 between 1971 and 1981, revealed a high degree of heterogeneity in social polarization.[43] Professional and managerial occupations were dominating mobility into the smallest villages, where growth had been strictly limited, and there was a tendency for these groups to gain at the expense of skilled and semi-skilled households. The latter were segregated off in the larger settlements and had become marginally more dominant in these. The process of social and spatial selection occurring in many other commuting areas was affected by the allocation of private and public housing, which has tended to be more generous in larger settlements in contrast to the smallest villages where planning restrictions have forced up house prices and encouraged the migration of higher income groups who buy up older 'desirable' properties. Only in medium-sized villages was the balance between social groups found to have improved somewhat — but mainly because they were dominated by less affluent groups at the start of the study.

The process of 'gentrification' is hence not entirely an inevitable one. The scale and rate of population change in rural settlements is strongly influenced by planning policy and constraints on access to housing in the private and public sectors. The combination of variable scales of land release (and their consequent effects on house prices) and variable degrees of estate development (and their effects on the quality of environment and house-type) are critical influences on patterns of social segregation, and must surely continue to be so given a continuation of past planning strategies in the commuting hinterlands. Improved opportunities for lower-income households to move into these restricted-growth areas must lie in adjustments to the supply of private housing and the provision of public housing. The Leicestershire research showed how both conditions could effect a degree of downward social mobility in both large and small villages. However, the degree of reduced social polarization which can be achieved under the stringent planning condition operating in other inner and outer commuting areas is probably more limited. Studies in 1960s of social segregation in the Surrey villages of the London metropolitan Green Belt revealed 'little evidence of higher class residents giving way to lower class residents even in the villages with the cheapest house prices . . . the invasion process is still entirely uni-directional as residents from higher status classes take over the homes of lower class groups.[44] Studies of social change in 13 West Suffolk villages between 1965 and 1976 showed little noticeable reduction in social polarization in villages that had known a disproportionate increase in housebuilding.[45] In other areas constrained by a legacy of strong planning control, it seems reasonable to expect gentrification to continue for some time and that adjustments to planning policy will have only a marginal indirect influence upon the degree of social polarization.[46]

The selective in-migration of non-local population into smaller towns and villages near the cities has had enduring social consequences. Relatively affluent commuters and retirees have effectively changed the social structures there by ousting established residents and creating a demand for private dwellings that has made it much more difficult for local people to acquire a house if they want to stay. Furthermore, the rapid increases of population in larger settlements have put strain on social services, disturbed the balance of provision, and deprived some groups of access to services. The problems of planning a more equitable distribution of housing and service provision are indeed massive ones. Access to housing for lower income groups has, if anything, become more difficult; they have to compete with other commuters who can afford more expensive housing. Some lower-paid, key service workers cannot compete in Green Belt towns with London commuters for owner-occupied housing, though the former are 'reluctant commuters' who have moved out from the cities not because they want to live in the countryside but simply because they could not afford a house in the city.[47] The decline of the rented sector, both public and private, further exacerbates polarization. While the inner city suffers too, the outer cities contain a much smaller initial base of rented housing, and so even slight losses will have a relatively large impact on the housing mobility of lower-income groups. Council housing made up 32 percent of the housing stock of the United Kingdom in 1980 (compared with 13 percent in the privately rented sector and 55 percent owner occupied), but the proportion was generally much lower in shire counties adjacent to the large cities — for example, in April 1981 it was 16.6 percent in Lancashire, 23.9 percent in Cheshire, 17.0 percent in Surrey, 18.8 percent in West Sussex, 23.9 percent in South Glamorgan, and 22.6 percent in Warwickshire [48] though it was higher in the North East and central Scotland. The rate of council house building has not been sufficient to offset the decline in the privately rented sector nor prevent a gradual decline in council housing as a proportion or rural stock. The end of planned overspill schemes brought about a cut-back in public housing in the New and Expanded Towns, and the government policy of selling off council housing is also having its effect. Between 1980 and 1981 sales or leases of local authority dwellings, including in the New Towns, accounted for more than 2 percent of total local authority-owned housing stock in Northhamptonshire, Berkshire, Buckinghamshire, Essex, Kent, Cheshire and Lancashire — a much higher relative rate of sale than in the conurbations. Bearing in mind the discrepancy between average incomes and average house prices in these outer commuting areas, particularly in the outer South East, it seems likely that low-income groups will face increasing difficulty in becoming owner-occupiers.

The problems of providing houses for local people in the smallest villages are made more difficult because public housing is invariably concentrated in the larger settlements, where there has been a virtual moratorium on council building in recent years. Also as the council housing stock is sold, it proves difficult to replace it with new low-cost housing settlements where environmental and planning restrictions restrict land available for new building. The high price of existing stock prevents potential first-time buyers from being able to purchase locally, and the council houses which are sold may not go to local people at all. Moreover, there is evidence that council houses are generally acquired by the younger and more affluent tenants, with the result that spatial and social segregation between tenants and owner-occupiers is likely to increase. Although the resale of properties can be controlled by local authorities in certain designated areas like Areas of Outstanding Natural Beauty, many of the more attractive commuting villages lie outside such restricted zones; indeed there is some evidence to suggest that it is precisely in these villages where most sales of council stock occur.[49]

Clearly the relative position of lower socio-economic groups depends upon government support for low-cost housing initiatives and local authority housebuilding.

A variety of different measures now available offer the prospect of some mitigation of social polarization in the outer cities. There is evidence to show that more developers are now willing to build starter homes for single people on lower incomes, although the pattern of supply is still dominated by three-bedroomed or four-bedroomed housing especially in smaller villages. Undoubtedly, the greatest need for housing exists among one-person and two-person households especially those which are young and elderly. Recent household projections by the Department of Environment and Office of Population Census and Surveys, based on the 1979 mid-year estimates, forecast the formation of 505,000 new households in the Rest of the South East (outside Greater London) between 1981 and 1991, of which 275,000 will be one-person households (54 percent), 183,000 will be married-couple households (36 percent), and the remaining 40,000 will be lone parents households (8 percent). Yet while it is expected that 540,000 new dwellings are to be built over that period only 79,800 (15 percent) will be one-bedroomed, 121,000 (22 percent) will be two-bedroomed, and the majority, 339,000 (63 percent) will be three or more bedrooms in size. 'Having regard to the evidence that most single people (and many older small households) find themselves excluded from owner occupation, it becomes clear that the majority of the new housing to be provided in ROSE [the Rest of the South East] during the decade will not meet the majority of additional needs.'[50] A static population with a growing number of small households will pose a major challenge to housebuilding policy in the outer cities, and the degree to which social polarization can be alleviated will partly depend upon the response.

A reduction in house prices could be affected by a relaxation of restraint in planning policies, the substantial opening up of the Green Belt, or the greater provision of housing in smaller villages in non-Green Belt areas. Containment policy has by and large been socially regressive, permitting the richer groups to purchase housing and leaving the poorer residents unable to move. It could be argued that if housebuilders are successful in forcing greater releases of housing land in the outer city, as they appear to have been so far, it could have a beneficial effect on lower-income groups, who would then be able to afford the cheaper housing provided. The argument turns, however, on the structure of local housing markets and the scale of development proposed. It might not be the case that prices would fall, but simply that developers would build more exclusive houses at the upper end of the market at lower densities and to a higher specification. In this situation, additional speculative housing would not lead more first-time buyers into the outer city unless there were to be careful control of housing mix by the planning authorities, and it is very unlikely that stronger controls of that kind would be politically acceptable at present. DoE Circular 22/80 makes it clear that this aspect should be left up to the developers themselves to determine.[51] Speculative housing could reduce social polarization in a relative sense by allowing a greater number of the 'middle bands' of the workforce to gain access to cheaper housing. But these are most likely to include the intermediate, skilled, and possibly semi-skilled groups rather than those in greatest housing need. The effect would probably be to reinforce the tendency for the more highly-skilled groups to move out. Some smaller settlements might benefit from a more integrated social structure. But the problem of housing need would not necessarily be touched.

Finally, we must not forget the impact which social polarization has upon the problem of providing social services and upon relative access to them. In the first place segregation between rich and poor is frequently associated with segregation between old and young. Growth settlements have attracted lower-income and generally younger families, as in many overspill housing areas, whereas higher-income and generally older households are drawn to the more exclusive settlements. Decisions to provide or not to provide educational services, for example, are closely related to these socio-demographic patterns. School closure is less likely to occur in rapidly growing settlements; indeed new schools may need providing. In contrast, primary schools in Green Belts are at risk because constraints on new housing have limited the possibility of increasing the size of young population. There may hence be an argument for further dispersal of urban development based upon the case for maintaining small schools, although the average unit costs of school provision rises where the number of pupils falls below 50 because the staffing and capitation allowances are higher per pupil in small schools.[52] Some observers argue that schools, health clinics, and local shops have been declining in number regardless of population size or the scale of new development permitted in settlements, a reflection of service rationalization which cannot be affected by adjustments in housing supply.[53] There may well be some truth in this, although clearly some services — shops for instance — are sensitive to changes in the scale and structure of local demand. Nevertheless, it is predominately the higher-income, more mobile, and older populations that have decentralized, and they demand a different and lower level of service provision than their youthful counterparts in the growth centres.

Access to social services is a problem for lower-income, and for some higher-income groups, wherever they live.[54] It cannot be assumed that the greater distances which people have to travel in the metropolitan villages impose greater hardship since distance is relative to age and social class. Older people will generally make less frequent visits for shopping and services than younger people. Similarly, high-status groups will travel further for non-durables. The number of cars in the household and the availability of local public transport will determine which members of a family have access. There is a complex association between frequency of use of services and variables such as distance from large centres, social class and life-cycle.[55] Over time, education, health and transport service policies have proved somewhat rigid in location. The larger metropolitan settlements have generally gained facilities at the expense of the smaller, but ironically there is likely to be greater relative deprivation in the 'key' centres.[56] This is because their rapid build-up of population has increased the number of young and old who require support. Similar problems were associated with the early phases of the New and Expanded Towns,[57] but special arrangements have made it easier to improve access to services than in the smaller overspill settlements. Problems of service access would hence appear to depend quite strongly on the scale, rate and type of housing provision in so far as this effectively changes socio-demographic structures.

A solution for the problems of social polarization will not be easy. The relaxation of planning controls, more flexible approaches to housing programmes, and, possibly, new initiatives in service provision, are all likely to be necessary. Undoubtedly, the question of the relative spatial concentration or dispersal of populations is important, although not the only factor. Greater dispersal is unlikely to improve social mix if nothing is done to improve the availability of low cost housing; and while a lower-income and more youthful population might stimulate the retention of existing services and the provision of new ones, this would not necessarily be the case. Either way, very complex political judgements are involved in securing a more equitable social balance in the provision of housing and services. Greater dispersal might involve the continued physical urbanization of the countryside and thus add to conflict over the environment especially over loss of food resources and wasteful land utilization, bearing in mind inner city vacant land. Furthermore, substantial and even small-scale speculative housing developments already face local political opposition and might simply reinforce existing patterns of social segregation. Some of these environmental objections might be overcome through, for example, demanding higher standards of residential design and layout in smaller metropolitan villages. But this would require stronger controls over developers, tend to raise development costs, and increase social polarization through its inflationary effect on house prices. A further consideration for central and local government must be the public and private sector costs involved in securing a more dispersed pattern of housing and the political tensions that too could create.

Political tension

The balance between preservation of existing amenities and the provision of land for future development has invariably fallen down on the side of preservation in rural areas. Locally elected representatives are often anti-development in attitude. Conservative councillors set out to defend existing ratepayers against newcomers, especially in the South East, and Labour councillors in the North have jealously guarded their territories. Each approach has tended to encourage social polarization since the poor are thereby denied access to the countryside. Conflict over the environment has been kept in check because growth has been kept at bay.

Although one might take issue on social grounds with the Conservative stance to the pressures for dispersed growth, and attempt for economic reasons to bring about a more permissive response to land provision in restraint areas, it has to be acknowledged that shire counties surrounding the big cities face a number of obvious political difficulties in meeting the challenges for more growth being made by central government, the districts, and the housebuilders. The first difficulty is the long-standing history of containment. Containment has received virtually unanimous political support at both local and national level from Conservative and Labour Councillors alike. The Green Belts have for this very reason become in 'truth, the jewel in the crown of the planning system, and the envy of the world'.[58] To change the balance in favour of development inside and outside the Green Belts may be to open up the floodgates still further, provoking enormous opposition and threatening the balance of political power in the outer cities. The second difficulty is that when councils are faced with the option of adding to the already considerable scale of development in 'growth locations' they must take into account the rising cost of providing the necessary social infrastructure, bearing in mind future rates of population growth and their own desire to cut back public expenditure. The third, and related difficultly is that they must satisfy themselves that these public social costs can be met — clearly a difficult task in view of diminishing resources and recent government cutbacks in financial support. Many councils have achieved considerable economies in local government. Councils located in potentially the most dynamic growth areas of Britain feel an obligation to provide land and buildings for industrial production. It is perhaps not surprising that local political opposition should have surfaced in the shire counties, which have to bear the brunt of the pressure for dispersed urban growth, nor that relations between local (county) and central government have reached an all-time low, especially counties who long felt they had political support for urban containment.

The land issue has been fully exploited by the housebuilders. They claim they have a powerful case based upon the intransigence of the county authorities over the release of land, the lack of suitable land already allocated, and short term blockages to the exploitation of inner city sites.[59] The developers also claim delay in bringing forward land for public housing that might otherwise be available for private development. The developers' allegations about insufficient land release are not confined to Green Belts, but these are obvious targets because at a time when house prices are rising again and other sites within the conurbations are more expensive to develop, they present opportunities for considerable speculative development. It is of course no accident that greenfield sites are favoured by private housebuilders — and successive governments have encouraged construction by issuing many guidelines to local authorities containing a presumption in favour of development. Central government may also be blamed for raising political tension in the outer cities by its decision to abolish the development land tax by which the previous Labour government had tried to contain speculative land deals. Notwithstanding the rationale behind recent events, the developers' case for releasing greenfield sites in the restraint areas is not clear cut.

The main debate should focus on the degree to which local planners have already been permissive within the Green Belts. The original boundaries were drawn to allow for considerable expansion of large villages and the 'infill' of smaller ones on 'white' land. These areas have been substantially developed. But other open land covered by Green Belt notation has also seen development granted, including after appeal. Green Belt policy, measured in terms of the amount of land released or population change, has not always been effective.

In the London Green Belt very substantial growth took place between 1951 and 1961 in the inner ring (averaging about 14 miles around the edge of London and including almost the whole of the approved Green Belt). Between 1966 and 1971 this inner ring accounted for nearly 40 percent of all population growth in the Outer Metropolitan Area (extending 30–40 miles out). In the period 1971–1974 just over 10 percent of the total acreage approved for housing in the South East outside Greater London (40,000 acres) fell within the originally approved Green Belt and a further 14 percent occurred in the extended Green Belt ring — a total of 24 percent (9,674 acres). It might be expected that the bulk of this development would take place on land without a Green Belt notation, and in fact it did; however, 9 percent was approved on land which was strictly Green Belt.[60] Evidence from the West Midlands covers the slightly earlier period 1968–1973, and includes a smaller corridor of land extending south-west from Birmingham through the Green Belt to the area beyond, including part of an Area of Outstanding Natural Beauty. Here the position was different, with approximately 9 percent of all land on which planning permission for housing was granted falling into the 'white land' category and 12 percent in the Green Belt. Looked at in the context of the study area as a whole, the figure of 12 percent (63.3 ha) represents a considerable relative increase in residential development and subsequent population growth, assuming average residential densities.[61]

One of the underlying problems has been the general trend for planning permission to outrun housing completions especially in greenfield locations. In 1976 there were reported to be at least 400,000 outstanding planning permissions for dwellings in the South East outside Greater London, tending to vitiate any overall restraint policies both inside and outside the Green Belts.[62] Similarly, the legacy of earlier planning permissions in some districts within Greater Glasgow is likely to make it very difficult to step development in the outer commuting areas, at least over the short term, despite a reported increase in the number of planning approvals and dwelling completions on vacant and 'infill' land.[63] Local exceptions to blanket Green Belt controls have become more commonplace; while they do not open the floodgates, they have allowed a considerable volume of small-scale building entirely in restraint areas.[64] Until the late 1970s there was slight evidence of any general shortage of available land, although it is true that housebuilders' views were not always closely monitored at this time. The more recent post-1979 surveys of land availability, conducted jointly by builders and planners, indicate no compelling case for releasing more land in the London Green Belt.[65]

Other arguments against releasing more land for housing in Green Belts bear examination. It threatens to place a great burden on the provision of social services at a time of financial stringency. There is a danger too that in the absence of any commitment to regional planning, infrastructure provision and countryside policy will be uncoordinated between adjoining authorities. Opposition to growth among the residents of the inner commuting areas is likely to surface under the threat of any substantial release in Green Belts, just as it has done in those outer commuting areas, like central Berkshire, where substantial development has been a long-established planning commitment. If the balance were to tip too far towards the developers it would surely be pious to hope that 'the skills of this generation of planners and architects could make certain that the hideous inter-war urban sprawl was never repeated again'.[66] Indeed in the long run the developers themselves might lose the chance of realizing the speculative gains they now enjoy under (relatively) strong planning control.

Equally forceful if belated anti-growth arguments spring from the massive public expenditure involved in meeting the pressures of urban development in the New and Expanded Towns and other growth settlements beyond the Green Belts. The official end of planned decentralization has not meant the end of conventional planning policies for concentrating major development into large compact settlements rather than allowing it to disperse more widely among smaller ones. Indeed many New and Expanded Towns will continue to grow substantially in the future — the only difference being that private rather than public investment will be allowed to determine the future scale of growth.[67] Also, 'growth points' still find favour in most structure plans in the context of strategic land allocations and rural settlement policy. In 1980, the Secretary of State, 'Michael Heseltine' made it known that in order to achieve savings in public expenditure, planning authorities should continue to concentrate new housing in areas with existing services and infrastructure, that is those already designated and thus committed to growth.[68] This is not the place to discuss the detailed case for planned growth. Suffice it to say that concentrated urban development has increasingly been preferred by central and local government since further marginal increases in development can be accommodated by existing public utilities (electricity, gas, water etc.) whereas dispersed greenfield sites require very substantial initial investment in water and drainage and roads prior to housebuilding, and there is always a risk that delay in building infrastructure will delay private housing construction, an increasingly important factor in the political calculus at the present time.[69]

The original selection of sites for town expansion was partly influenced by the ability of local authorities to provide the necessary services, often without much support from the 'exporting' authority. Places of medium size (20,000–50,000 inhabitants) were selected according to whether their population could be doubled without placing too much strain on services and whether new industry could be attracted to provide some financial return to the authority. Similar arguments were used in favour of much larger-scale expansion settlements with populations of 100,000 or more, as in the Mark II and subsequently Mark III New Towns. The chief advantage of planned town expansion programmes was that while the financial burden for their implementation lay with the local authority and the Development Corporation (in the New Towns), the direct and indirect costs — of land assembly, transport networks, water and sewerage facilities, new schools, clinics and day nurseries, and so on — could be met cheaply. Central government grants helped to offset the necessary expenditure. Moreover, industrial and commercial development produced new rate income, reducing the additional local expenditure required to service a larger population. However, central government has now reduced its financial support. The winding up of New Town Development Corporations has placed extra financial burden on the local councils. Ending the town expansion programme has had a similar impact. But the towns have not stopped growing and nor has the necessity for additional infrastructure spending. Furthermore government has given little indication of how this can be achieved.

With hindsight, we can see that the long term and indirect public costs of urban expansion in the outer cities were largely underestimated in the programmes for planned decentralization, a point taken up in Chapter 4. In the case of the town expansion schemes, the question of which towns should grow (and by how much) was left largely to the local authorities, with each council negotiating for what was then relatively small-scale development. Decisions about the location of New Towns were similarly constrained by local opinion. In neither case was an attempt made to coordinate plans at an intra-regional scale, with the result that the cumulative and indirect social cost of allowing so many planned growth centres in close proximity to each other are now only too obvious in the sphere of transport infrastructure. The growth of domestic and commercial traffic associated with the development of New and Expanded Towns in the counties of Buckinghamshire, Bedfordshire, Northampton and Cambridgeshire, has been so great that the entire traffic network is likely to be overloaded within ten years. The New Towns of Peterborough, Corby, Northampton, and Milton Keynes, are all located in this area (Hemel Hempstead and Stevenage are on the border) and there are several Expanded Towns too (Daventry and Wellingborough for example). Several motorways and trunk roads criss-cross the region, attracting heavy commercial goods traffic onto less important roads. The local traffic highway authorities thus face the financial burden of relieving congestion created by both through and local traffic. Planned county council expenditure (capital and current) on roads in the affected counties between 1979 and 1984 was estimated at 1977 prices to be in the order of £126 millions,[70] a very considerable sum bearing in mind that in 1980–81 *total* spending on local roads in England and Wales was £1271 millions.[71].

It is not only major growth that involves rising public expenditure. The dispersal of population into many smaller towns or villages can raise the costs of service and infrastructure and adds weight to the economic arguments for limiting the spatial spread of housing estates, especially at a time of severe limitation on public expenditure. The trouble is that for a variety of reasons, some of which bear on the strategies of different authorities, it has not proved easy to relate public to private investment in settlements under great pressure for private housebuilding. In theory, the rate of new planning permissions can be controlled so that lower-cost sites are developed first. In practice, long-term infrastructure costs have not been factors that private developers have needed to account for, at least while the public sector paid the bill for off-site water, sewerage and roads. This is probably one reason why applications in supposedly restricted areas have remained at such a high level. Nor, it should be added, has the lack of infrastructure always been used by planning authorities as a primary determining reason for refusing permission for development.[72] The need to economize on construction costs has forced private and public developers to look much more carefully at the question of infrastructure in recent years. District councils have been placed in an increasingly difficult position by central government which urges that applications for residential development should generally be granted unless there are overriding planning objections. Although absence of infrastructure could be a legitimate objection, and one which might be upheld on appeal, Circular 22/80 makes it clear that local authorities must not refuse permission without first negotiating with developers about the provision and financing of facilities, possibly using a Section 52 Agreement.[73] But legal and technical problems may arise that make negotiation difficult, and builders are not prepared to meet all the costs of infrastructure. One special cause for concern is that land being committed now for future development could be built on later when and if the recession ends. This would mean that some outer-metropolitan areas would suffer from excessive overload.[74] The likelihood of such infrastructure shortfalls must surely remain a possibility given the extent of housing land allocation recently approved by the Secretary of State, often well in excess of proposals in structure plans which were presumably predicated on the need to balance future population growth with the existing and planned capacity of infrastructure networks.

Political tension between local and central government must grow unless the latter shows a greater willingness to help pay the cost of concentrated and dispersed growth in the outer cities. As long as central government could raise the essential finance from taxes, the authorities did not need to grumble too much; but with national economic recession and the cuts in public spending by government, they have a stronger case to put, especially since they can claim to be relatively low spenders and to have fulfilled many of the rigorous targets imposed on them by recent DoE policy. Despite its insistence that local councils should implement national economic strategy, and that economic and employment-generating developments should take priority,[75] central government has backed away from the financial implications involved. Admittedly, the introduction of the block grant system of central financing produced a sharp reduction in the relative level of per capita aid to the inner areas, which favoured the shire counties.[76] But this hardly compensates for the rising direct and indirect public costs associated with the massive redistribution of population taking place in the outer areas. Little wonder that political protest is fierce,[77] or that when local pressure groups oppose urban growth on environmental grounds, the financial implications are very much in the minds of objectors.

Conclusion

The pressures for dispersal are strong and growing, partly in response to economic recession. The key question for government is whether dispersal is the *sine qua non* for future economic growth. The only growing sectors are the tertiary and quaternary ones. Since in the main these require the most skilled and educated labour force, and it is the outer city which can supply these, it would appear logical that industrial development should be encouraged there rather than anywhere else. But there are two cautions to this argument. First, although these sectors could expand more if allowed to do so, there is no guarantee that employment growth would result. Indeed, new factories, warehouses and 'science parks' are unlikely to produce more than a marginal increase in the rate of job growth. This raises a more serious and fundamental philosophical objection to 'growth at any price'. The high technology route to growth implies a diminishing workforce in the production of high value goods, and can never be, of itself, or for very long, an acceptable or sufficient political goal. Second, it is important not to forget the social costs which arise from economic growth in the outer city: the physical urbanisation of the countryside, increased social polarization, and massive public sector expenditure. It would be wrong to overemphasize the importance of economic growth as a solution to social, environmental and political issues. In theory, long-term recovery might permit greater public expenditure on housing, jobs and transport, thus making it possible to plan for dispersal in an acceptable way, but in reality one suspects that economic growth strategy will come too late to solve the problems facing planners in the outer city, which are growing daily more acute.

Although employment-generating development might seem to represent the greatest challenge to urban containment, we must not lose sight of the fundamental importance of housing development. Housebuilding programmes encouraged population dispersal *in advance* of employment decentralization, and have since been actively managed by central and local government. The ending of the publicly planned overspill scheme does not mean that housing could not be used as a lever for the management of dispersal. Moreover, in some respects, socio-demographic rather than economic change is the more potent cause of the environmental, social and political conflicts outlined in this chapter. Housebuilding has stimulated in-migration. Housing rather than industry accounts for the greater loss of farmland. Speculative housing has tended to exacerbate social polarization within the outer city and between inner and outer areas. The resulting population growth has put pressure on social services and infrastructure, thus raising public expenditure. Of course, land for housebuilding need not be released; a more equitable mix of housing types and tenures could be provided; and the social costs of community development could be reduced or spread over a much longer time span. Public policies for the containment of housing are as necessary as those for the containment of industry if the adverse social consequences of dispersal are to be avoided. But for these things to happen there would have to be a clearly defined national consensus in favour of restraint and conservation. It is by no means clear that the state planning strategies now being developed are moving in this direction. We must now turn to these and consider why this should be so.

Notes

1.   A. W. ROGERS (ed.), *Urban Growth, Farmland Losses and Planning*, Rural Geography Study Group (Institute of British Geographers, 1978).

2.   R. H. BEST, 'The extent and growth of urban land', *The Planner*, vol. 62, 1976; and 'Agricultural land loss — myth or reality?', *The Planner*, vol. 63, 1977.

3.   See the writings of A. COLEMAN, 'Is Planning really necessary?', *Geographical Journal* vol. 142, 1976; 'Land use planning: Success or failure?', *Architects Journal*, vol. 165, 1977; 'The countryside endangered', *Country Life*, 2 July 1981.

4.   Centre for Agricultural Strategy, *Land for Agriculture*, C.A.S. Report 1, 1976; *Strategy for the U.K. Forest Industry* C.A.S. Report (University of Reading, 1980).

5.   Department of Environment, *Land for Housing*, Draft Circular, July 1983.

6.   Council for Protection of Rural England, letter from the Director to the Rt. Hon. Peter Walker, Minister of Agriculture, Fisheries and Food, 26 August 1982; reported in 'More farmland lost to urban sprawl', *Times*, 30 August 1982.

7.   M. ELSON, 'Farmland loss and the erosion of planning', *Town and Country Planning*, vol. 50(1) 1981.

8.   For a full discussion of the land issue see R. BEST, *Land Use and Living Space* (Methuen, 1981).

9.   *Hansard*, House of Commons Written Answer, HC Deb Col 128, 6 May 1982.

10.   M. ELSON, *The Urban Fringe: Open land policies and programmes in the Metropolitan Counties*, Report commissioned by Countryside Commission, December 1977; also M. ELSON, 'Research review: land use and management in the urban fringe', *The Planner*, vol. 65, no. 2, 1979.

11.   See for instance S. RETTIG, 'An investigation into the problems of urban fringe agriculture in a Green Belt situation', *Planning Outlook*, vol. 19, 1976; N. LOW, 'Farming and the Inner Green Belt', *Town Planning Review*, vol. 44, 1973; R. MUNTON, 'Agricultural land use in the London Green Belt', *Town and County Planning*, vol. 50(1), 1981.

12.   See for instance G. MOSS, *Britain's Wasting Acres: Land Use in a Changing Society* (Architectural Press, 1980).

13.   R. BEST, op. cit., chapter 7.

14.   R. BEST, ibid, p. 68.

15.   Department of Environment, *Commercial and Industrial Floorspace Statistics England 1977-1980*, No. 9. (London HMSO).

16.   J. WILLIAMS, *A review of Science Parks and High Technology Developments* (Drivars Jones Planning Consultants, 1982).

17.   G. STEELEY argues that Software Valley exists; 'the Thames valley is replacing California as a focus of world growth. Silica valley is being challenged by software valley'. 'Information technology: Supply and demand', *Town and Country Planning* vol. 51, no. 8, September 1982.

18.   See the report 'Business Park at Swindon', *Planning Bulletin*, 17 September 1982.

19.   See for instance 'Britain's sunrise strip', *Economist*, 30 January 1982; 'Western corridor: a look at why high technology companies are being drawn to locations west of London along the route of the M4 motorway', *The Times*, 30 June 1983.

20. H. BAXTER, 'Sunrise Parks', *Local Government News*, June 1982.

21. Standing Conference on London and South East Regional Planning, *The Impact of the M25*, Report by the Industry and Commerce Working Party of the Regional Monitoring Group, SC1618R, January 1982.

22. Avon County Council, *County Structure Plan: Situation Report, Employment* (Avon C.C., May 1976).

23. See report on 'The location of DIY retail warehouses', *Surveyor*, vol. 5, 1980.

24. See for instance The Unit for Retail Planning Information, 'Hypermarkets and Superstores: Report of a House of Commons Seminar', May 1976; and P. M. JONES, 'Trading Features of hypermarkets and Superstores', *Urban and Retail Planning Information*, June 1978.

25. See for instance D. HARRIS, 'More big stores win planning consent', *The Times*, 8 December 1981; 'Battle of the superstores', *The Times*, 22 June 1981.

26. R. SCHILLER, 'Superstore impact', *Planner*, vol. 67, no. 2, 1981.

27. Avon County Council, *Carrefour: A Study of the Impact of a Hypermarket*. (Avon CC, 198).

28. M. BELL, *et al.*, 'Agricultural land — take for new roads', *Town and Country Planning*, vol. 46, no. 3, March 1978.

29. Nathaniel Lichfield & Partners and Goldstein Leigh Associates, *The Property Market Effects of the M25*, January 1981.

30. British Road Federation Conference, *Impact of the M25: Summary of Papers and Discussions*, (BRFC, 30 October 1980).

31. See for instance M. ELSON, 'Structure Plan policies for pressured rural areas' in A. W. GILG (ed.), *Countryside Planning Yearbook*, vol. 2 (Geo. Books, 1981).

32. Council for Protection of Rural England, *Planning — Friend or Foe?*, (CPRE, 1981).

33. 'Will the Thatcher policy mean a further ring of detached houses in exurbia?', *Guardian*, 20 July 1982.

34. Royal Town Planning Institute, 'The Planning Response to Social and Economic Change', First report of an RTPI Study Group, 1982.

35. See for instance M. BARKE, 'Some aspects of population and social change in Glasgow, 1961–1971', *Professional Geographer*, vol. 30(1), 1978.

36. A. TOWNSEND, 'The scope for intra-regional variation in the 1980s', *The Planner*, vol. 69, no. 4, July/August 1983.

37. C. G. BENTHAM, 'The changing distribution of low income households in the British urban system', *Area*, vol. 15, no. 1, 1983.

38. The effects of town expansion on housing mobility among skilled and unskilled groups is discussed in M. HARLOE, *Swindon: a Town in Transition* (Heinemann, 1975).

39. Cheshire County Council, *Structure Plan: Report of Survey Summary* (Cheshire CC, February 1977).

40. R. E. PAHL, *Urbs in Rure: The Metropolitan Fringe in Hertfordshire*, Geographical Paper No. 2, (London School of Economics, 1965).

41. P. AMBROSE, *The Quiet Revolution: Social Change in a Sussex Village, 1871–1971* (Chatto and Windus, 1974).

42. M. PACIONE, 'Differential quality of life in a metropolitan village', *Transactions of Institute of British Geographers*, vol. 5(2), 1980.

43. J. M. HERINGTON, 'Rural settlement policy and housing mobility: a discussion of research findings', Report for SSRC Department of Geography, Loughborough University, Research Paper No. 6, 1981.

44. J. H. CONNELL, 'The Metropolitan village: spatial and social processes in discontinuous suburbs' in J. H. JOHNSON (ed.), *Suburban Growth* (Wiley, 1974).

45. I. M. GILDER and B. P. McLAUGHLIN, 'Rural Communities in West Suffolk', Chelmsford, Chelmer Institute of Higher Education, 1978.

46. D. J. PARSONS, 'Rural gentrification: the influence of rural settlement planning', Department of Geography, University of Sussex, Research Paper No. 3, 1980.

47. R. E. PAHL, *Whose city? And further essays on urban society* (Penguin Books, 1975).

48. Central Statistical Office, *Regional Trends* (HMSO, 1982).

49. See for instance M. BEAZLEY *et al.*, 'The sale of council houses in a rural area: a case study of South Oxfordshire', Oxford Polytechnic Department of Town Planning, Working Paper No. 44, also D. PHILIPS and A. WILLIAMS, 'Council house sales and village life', *New Society*, vol. 58, No. 993, 1981; S. GILLON, 'Selling rural council houses', *Town and Country Planning*, vol. 50, 1981.

50. E. TURNER, 'Housing Policy — the need to think small', Unpublished Diploma thesis, Polytechnic of Central London, April 1982.

51. Department of Environment, Circular 22/80. *Development Control — Policy and Practice* (HMSO, 1982).

52. Association of District Councils, *Rural Deprivation* (ADC, September 1979).

53. M .SHAW and R. STOCKFORD, 'The role of Statutory agencies in rural areas: planning and social services', in J. M. SHAW (ed.) *Rural Deprivation and Planning* (Geo. Books, 1979).

54. M. J. MOSLEY, 'Is rural deprivation really rural?', *The Planner*, vol. 66, no. 4, p. 97, 1980.

55. The problem of access to services is discussed in T. LILLEY, 'A comparative study of the social geography of selected rural settlements in parts of Shropshire, Staffordshire and Cheshire', Unpublished M.A. thesis, Department of Geography, University of Keele, 1981.

56. G. MOSS Associates, *Rural Services: Report of a Pilot Study of Statutory Provision and Accessibility in Leicestershire* (Graham Moss, 1982).

57. G. ARMEN, 'Programming of social provision in new communities — some case studies and conclusions', *Town Planning Review*, vol. 47, no. 3, 1976.

58. Reported as 'Green Belts: a neat adjustment', *Sunday Times* leading article, 7 August 1983.

59. See for instance B.PHILLIPS, 'Should green belts change their shape?', *The Times*, 30 June 1982; 'Eyeing open spaces', *Planning Bulletin*, 30 July 1982.

60. Standing Conference on London and South East Regional Planning, *The Improvement of London's Green Belt* (SCLSERP, SC 620, July 1976).

61. Joint Unit for Research into the Urban Environment, *Land Availability and the Residential Land Conversion Process*, (University of Aston, 1974).

62. South East Joint Planning Team, *Strategy for the South East: 1976 Review* (HMSO, 1976).

63.   T. J. PARKE, 'Peripheral expansion or urban regeneration? The Strathclyde Experience', Unpublished paper, Department of Physical Planning, Strathclyde Regional Council, May 1983.

64.   These points are developed by I. GAULT, 'Green Belt policies in Development Plans', Oxford Polytechnic Department of Town Planning, Working Paper 41, 1981. See also P. HEALEY, 'Regional policies in the South East', *Town and Country Planning*, vol. 49. no. 11, December 1980.

65.   Standing Conference of London and South East Regional Planning, *Housing Land in South East England* (SCLSERP, November 1981).

66.   J. COLLINS and M. ROSS, 'Green Belts: How sacrosanct?', *Planning*, vol. 482, 20 August 1982.

67.   When the New Town Development Corporations are wound up in England, the population of the 'third generation' towns will be as follows: Northampton 170,000, Milton Keynes 150,000, Peterborough 150,000, Telford 130,000, Central Lancashire 270,000, Warrington 160,000. The figures are not regarded by the Secretary of State as targets. *Planning*, vol. 405, 13 February 1981.

68.   Secretary of State's letter to the Chairman of the Standing Conference on London and South East Regional Planning, 7 August 1980.

69.   See for instance J. GARRATT, 'The relationship between builders and statutory undertakers which provide essential services', *Building*, vol. 238, no. 7127(8), 1980; S. BLOOMFIELD, 'Problems in the pipeline', *Building*, vol. 237, no. 7109, 1979; also reported, 'Builders spot the infrastructure gap', *Planning*, vol. 428, 24 July 1981.

70.   British Road Federation, *County Roads Needs in Bedfordshire, Cambridgeshire and Northamptonshire* (BRF, 1978).

71.   Central Statistical Office, *Social Trends*, (HMSO, 1982).

72.   N. BATHER, 'The speculative residential development and urban growth', Department of Geography, University of Reading, Geographical Papers, No. 47, 1976.

73.   See for instance R. W. SUDDARDS, 'Section 52 agreements: a case for new legislation', *Journal of Planning and Environment Law*, October 1979.

74.   Standing Conference on London and South East Regional Planning, *Emerging Issues in the South East Region* (SCLSERP, SC 1640, 23 March 1982).

75.   R. COWAN, 'Mr. Heseltine's Budget', *Town and Country Planning*, vol. 50, no. 4, April 1981.

76.   P. A. WATTS, 'The new block grant and controls over local authority capital payments', *Local Government Studies*, vol. 6, 1980. For a full account of financing systems see R. BENNETT, *The Geography of Public Finance: Welfare Under Fiscal Federalism and Local Government Finance* (Methuen, 1980); and R. BENNETT, *Central Grants to Local Governments* (Cambridge University Press, 1982).

77.   Recent opposition reported in 'Tory County Councils set to revolt over spending cuts', *The Times*, 3 November 1982.

PART TWO

THE STRATEGIES

4   The Role of Central Government

> The government remains committed to the continuing protection of the Green Belts.
> They are essential to contain urban sprawl . . . but if Green Belts are to last authorities
> must make adequate provision for development.
> (Rt. Hon. Patrick Jenkin, 1983).

For at least thirty years successive British governments have advocated control over the growth and development of the outer cities. This so-called strategy of urban containment has commanded widespread support from politicians of both major parties.[1] Local authorities have sought to protect the countryside by safeguarding the better agricultural land, to conserve attractive landscapes, and to minimize public expenditure by channelling urban developments away from smaller rural settlements, all in the name of urban containment.[2] Regional urban policy has combined physical restraint with planned development of single settlements such as New and Expanded Towns. Central government, performing at times a careful balancing act between national requirements and local interests, has encouraged the shire counties to be protective whilst at the same time assisting the metropolitan authorities in their search for housing land and thus taking initiatives on land release and development that have proved unpopular with the counties.

Underpinning central government's commitment to urban containment was a belief that peripheral urban expansion should not be allowed to take place under market conditions, and that the existence of a strong yet locally accountable planning system was essential. After all, it was the failures of the market system that first alerted politicians to the importance of countryside protection — the break up of agricultural estates in the 1920s, the lowering of residential densities, the ribbon growth of housing along arterial roads leading out from the cities, and the mounting pressures for recreation in the countryside. Moreover, the absence of planning control was a factor in the rapid relative rate at which agricultural land was being lost. This was particularly high in the counties of central and southern England surrounding London and Birmingham, reinforcing public awareness of the need to protect farmland. The wartime planning legislation based on the reports of Scott, Uthwatt and Barlow stressed the need for strong national planning control to protect farmland and countryside and contain urban development, yet disperse jobs and people away from the large cities.[3] To implement such a containment policy effectively, central government clearly needed to be able both to guide and regulate local development and to coordinate and channel national expenditure into the growth locations. (It also required a regional planning dimension, but that is in an issue we turn to in the next chapter).

If the dispersal of population and employment is to be checked today, it is clearly essential for central government to play a leading role. In practice, however, containment has proved effective only in the management of the use of land.[4] In many other activities of central government, there is no obvious commitment to urban containment *per se*. The Department of Transport's motorway programme has encouraged the dispersal of industrial activity. The Department of Industry has actively promoted industrial development in the outer areas. The Department of Environment has urged a greater release of housing land and sought to assist rather than prevent private housebuilding programmes. Many commentators insist that no government agency is any longer really concerned with urban containment. 'There is clear evidence of a government philosophy which runs counter to the traditional social and environmental objectives of planning by favouring development at all costs'.[5] If this is true, it is likely to prove increasingly difficult to manage growth in the outer areas in future, let alone seek a redirection of resources to the inner cities.

The most important government agency is undoubtedly the Department of Environment since it has overall responsibility for the formulation and supervision of plans for urban development in the countryside. But there are many divisions of responsibility within the DoE, some of which are more directly concerned with infrastructure issues and investment expenditure bearing on the growth areas. Most other national ministries impinge on the spatial policies of the DoE, especially the Department of Industry and Trade (DoI), the Department of Transport (DoT) and the Ministry of Agriculture, Fisheries, Forestry and Food (MAFF), and it is relevant to examine the way in which some of their operational policies and programmes affect the DoE's attempts to manage and restrain growth. It would be misleading to argue that any one ministry has exclusively influenced peripheral urban expansion. Their cumulative impact on the dispersal process is considerable. The government's overriding preoccupation with economic regeneration is discernible in the attitude of all these different government agencies towards urban containment. Indeed, we must seriously question whether a national approach to the twin objectives of restraint and planned growth is still possible.

The Department of Environment

The DoE was created in 1970 as a super-ministry to bring together previously disparate policy in the planning of transport and local government.[6] Although potentially capable of formulating a clear and consistent strategy for the containment of urban areas in Britain, its policies for the use of land have in practice been blunted over a number of years by the force of economic and political circumstances and by problems of coordination between territorial planning objectives and other sector policies, notably those of housing, water, transport, and industry, the latter two being the responsibility of the DoT and the DoI. In some respects the DoE has acquired a more important role in economic than in spatial management through its growing involvement in the administration of local authority finance.[7]

The Department's activities are divided between the directorates of planning, inner cities and New Towns, environmental protection and rural affairs, housing and construction, water, finance, and Local Government. There is much ambivalence about the direction of policy and there are clearly problems in bringing together the separate interests involved.

The relationship between the planning of the use of land and the planning of transport, for example, has always been an uneasy one. It has not been helped by the decision in 1976 to hive off transport, an issue we take up later. Nor would it seem helpful to separate; as from 1982, the activities of the Countryside Commission. The latter has an important and direct role in the protection and management of urban fringe areas including the Green Belts and Areas of Outstanding Natural Beauty. Moreover, the Countryside Commission's remit is changing in a subtle way, with more emphasis given to local initiatives perhaps to the neglect of broader strategic issues.[8]

Yet there is a strong case for arguing that 'the changing role of statutory land use planning, possibly from that of containing urban development to one of facilitating private investment, with less locational controls, is a serious issue which the Countryside Commission should involve itself in nationally'.[9]

The relationship between the planning of the use of land and the planning of housing is similarly problematic. Responsibility for liaison with the private-housebuilding industry, mortgage finance, and policies for home ownership and low-cost housing, all rest with the DoE's directorate of housing and construction. Approval for development plans and policy on large-scale urban developments, including New Towns, lies with its planning directorate. There is actual and potential conflict between the strong encouragement being given by the government to speculative housebuilding and its expressed desire for restraint in regional and structure plans. Moreover, the overwhelming priority being given to private home-ownership makes it difficult to redress the social imbalances stemming from restrictions on housing development in some of the outer areas. Admittedly, the DoE's housing mobility scheme permits local authorities to waive their residential requirements for council-house waiting-lists and open up one percent of their stock to tenants from outside their local area. But the purpose is to foster greater mobility of labour. As a tool for relieving social hardship or enlarging the housing opportunities in the outer cities it is likely to have an extremely marginal impact.

There are also contradictions between land-use strategies and the operational programmes of the regional water authorities. These agencies, created at the time of the reorganisation of English local government in 1974, have a powerful indirect influence on the direction of future private investment in the outer cities since they control water supply, sewerage, and sewage disposal, all of which are critical to industrial expansion. The operational programmes of the regional water authorities, which are based on national spending targets and estimated regional requirements, frequently conflict with more local policies for location of development proposed by the local authorities.[10]

The present division of responsibilities within the DoE clearly makes it difficult for it to coordinate the twin policies of countryside protection and urban growth. National policy on the interrelationship between land-use, transport, housing, and other aspects of urban policy, is undeveloped. There is no national land-use plan. Advice is handed down to local authorities in the form of circulars, advice notes and other central guidance. Support or otherwise for regional policy is expressed through government statements on submitted strategies and structure plans. These may be used by different agencies in support of their proposals for restraint or for development. It is by approving or modifying structure plans and adjudicating planning appeals that the DoE exerts considerable influence on spatial change in the outer areas. The DoE may 'call-in' developments considered to be of strategic importance and will arbitrate on 'departures' from approved development plans. But appeals are much more important than 'departures'. They arise where speculative developers or property companies challenge the restraint policies of local authorities. On the other hand, the appeal decisions of the DoE reflect no clear and consistent national policy — very often they will back up the local planning authorities, but each case is dealt with on its own merits.[11] Although the Inspectorate in the Department of Environment may uphold local policy as being in line with national policy, there is recent evidence to suggest this is happening less frequently. The result is that local government policies at county and district level may be overruled by the DoE, a point to which we return in Chapter 7.

Land-use planning

The advent of the present Conservative regime in 1979 led to a shake-up of DoE planning procedures. The government's strategy was revealed in a number of ministerial speeches and the publication of several controversial circulars following the monolithic piece of legislation called the Local Government Planning and Land Act 1980. The main impact of these new measures on the outer cities has been to strengthen central government's hand in the regulation of development, but to reduce the powers of regulation in a way that assists private-sector interests.[12] In 1979 and 1980 the government introduced and promised many policies that encouraged private development in the outer areas. These included extra encouragement for private housing,[13] the sale of council housing discussed earlier, the sale of public land,[14] including the sale of the industrial and commercial assets of the New Towns,[15] and promotion by the Department of Trade of those sectors of the economy that have shown most favourable growth prospects, especially micro-electronics and other forms of high technology.

The government's re-appraisal of the public planning system has involved modifications to the local development plan system and the relaxation of planning controls associated with the transfer of planning powers from counties to districts under the 1980 Planning Act.[16]

The modifications to the development plan system are discussed fully later on in this book since they have special implications for local government strategies both at the county and district levels. DoE policy guidance was given in two circulars issued in 1977 and in 1979,[17] just before the Tories came to power. These circulars sought to speed up the system of structure and local planning which had run into difficulties after the reorganisation of local government and was now proving something of an obstacle to the achievement of the government's industrial strategy. In 1981 and 1982 the DoE continued to urge local authorities to simplify and streamline their procedures for structure and local plans in order (ostensibly) to reduce costs and enable overall savings to be made.[18] Streamlining means spending less time preparing plans, cutting back on public consultation, and reducing the number of local plans. The then Secretary of State, Mr Michael Heseltine, claimed in 1980 at the National Housing and Town Planning Conference in Harrogate that 'my purpose is not to dismantle the planning machine, but the leisurely, over-complicated, negative approach of our planning system must be changed. Planning policies must be made more responsive'. Yet what does a more responsive development plan system involve? The latest draft memorandum states that 'Structure Plans should guide social and economic change over a fairly long time and only be changed when fundamental alterations are needed'. A fundamental switch in central government policy or a failure to implement local plans, might occasion the need for such an alteration. Both conditions have become probable since the effect of the 1980 legislation has been to vest more power with central government and the districts respectively. But the DoE's reaction to structure plan alterations is by no means clear. Given the government's overriding priority of regenerating the economy, the DoE is tending to adjust global targets for housing and employment more closely to the requirements of the development industry, particularly where it feels local plans are too rigid or where development has been held back in the past. The responsiveness of structure plans is being judged by the degree to which they meet economic requirements, and modifications or alterations to structure plans are the government's main tool for achieving higher levels of private investment in the outer cities.

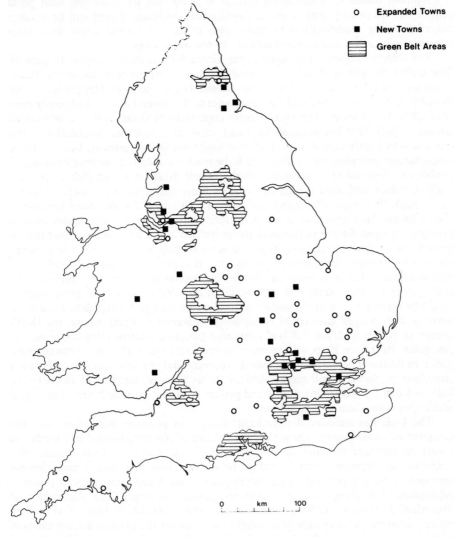

Figure 7.   Green Belts, New and Expanded Towns in England

The DoE's growth-orientated stance on development plans is not a recent one. The DoE persistently pressed for the allocation of more housing land during the late 1960s and early 1970s. Additional land was to be found in specially defined areas of the Green Belts and Areas of Outstanding Natural Beauty.[19] The 1973 guidelines on housing land clearly encouraged developers to apply for planning permission in restraint areas since they knew that central government was more likely to uphold their argument on appeal.[20] Circular 122/73 pointed out, moreover, that 'a good deal of housing land can be found by infilling of villages, and by further modest expansion'. In the late 1970s the DoE sought a more explicitly cooperative approach with the development industry. While being careful to stress that structure and local plans provide the framework within which development decisions should still be made,[21] nevertheless the modifications to these same plans cast further doubt on central government's commitment to containment in the outer areas.

The changed policy stance towards the Green Belts is most worrying (Figure 7). The DoE's attitude is shown in its modifications to structure plans in the Home Counties around London. Attempts to extend Green Belts in Hertfordshire and Berkshire have been resisted and the boundaries of the Green Belts have generally been cut back to 12–15 miles. The DoE remains committed to Green Belts but in its draft circular of July 1983 has asked all local authorities to review their boundaries.[22] The purpose is to ensure that their protection is long-term and permanent. But to achieve this, adequate provision would also have to be made for long-term development needs. Authorities were asked to consider whether small detached Green Belt areas were really necessary (although if such land was excluded they may compensate elsewhere for its loss). 'It is especially important', says the circular, 'that the inner boundaries should be carefully drawn so as not to include land which it is unnecessary to keep permanently open for the purposes of the green belt'. And there is a warning that 'if green belts are drawn excessively tightly around existing built up areas it may not be possible to maintain the degree of permanence that green belts should have'. These guidelines are widely interpreted as a further concession to development interests: 'the consequence for the countryside near many of our cities', writes one commentator, 'could be serious . . . and the ability of local authorities to restrict development on sensitive undeveloped sites could be seriously weakened'.[23] Furthermore, the DoE's change in policy in favour of less restrictive planning control casts doubt on the possibility that Green Belts will remain effective instruments of strategic containment policy in future. The desire for economic recovery and the reluctance to take power away from the districts, will make it difficult, to say the least, for the DoE to use Green Belts as a tool for redirecting public and private resources into the inner cities, a goal which they now claim to take seriously.

The DoE has announced significant changes in planning legislation since the Conservatives took power. These shift the balance of planning control still further in favour of development and against protection and restraint. They require less restrictive development control practice by district councils,[24] and a more flexible approach to the number and type of developments which can occur without planning permission. The former has provoked the greatest outcry.[25] The Association of Municipal Authorities (AMA) argued with some justification that 'it is written entirely from the point of view of developers and ignores the positive achievements of planning over the years'. Predictably the House-Builders Federation (HBF) claimed that 'this excellent document will be welcomed . . . as bringing a breath of fresh air into a planning system which was becoming increasingly negative and obstructionist'.[26] The Council for Protection of Rural England (CPRE) drew attention to the divergence of standards which would apply when nationally designated areas, like National Parks, or Areas of Outstanding Natural Beauty, are given more protection than remaining areas. Special designations will be subject to stronger controls under the Town and Country Planning, Special Development Order of 1981. Yet the status of other attractive countryside, such as the High Weald and Wiltshire Downs, proposed but are not yet approved as AONB's, remains unclear.[27] There would seem to be a presumption in favour of development over the 70 percent of England and Wales not covered by special designation. Many pleasant landscapes near large cities in lowland England fall into this category, where permission for new development will not be refused by the districts unless there are, in the words of Circular 22/80, 'clear planning objections'.

A useful indicator of the government's more relaxed policy stance is the number of appeals made by developers against refusal of permission. The DoE reject claims by the CPRE that both the number and proportion of appeals allowed has risen since 1979, but their own Chief Inspector's annual report for 1981 gives data which suggests this to be the case.[28] It is not yet clear whether developers are increasingly getting all their own way. Green Belt policy is still being upheld on appeal,[29] and keeping green wedges of open countryside between settlements is still favoured.[30] But several cities have not used Green Belts as a device for urban containment. Here, as in areas beyond the Green Belts, recent development pressures challenge the effective implementation of settlement policy — an aspect discussed in Chapter 7. Attempts to divert development away from small to larger settlements in the interests of restraint of low-growth strategies *have* been thwarted by central government on appeal. In several recent cases the local authorities' arguments have not stood up on appeal.[31] As a result, the power of the local authorities is diminished and the development of the outer city is allowed to take place without a strategic framework. This makes it more difficult to implement a spatially selective containment strategy. Restraint may no longer be sustained in the face of national and regional policy, compounding the difficulty of confining development to the growth locations. Moreover, this more incremental and short-term philosophy towards planning increases political tension. Central government thus assumes a dominant role in the policy process. County structure plans are no longer overriding considerations when new developments are being considered.[32] Of course, even if proposals for small-scale industries are made outside the areas allocated on development plans, this is not in itself a reason for refusing them, bearing in mind the government's desire to support small businesses.[33] A district council may not be justified in refusing permission for housing just because the site is not shown on the structure plan or because there is no local need: 'a reasonable surplus of sites is necessary to provide continuity and choice'.[34] Local authorities may not like these decisions, but there is little they can do about them. They may try to appeal themselves, with a limited success.[35] More rarely, a developer, sensing the political climate is sympathetic, finds it worthwhile to take a local authority to High Court over the provisions in their structure plan.

It would be misleading, however, to imply there is no outer-area dimension to DoE land-use planning. In the restraint areas there are still many refusals and subsequent appeals which are dismissed. Some modifications have led to a tightening rather than relaxation of restraint. But recent experience shows a stronger shift in the direction of growth and development in all outer areas. The DoE seems more prepared to undermine some local policies for the containment of urban development and to put at risk some of its own growth area policies and programmes. Many local authorities who are themselves wanting a less rigid approach to land-use policy may welcome greater centralization of decision-making, regarding the pre-emption of their own restraint policies as inevitable and desirable. The more thoughtful, on the other hand, must surely look with dismay at what the DoE is doing to the outer cities for the sake of economic recovery.

Planned growth programmes

Central government commitment to containment always stood to be judged by its resolve to achieve a planned distribution of population and jobs in the outer cities. The Ministry of Housing and Local Government and later the Department of Environment have been instrumental in developing and financing the New and Expanded Towns programmes as a counterpart to restraint in the outer cities. The Expanded Town programme began after the introduction of the Town Development Act 1952. Although many Expanded Town agreements are now concluded, the DoE remains responsible for local authority financial support and the DoE's Directorate of Environmental Protection and Rural Affairs (DEPRA) has a direct interest in government development agencies like the Council for Small Industries in Rural Areas (COSIRA) and the Development Commissioners which help to promote the selective expansion of these and other towns in rural areas. The DoE's commitment to New Towns, on the other hand, had been weakened by the government's desire to reduce public expenditure and by the official ending of planned decentralization policy. As mentioned earlier, substantial disposal of completed assets to the private sector is being encouraged in an attempt to reduce public spending. The New Towns, created in 1946, were administered by state-run Development Corporations. In England, eight Development Corporations had been dissolved by 1983. A further seven will be wound up by the mid-1980s and the remainder by 1990. The Scottish Economic Planning Department announced in September 1981 that three of the five New Towns — Livingston, Cumbernauld and Irvine — will lose their Development Corporations by the end of the century; the future of the Welsh New Town is still under review.[36]

The apparent redirection of national policy implied by the DoE's recent inner city initiatives should not be mistaken for a conscious dismissal of the virtues of town expansion or planned growth areas. Nor should we underestimate the scale of growth already committed to the New Towns (Table 1). It will not be easy for the government to shake off the legacy of past policy even if, as seems unlikely, steps are taken to slow down future private investment in the growth schemes. The demise of the New Towns is certainly not a necessary corollary of current DoE thinking, despite the more alarmist views of the Town and Country Planning Association (TCPA). In any case, plans for private enterprise New Towns have been made in the past.[37] The continued development of the Expanded Towns is looked on favourably by the DoE, as witness the rapid growth of Swindon which has resulted from allowing a number of planning appeals for residential development in the absence of an approved structure plan. It is important to remember the variety of public goals which have lain behind the long history of post-war attempts to plan growth. Planned dispersal has not been conceived simply as a panacea for the problems of the cities. Indeed it has been viewed, especially by some local authorities, as a rather desirable way of increasing, through the build up of employment and people, the wealth needed to provide additional rural services. Both push and pull factors have lain behind central government's commitment to some form of planned dispersal, although the nature of the programmes adopted have been very disparate and frequently devised as responses to narrowly perceived problems.[38].

Although commitment to New Towns policy is changing in England, government investment in them rose slightly from £161 to £163 million between 1979 and 1980. In some of the large 'third generation' New Towns the effects of the reduction in planned growth targets is rather limited, as Table 1 demonstrates. All of these grew between

Table 1: *Population growth and targets of the 'third generation' New Towns*

	Date of Designation	Population		Population Target	
		Original	1981	When Designated	Current
Central Lancashire	1970	234,000	247,200	420,000	285,000
Warrington	1969	122,300	134,300	225,000	170,000
Telford	1968*	70,000	103,400	250,000	150,000
Milton Keynes	1967	40,000	96,100	250,000	180,000
Northampton	1968	133,000	156,900	260,000	180,000
Peterborough	1967	81,000	114,100	180,000	160,000
Total	—	680,300	852,000	1,585,000	1,125,000
		171,700 [1]		273,000 [2]	

Planner News, July, 1982.

[1] *Difference between the original and 1981 population.*

[2] *Difference between the 1981 and currently estimated target.*

* Originally designated as Dawley in 1963

their date of designation and 1981, and current 'target' figures show that substantial additional growth will take place over the 1981 figure especially in Milton Keynes (+83,900) and Telford (+46,600). It is ironic to note that among this sample of English New Towns the DoE's proposed scale of population growth in the post-1981 period (+273,000) is considerably higher than the recorded growth between the designation dates and 1981 (+171,700). No time limits are imposed on future growth, nevertheless it must be conceivable, given the spur to private investment, that some New Towns will grow faster in the 1980s than they did in the 1970s. The prospect certainly makes it more possible to see a continuing DoE commitment to New Towns — although the reverse of the coin is that it raises some embarassing questions for inner city policy.

The Scottish Office takes a rather different position from the DoE on New Towns. This is because they attach more importance to the economic role of New Towns rather than to their containment role. They do not want to dissolve the Development Corporations before the end of the century and they have confirmed that their primary role will remain the provision of housing and industry — in other words, a continuation of previous policy.[39] They appear to see the New Town programme as a complement rather than an alternative to inner city initiatives. The strong commitment to planned growth in Scotland is explained by the depressing industrial context and the legacy of earlier regional economic planning which pinned its hopes on 'growth points' in Central Lowlands. Although containment is a secondary priority, it appears that Scottish New Towns have been able to both promote regional development and contain urban growth more effectively than their English counterparts.[40] In England it is less easy to see how the 'third generation' New Towns, for example, can fulfill their containment role given the government's abandonment of planned overspill and much more limited control over public housing development. This does not mean that New Towns (or Expanded Towns) could not become effective vehicles for managing the spatial redistribution of private-sector housing in the outer cities, although this would obviously depend on the government having a strong restraint policy for neighbouring countryside areas.

The outer-area dimension in central government thinking about planned growth has been very limited. Over a period of time New and Expanded Towns have exported a part of their growing population to adjacent settlements. There has been no administrative mechanism for resisting the upward social mobility associated with residential development in neighbouring towns and villages. As a result, planned towns have proved unable to contain the dispersal of population. Could DoE policy respond to this trend? Moreover, could the social polarization between planned towns and those outlying settlements be overcome? Paradoxically an enlarged role for the private sector in housebuilding might mitigate social polarization somewhat. There is some evidence that increasing the supply of private housing in the New and Expanded Towns has increased the opportunity for upward social mobility among both newcomers and residents.[41] Furthermore, it might help to broaden the social base of towns where expansion has been associated with an over-emphasis on council housing.[42] But a socio-spatial policy of this kind would require careful monitoring of the balance between private and public housing provision, and this must seem a rather vain hope given the DoE's intention to cut back on public housing and encourage council house sales. It would require much tighter land use planning in the restraint areas to ensure that private housing was channelled to the planned towns. As argued earlier, the DoE has backed away from this issue, leaving the local authorities to control small settlement change. Counties have been told to work out their own urban containment strategies which the districts will implement. DoE advice is limited to the location and management of investment in the New Towns or planned growth areas. The interrelationship between these growth policies, land-use planning and the settlement strategies of local authorities is remarkably unclear; and the absence of a regional dimension must surely make it less likely that the planned growth areas will be effectively managed by the central government.

The link between central government investment programmes and the planned growth areas is also complex and unclear. A major problem with overspill was the relationship between housing policy and employment policy. When the DoE was created, it was thought that policy for the regional location of industry would become one of its tasks, thus in theory allowing some coordination with the planned programmes. In practice, however, the Department of Industry has remained separate and pursued policies that hinder town development. The Assisted Areas received priority for manufacturing industry over New and Expanded Towns, and since 1978 the inner cities take second priority to Assisted Areas. The Employment Transfer Schemes work in the opposite direction to regional policy, encouraging the movement of labour into the prosperous regions. Between 1977 and 1978, the eastern and southern regions, as defined by the Manpower Services Commission (broadly coincidental with outer London), had a net gain of 3,382 workers (36 percent) out of a total of 9,295. London took 4,666 (50 percent).[43] Employment Transfer Schemes are an attempt to relieve unemployment through labour mobility. They may be criticised for failing to match job skills with jobs available in reception areas; and they have certainly not been used directly as an instrument of the planned programmes for employment distribution in the outer city.

The Department of Industry's regional economic policy has no apparent outer-area dimension. Indeed some commentators have claimed that the New Towns attract only a relatively small proportion of new manufacturing industry.[44] However, the position is not so straightforward when the allocation of the DoI's regional development grant is analysed. This grant is a subsidy to manufacturing companies moving to, or expanding in, the Assisted Areas. The relative proportion of the grant varies between different categories of development area. Between 1981 and 1982 the proportion of total expenditure claimed by the New Towns varied quite widely in Scotland. Apart from Cumbernauld, all other towns did better than Central Glasgow as might be expected. Moreover, many of them performed relatively well compared to free-standing industrial towns like Renfrew and Hamilton or Dumbarton. In the North West the position was less clear. The effect of Merseyside's Special Development Area status was noticeable in the high levels of investment allocated to Runcorn and Kirkby. Other New Towns in the Intermediate Area performed less well.

The experience of both areas, whilst by no means conclusive, does suggest that the DoI is demonstrating more awareness of the New Town programmes than some critics give them credit for. However, this interpretation would seem less appropriate in the case of the Expanded Towns in England, which have received no special financial support.[45] Moreover, the activities of the Council for Small Industries in Rural Areas (COSIRA) and the local authorities, encouraged by central government support for small businesses, have tended to work in favour of the economies of the small towns but not necessarily the expansion schemes. Such promotional activities have helped to bring about employment growth in the outer areas. The industrial expansion of small towns was and still is regarded as a desirable objective of central and local government planning.[46] In the 1960s and early 1970s an industrial dispersal policy of this kind seemed an acceptable way of relieving growth pressures on the inner commuting areas: 'without any major conflict with rural resources, there is scope to expand many towns, and to increase the population of the rural regions. The role of the rural regions should be to offer an alternative place of residence and work to the conurbations . . . a full life in the country should be a reasonable prospect for an increasing number of people'.[47] Such sentiments may have reflected the mood of the time but the provision of land and buildings for industry has and still does encourage the trend toward a more dispersed pattern of employment outside the planned growth areas, which we now associate with the 'urban-rural shift'. Central government has not been unmindful of the potential contradiction between a planned growth programme and a more widespread dispersal of industrial activity, arguing in the past with the counties for a smaller number of large expansions, well spaced out. But the political difficulties of administrative machinery like the Development Corporations, and the rising cost of New Town Schemes, led them quickly to jettison a comprehensive national programme for urban dispersal.

Finally, mention must be made of water services investment. This is a DoE responsibility, and it has a critical bearing on growth and restraint policy in the outer areas. Government expenditure on water supply and sewerage exceeded £600 million in 1982–3 and was estimated to exceed £750 million by 1984–5.[48] The nine regional water authorities, covering several counties, have a statutory duty under Section 24(8) of the Water Act of 1973 to consult and 'have regard to' the structure plans for their area, but their responsiveness to local planning forecasts is variable and uncertain. The water authorities' individual annual plans are set within DoE targets for capital expenditure, but the separate plans do not represent a national strategy.[49] While much attention focusses on the interrelationship between local authority strategies and water programmes, an equally important question is the degree to which water investment is being channelled to the planned growth settlements or areas. Past and future capital expenditure data is broken down to individual river, water supply and drainage divisions. While clearly unrefined for the purposes of direct comparison with planning policy sub-divisions they do provide some indication of current investment commitment in the outer areas.

Table 2 shows the pattern of planned capital expenditure on sewerage and sewage disposal in a number of drainage divisions in the Thames Conservancy and the Anglian Water Authority. The data is difficult to evaluate since estimates of future spending are sometimes based on slightly different start dates. It must also be remembered that programmes vary from year to year and that some will reach fruition sooner than others. Notwithstanding these reservations, Table 2 shows that some planned-growth areas will have investment pruned, notably the Expanded Towns of Swindon, Banbury and Aylesbury, a 'medium-growth' location in the 1971 Strategic Plan for the South East. On the other hand, Central Berkshire, a major growth area, receives a considerable boost in expenditure. However, the neighbouring Chilterns, predominately a restraint area, will also have a substantially increased rate of investment. Northampton, one of the 'third generation' New Towns will see a falling rate of growth, as will Essex which contains many Expanded Towns. Perhaps most striking is that London's position is worse than all other areas with the exception of

Table 2: *Planned capital expenditure on sewerage and sewage disposal in South East England, Thames Conservancy and Anglian Water Authority.*

Drainage areas	1981–1982 £000	Forecast expenditure per annum[1] £000	Total per annum change £000	Percentage per annum change
Metropolitan London	12,535	3,642	−8,893	−70.9
Southern (E. Hants, Surrey	5,451	1,534	−3,917	−71.8
Cotswold (Swindon, Moreton)	3,349	1,482	−1,867	−55.7
Essex	13,000	7,346	−5,654	−43.5
Vales (Banbury, Aylesbury)	8,150	4,835	−3,315	−40.6
Northampton	6,177	4,947	−1,230	−19.9
Bedford	9,000	10,905	+1,905	+21.2
Chilterns	1,886	3,033	+1,147	+60.8
Lambourne (Bracknell, Reading)	2,608	4,806	+2,198	+84.0

Water Services Yearbook, 1982.
[1]1982 base has been assumed.

Surrey and parts of East Hampshire, areas tightly constrained by Green Belt policy. Data for the South East indicates some limited but rather inconsistent commitment to growth and restraint policy. The evidence from the other metropolitan regions is less happy. The North West Water Authority plans to increase investment by £7,694 million in the Manchester/Salford area over an unspecified period after 1982. But a massive £10,900 million is to be spent between 1982 and 1984 in the southern area which includes the Cheshire towns of Northwich, Crewe, Congleton and Nantwich. In Strathclyde only 39 percent of expenditure on sewerage programmes under construction or planned to take place after 1982 will affect Central Glasgow. The pattern in the remaining 61 percent shows no special discrimination in favour of the New Towns.

The Department of Transport

By the early 1980s the Department of Transport was spending over £700 million pa on motorways and trunk roads in England.[50] Between 1982 and 1984 most of this investment will be allocated to about 400 miles of new road, including a remaining 55 miles of the M25 route running through the London Green Belt. Other motorway links in the Midlands yet to be completed are the M42 (Birmingham–Nottingham), the M40 (Birmingham–Oxford) and the M54 (Birmingham–Telford link). The M40 is intended to relieve congested towns and villages in Warwickshire and provide an alternative route for the M1 (Birmingham–London). Part of the southern section runs through the Oxford Green Belt. Investment in all these locations reflects the government's priority to aid economic recovery and assist industrial development as well as to bring some environmental benefit.[51]

Tory and Labour administrations have presided over a steady increase in major road-building programmes, especially since the early 1960s. Expenditure on the primary road networks (predominately the inter-urban trunk roads) grew from £190 million in 1964-5 to £504 million in 1970-1 and was forecast to grow from £524 million in 1980-1 to £702 million in 1982-3. In general, motorway and trunk-road spending, together with local authority spending on roads, has risen faster than was anticipated in Labour's 1977 White Paper.[52] The present government has emphasized that the principal inter-urban network will be completed by the late 1980s and it wishes to see investment directed towards the improvement of existing routes (the IER strategy) which will relieve local bottlenecks.[53] In 1982, the Department of Transport duly announced a programme of 220 additional bypass schemes to be built between 1982 and 1987.[54] It remains to be seen whether this switch of emphasis in road planning results in any overall pruning of government capital expenditure on transport. The indications from recent spending plans are that it will have only a marginal effect.

While the main thrust of the motorway building programme may be coming to an end, there can be little doubt that existing and planned projects will continue to have a major impact on the relocation of industry and population in the outer areas. The effects of the West Midlands motorway system on actual and perceived industrial opportunities have been systematically analysed.[55] The motorway programme has greatly assisted peripheral economic expansion and hence been a crucial influence over the dispersal of employment. There can be little doubt that DoT strategies will increase the pressure for a variety of manufacturing, warehouse, office and other forms of enterprise in the outer areas. Recent DoE approval for high-technology firms located near existing and proposed motorways strongly suggests these pressures may prove irresistible in the case of certain stretches of the M25 and M40. Moreover the potential impact of the IER programme on industrial expansion cannot be underestimated since many of the schemes announced are located in outer commuting areas most attractive to some industrialists.

The DoT has been uninterested in the spatial impact of its programmes on the relocation of population in settlements within and beyond the Green Belts. Yet the pressures for housing have proved irresistible in many smaller towns and villages in close proximity to motorways. The government's present encouragement of the private housebuilding industry must surely accelerate this trend in the future, thus assisting the dispersal process. But the issues go beyond this. When the Ministry of Transport was absorbed into the DoE in 1970 greater coordination between road and land use planning seemed in prospect, as did a greater degree of integration between private and public transport investment. But the Labour Government agreed to separate the DoT from the DoE in 1976, making it more difficult to achieve an integrated national transport programme, thereby changing the bias in favour of private transport — a consistent strand of government thinking in the post-war era. Commitment to private car ownership has been accepted without any appraisal of the implications of greater household mobility for settlement change in the outer areas. Possible alternatives such as road pricing, or measures to limit car ownership and use, have never been seriously entertained — they would prove both costly and politically contentious. An additional and related point is that the DoT has tended by default to foster a greater use of private cars, being reluctant to adequately support the (rising) public expenditure needed to secure an effective road and rail network. In recent years both national and local spending have been increased at a faster rate than have subsidies to the transport industry.[56] The effect of greater investment in road building is to encourage the switch from public to private commuting, especially in the outer South East.[57] Similar trends may be noted in other outer metropolitan areas where the existing provision and the use of public transport is greater. There are signs that the British Railways Board is now alert to the passenger implications of further population growth in the outer areas and the possible readjustments to the demand for rail commuting that may follow further decentralization and associated motorway building.[58] Sadly, these investment decisions are not being coordinated at a national or regional level. The Passenger Transport Authorities (PTAs) may have helped, but they were intended to improve transport policy in metropolitan authorities only. No parallel mechanism exists for the outer commuting areas, although shire counties have a duty, under the 1968 Transport Act, to prepare integrated transport policies.

The DoT's inter-metropolitan road programmes, on the other hand, have been executed by central government with comparative smoothness. This contrasts with the DoE's land use policies which have relied in large measure on the support of the local authorities for successful implementation. The absence of effective political opposition to rural motorway building has probably helped, as has the rising cost of the urban programme. Local government resistance to road proposals has proved rather half-hearted. Admittedly, the counties have fought proposals which contradicted local land-use containment policy or threatened areas of high landscape value, but this has usually led to a readjustment of the routes rather than the plans being scrapped. Districts often give their support to new road building, particularly bypass schemes which offer to relieve lorry traffic and possibly create new opportunities for economic development. The recent announcement of further bypass schemes will be generally acceptable to both counties and districts. Other central government departments have been surprisingly mute in their opposition to new roads. The DoE, for example, strongly supports the M25 which runs for its entire length through London's Green Belt. The MAFF has recently abandoned its opposition to the proposed M40 extension from Oxford to Birmingham. This M40 extension exposes the contradictions and interactions between a number of central and local agencies. Warwickshire wants the road. Oxfordshire is split, some people arguing it will bring much needed relief to Banbury, others that it is not sufficiently close to Oxford to solve the city's traffic problems. Buckinghamshire firmly resists any eastwards movement of the line in its direction. Cherwell District, which includes Banbury and Bicester, sees the motorway as essential in redirecting the present high levels of through and local traffic. The CPRE, rightly viewing the issue in much broader terms, wants the DoT to drop the present plan for the M40 and apply the investment in existing roads, a strategy which they claim will reduce farmland loss *and* permit much greater relief for local traffic.[59] There have of course been some classic battles fought between local action groups and the DoT when rural motorways have been proposed — the Aire Valley motorways around Leeds, the M3 at Winchester, the M25 in the Darent Valley, the M42 in the Forest of Arden, and now the M40 in Oxfordshire. But the opposition to all these motorways has come too late to be effective since many were long established elements of the old Ministry of Transport's inter-urban road strategy.[60]

Finally, many commentators on the government's inner city initiatives point to the difficulty of 'bending' on transport policies in ways that will exclusively benefit the urban communities. The road programmes in progress or proposed invariably benefit the outer cities. For instance, there is considerable uncertainty about the building of a motorway link between the M25 and London's docklands area. A related point is that while major national road building programmes may slow down in the future, there is still substantial impetus to road investment in the shire counties, especially in the growth locations, as we saw in Chapter 3. Recent cut backs in capital funding have stopped certain projects, but an examination of local transport policy programmes still reveals a high relative level of public investment on county roads.[61] The cumulative consequences of all these central and local decisions are given little critical analysis. The need for an effective national and regional framework for planning road investment in the outer cities seems beyond doubt. DoT strategies must be seen to challenge the principal of urban containment since they have indirectly assisted peripheral urban development and thus promoted the dispersal process. Yet more than any other activity of central government, transport programmes provide a positive tool for shaping containment strategy, through the influence they have on the location, direction and scale of private and public investment and on the decisions of development agencies and local authorities.

Conclusion

Any serious commitment to the management of growth in the outer areas requires a coherent central government strategy. Through investment programmes and controls over the use of land government can manipulate the physical form of urban development and the overall scale of population and employment growth. Analysis in this chapter shows that the Department of Environment is actively shifting its policy stance away from the traditional objectives of containment: firm control over the use of land in restraint areas and concentrated urban growth in planned centres. Present planning policies appear to be moving away from a specific outer-area dimension in the interests of economic regeneration; and the ending of the planned decentralization schemes has left a gap in official thinking about how to manage peripheral urban development.

Some of the Department of Environment's present policies appear to run directly against urban containment philosophy. While still officially prepared to uphold the need for Green Belts, structure plans have been modified to permit selective release of new housing land. It would be inaccurate to say that the Green Belts were being abandoned, but it seems that at a time of economic uncertainty the DoE is prepared to contemplate a greater degree of residential and industrial development in them. The Department of Transport has shown little hesitation in planning motorway routes which cross the Green Belts. Moreover, the DoE has treated the green belts as a 'stopper' to urban growth, failing to develop any strategy for changes in the use of agricultural land,[62] or for commercial agricultural developments like riding schools and farm shops.[63] The question of the degraded and despoiled areas in Green Belts[64] remains a very open one. The latest circular seems to imply that the inner fringes of the Green Belts will be asked to provide more land for residential development rather than for recreation or open space. There are misgivings too about the relaxation in the power of planning controls, a relaxation that may leave the specially designated areas less well protected than hitherto.[65]

It is difficult to expect that all land use pressures can be resisted in Green Belts and other restraint areas containing a mix of established county towns and smaller rural settlements. Inward migration has been considerable even with land-use planning; and for restraint to become a more effective tool for managing growth in the outer cities, it may now be necessary to contemplate overspill arrangements from settlements within the Green Belt to places beyond it.[66] The difficulties in pursuing a more rigorous policy are of course considerable. The continuation of a dual market in housing, and especially the cooperation with private housebuilding interests, have not helped. The reorganisation of local government in 1974, which led to the split in planning powers between counties and districts, hinders the smooth implementation of policy in Green Belts. The system of structure and local plans, established by the 1968 and 1971 Town and Country Planning Acts, allows for a great variety of approach to Green Belt policy and proposals for development, a situation which is of central government's making. While structure plans would seem to be obvious documents for expressing containment strategy at a local scale, the DoE do not altogether agree, arguing against the preparation of special Green Belt Subject Plans. While the counties might argue that a Green Belt around a large city must be coherently planned at a regional or sub-regional scale, taking account of related policies for housing, industry and retailing, their views count for little since the districts can claim that the boundaries of the Green Belt cannot be defined until *they* have produced local plans which show in detail where development will or will not occur. It is thus central government and the districts who determine development change in the Green Belts because the powers of direction and control have been taken from the counties. By doing so, central government has heightened political tension, both between itself and county government and between counties and districts — themes which are so important for the outer cities that we must return to them later.

We must conclude that central government is failing to implement containment strategy. Strong national coordination of departmental policies and programmes is missing. Instead we find an ambivalent commitment to growth and diminishing concern for restraint. Although the DoE may have a clear idea about the desirable physical form of urban regions, they have neglected to develop perspectives on the national urban system: 'Britain has an emerging national regional policy and a regional urban policy, but no national urban policy.'[67] The role to be played by outer cities and the exurban settlements within them remains problematic. So long as effective power remains with the local authorities the prospect for a resolution of problems of the outer city remains a bleak one. In the longer term the overruling of local decisions in order to accelerate change and assist economic development may well prove damaging to the relationships between central and local government and become more unpalatable than the introduction of stronger regional planning. Conservative governments have conventionally decentralized power to the local state, but this does not imply that they would necessarily find the cumulative impact of local change in the outer areas a desirable one if it threatened other agencies' interest in land-use protection and popular environmental values.

The objection to a new and streamlined national planning system, according to the political right, is the incompatibility of economic growth and control of the market. Planning is the *bête noire* of the private developer whether in the industrial or residential field. Planning, it is said, raises costs by imposing delays on essential development. Planning, it is said, has brought about a dreary uniformity in the visual environment. It would hence be logical to abolish the planning system altogether, provided there were some safeguards for nationally important areas like Green Belts.[68] Yet containment has always implied a planning system. It was the unhappy memory of urban sprawl in the 1930s that prompted the idea of a central government strategy. With hindsight, it can certainly be criticised for its rather rigid adherence to Green Belts and the planned-growth centres beyond. It may not be desirable, given the changed demographic conditions of the 1980s, to pursue this kind of long-range dispersal any longer. Carefully planned peripheral suburban development could be a better alternative.[69] But without strong control over development in the restraint areas and the growth locations there is no guarantee whatsoever that outer city expansion would not result. To prevent that, only a firmer control over the relative autonomous counties and districts would be needed, and probably some form of effective regional or sub-regional planning as well — options which, as the next chapter shows, appear positively utopian at present.

Notes

1.   D. H. McKAY and A. W. COX, *The Politics of Urban Change* (Croom Helm, 1979).

2.   Working Party on Rural Settlement Policies, *A Future for the Village*, Bristol (HMSO, 1979).

3.   This phase of commitment to national planning is fully examined by G. CHERRY, *The Evolution of British Town Planning* (Leonard Hill, 1974).

4.   Countryside Review Committee, *The Countryside — Problems and Policies*, (HMSO, 1976).

5.   K. STANSFIELD, *Local Government News*, January 1981.

6.   E. SHARP, 'Super-ministry: the first steps', *Built Environment*, April 1972.

7.   D. WALKER and B. DONOUGHUE, 'Tarzan tames his jungle: the changing role of the DoE', *The Times*, 20 January 1982.

8.   Countryside Commission, *Countryside Issues and Action*, CCP 151, April 1982.

9.   The view of the Royal Town Planning Institute expressed in *Planner News*, September 1982.

10.   A. J. WILLIAMS, 'The relationship between Regional Water Authorities and Local Authorities' in P. J. DRUDY (ed.), *Water Planning and the Regions*, Regional Studies Association, Discussion Paper 9, 1977.

11.   P. HEALEY *et al.*, 'The Implementation of Development Plans', Report for the Department of Environment, Department of Town Planning Oxford Polytechnic, 1982.

12.   Reviewed by P. WEATHERHEAD, 'Never a dull moment', *Local Government News*, December/January 1982.

13.   T. ANDERSON, 'Bill aims to boost private housing: Heseltine to sweep away red tape', *Building Design*, no. 452, 1979.

14.   See report 'Heseltine to force sale of public land', *Architects Journal*, vol. 171, no. 24, 1980.

15.   D. LOCK, 'Asset stripping the New Towns', *Town and Country Planning*, vol. 48, no. 7, October 1979.

16.   The 1980 changes are summarised by S. GILLON, M. DORFMAN, and A. MOYE, *The Local Government Planning and Land Act 1980 — A Layman's Guide*, (Town and Country Planning Association, 1980).

17.   Department of Environment, *Memorandum on Structure and Local Plans*, Circular 55/77 (HMSO, 1977); Department of Environment, *Memorandum on Structure and Local Plans*, Circular 4/79 (HMSO, 1979).

18.   Department of Environment, *Development Plans*, Circular 23/81 (HMSO, 1981); Department of Environment, *Structure and Local Plan Regulations*, Circular 22/82 (HMSO, 1981).

19.   Department of Environment, *Circular 10* (HMSO, 1970); Department of Environment, *Circular 102* (HMSO, 1972).

20.   P. HEALEY, op. cit.

21.   See for instance Department of Environment, *Private Sector Land Requirements and Supply*, Circular 44/78 (HMSO, 1978); *Land for Private Housebuilding* (HMSO, 1980).

22.   Department of Environment, *Land for Housing*, Draft Circular, July 1983 (HMSO, 1983).

23.   Reported in 'Green Belt crunch hits new phase', *Planning*, vol. 531, 12 August 1983.

24.   Department of Environment *Development Control — Policy and Practice*, Circular 22/80 (HMSO, 1982).

25.   See for instance 'Development Control: praise and abuse for draft circular', *Architects Journal*, vol. 172, no. 36, 1980; J. FINNEY, 'Biggest changes in development control since 1974', *Planner News*, December 1980.

26.   'RTPI hits the headllines on the DC Circular', *Planner News*, Royal Town Planning Institute, October 1980.

27. T. LONG, 'Rag-bag of control advice', *Planning*, vol. 412, 3 April 1981.

28. Report on 'Planning Inspectors', *Planning*, vol. 479, 30 July 1982.

29. See for instance 'Wait for Green Belt Plans', *Planning*, vol. 422, 12 June 1981.

30. See for instance 'Reacting to housing pressure', *Planning*, vol. 456, 19 February 1981.

31. Reports in 'Clear planning objections — the impact on appeal', *Planning*, vol. 490, no. 15, October 1980.

32. Statement by the Under Secretary for Wales, *Times Parliamentary Report*, 19 April 1982.

33. See the report 'Local freedom threatened by ministers?', *Planning*, vol. 401, 16 January 1981.

34. The case is examined in 'Connection'. *Town and Country Planning*, vol. 48(7), 1979.

35. A. ALESBURY, 'Planning appeals the other way round: the number of appeals against the Secretary of State seems to be on the increase', *Architect*, vol. 125, no. 12, 1979.

36. See for instance S. POTTER, 'The last of the New Towns', *Planner News*, July 1982.

37. R. W. ARCHER, 'Prospects for private enterprise new towns', *Official Architecture and Planning*, July 1971.

38. For a useful critique see M. ALDRIDGE, *The British New Towns: a Programme without a Policy* (Routledge & Kegan Paul, 1979).

39. Reported in *Planning*, vol. 489, 8 October 1982.

40. D. R. DIAMOND, 'The urban system' in J. W. HOUSE (ed.) *The U.K. Space: Resources, Environment and the Future* (2nd edn.) (Weidenfeld and Nicholson, 1977).

41. See for instance M. HARLOE, *Swindon: A Town in Transition* (Heinemann, 1975).

42. D. M. HUDSON (ed.), *The Future of the London Town Expansion Programme*, discussion on social polarisation, Regional Studies Association Discussion Paper, 5 March 1974.

43. J.H. JOHNSON and J. SALT, 'Population redistribution policies in Great Britain', in J. WEBB, A. NAUKKARINEN and L. A. KOSINSKI (eds), *Policies of Population Redistribution*, Geographical Society of Northern Finland, for the IGN Commission on Population Geography, Oulu, 1981.

44. S. FOTHERGILL, M. KITSON, and S. MONK, 'The impact of the New and Expanded Town programmes on industrial location in Britain, 1960–78, *Regional Studies*, vol. 17, no. 4, 1983.

45. J. WILLIAMS, *et al.*, 'Town Development Act', *Town and Country Planning*, vol. 45, no. 9, 1977.

46. Ivor H. SEELEY, *Planned Expansion of Country Towns* (George Godwin, 1968).

47. R. J. GREEN, *Country Planning: The Future of The Rural Regions* (Manchester University Press, 1971).

48. The Treasury, *The Government's Expenditure Plan 1982-1983 to 1984-1985. Vol. 1* Cmnd 8494-1 (HMSO, March 1982).

49. E. C. PENNING ROWSELL, 'Planning and water services: keeping in step', *Town and Country Planning*, vol. 51, no. 6, June 1982.

50. The Government's Expenditure Plan, op. cit.

51. Department of Transport, *Policy for Roads: England 1981*, Cmnd 8496, (HMSO, 1982).

52. Department of Transport, *Transport Policy*, Cmnd 6836 (HMSO, 1977).

53. Department of Transport, *Policy For Roads: England 1980*, Cmnd 7908 (HMSO, 1980).

54. D. HOWELL, Conservative Party Conference, 8 October 1982.

55. S. W. HAYWOOD, *The Determinants of Industrial and Office Location: Survey of Estate Agents and Property Development Companies*, Joint Unit for Research on the Urban Environment, Aston University, Research Note 1, 1979.

56. Central Statistical Office, *Social Trends* (HMSO, 1982).

57. See for instance Standing Conference on London and South East Regional Planning, *The Commuting Study*, SCLSERP, SC 1551 July 1981; A.H. BROWN, 'Commuter travel trends in London and the South East 1966–1979 and associated factors', *Department of Transport Statistics*, October, 1981.

58. British Rail has recently announced a new strategy for building perimeter inter-city stations; 'Inter-city's answer to M25', *The Times*, 4 August 1983.

59. See the report by T. LONG, 'Plans for wonderland motorway', *Planning*, vol. 484 3 September 1982:

60. Ministry of Transport, *Roads for the Future: the New Inter-Urban plan for England*, Chund 4369, HM 70, 1970.

61. County council expenditure on roads (excluding trunk roads) is given in the Transport Policy Programmes submitted annually to the Department of Transport. For comparison of capital expenditure on local roads and motorway/trunk roads see HM Treasury, *The Government's Expenditure Plan*, op. cit., March 1982.

62. R. MUNTON, 'Agricultural land use in the London Green Belt', *Town and Country Planning*, vol. 50, no. 1, January 1981.

63. See the report 'Not so Green Belt', *The Economist*, 14 February 1981.

64. Standing Conference on London and South East Regional Planning, *The Improvement of London's Green Belt*, SC 620, 21 July 1976.

65. See for instance M .ANDERSON, 'Planning policies and development control in the Sussex Downs AONB', *Town Planning Review*, vol. 52, no. 1, 1981.

66. D. GREGORY, 'Green Belt policy and the conurbation' in F. E. JOYCE (ed.), *Metropolitan Development and Change: The West Midlands — A Policy Review* (Teakfield, 1977).

67. L. S. BOURNE, *Urban Systems: Strategies for Regulation* (Oxford, 1975).

68. Adam Smith Institute, *Town and Country Chaos* (London, 1982).

69. D. L. SAUNDERS, 'The changing policy framework' in F. E. JOYCE (ed.) *Metropolitan Development and Change: The West Midlands — A Policy Review* (Teakfield, 1977).

5   The Regional Dimension

The new regional geography of Britain has become finer-grained: prosperous south and
peripheral north have been replaced by declining city and expanding shire. The intra-
regional perspective, not the inter-regional, is now a meaningful one.
(P. Hall, 1983).

The case for a clear *regional* stance on dispersed urban growth rests on three
developments. First, there are the substantial commitments to population and
employment growth made in existing approved development plans which, if
implemented, will greatly encourage the trend to dispersal and challenge containment
principles in the outer areas. Second, there is a deterioration of housing and industrial
building in the conurbations which, if allowed to continue unchecked, will make it
difficult to sustain the government's professed commitment to urban regeneration.
Third, very considerable public expenditure is needed in the medium term (three to
seven years), especially in new roads, water and sewerage, just to maintain existing
commitments. Moreover, the problems facing local authorities in managing the growth
pressures in the outer-metropolitan areas are becoming more acute as government's
drive for economic recovery gains momentum. In the South East, for example, the
present 'near frantic pursuit of local programmes scattered throughout the region . . .
add up to inconsistent and wasteful development as between the different counties and
their parts and in terms of the regional objectives to improve the attractiveness of
London.'[1]

Sadly, central government in England has retreated from its earlier enthusiasm for
urban regional planning which was so evident in the 1960s and early 1970s.[2]
Admittedly, demographic and economic conditions have changed. Pressure for
outward population dispersal has diminished (although the fall in household size has
not lessened the demand for housing land) and the contrast between prosperous and
less prosperous regions (the prime stimulus to regional policy) has been blurred by
overall economic decline. The attempt to steer industrial expansion away from the
Midlands and the South East seems less relevant as the spatial pattern of
unemployment becomes more complex. The Department of Industry's modifications
to regional policy announced in 1979, which included reductions in the areas receiving
financial assistance and the abandonment of the Regional Economic Planning Councils
(EPCs) created by the Labour government in 1964,[3] were ostensibly the result of the
government's commitment to prune public spending rather than a reaction to
economic deprivation. However, by 1983 the government was having to consider
further modifications to regional policy, in particular the redirection of funds towards
job creation rather than to capital formation in areas of the West Midlands hard hit by
recession.[4] But these changing conditions do not satisfactorily account for the present
lack of enthusiasm for an urban-regional dimension in central government thinking.
To asssess why this should be so we must examine the experience of regional planning
during the 1970s and ask how far it has had a significant impact on the outer areas.

Central government initiatives

The case for a unified and coherent national approach to the physical problem of urban expansion and the economic problem of regional decline was first mooted by the Barlow Report of 1940.[5] Barlow argued for the physical containment of London and the dispersal of industry and population to the then depressed regions of Britain. New Towns were proposed as a way of decongesting the capital and other conurbations. A single government department should have overall responsibility for coordinating physical with economic planning. The framework for subsequent direction of central government involvement in post-war regional planning was set: encouragement to industry to move away from London and the South East to peripheral regions (regional policy) and the accompanying planned dispersal of population from the cities (regional strategy). Although it was contrary to the main Barlow report, dispersal was to take place at the intra-regional scale in the now familiar package of Green Belts and New Towns.

Regional policy and urban-regional strategy have in practice never been satisfactorily married together, because they are the separate responsibility of the Department of Industry and the Department of Environment. The DoI has taken a broad national view of its economic and industrial role, and shown a limited interest in the regional or outer-area dimension to investment allocation, as mentioned in the previous chapter. The DoE, at least until the late 1970s, was actively engaged in and concerned about urban-regional planning and the implications of DoI policy within the regions. Nevertheless, the DoI's views have had a stronger influence on the spatial allocation of investment in regional plans; and the present government's overriding interest in national economic recovery has almost certainly strengthened the DoI's role in policy making. The government's desire to relax planning controls must in any case seriously undermine the DoE's ability to implement the strategies published in the 1970s. The local authorities played an important part in the early development of central government plans for the urban regions and present county-district strategies are having an equally significant impact on spatial change in the outer areas, a theme we develop in the following two chapters.

Urban containment was a central objective of the early regional plans encouraged by the Ministry of Town and Country Planning. These included the advisory plans for Greater London, the West Midlands and Clydeside, published between 1944 and 1945 (which owed much to the influence of Sir Patrick Abercrombie).[6] The main thrust of policy was strong restraint in Green Belts and planned dispersal to satellite and New Towns. The history of urban–regional planning demonstrates that some local authorities were reluctant to adopt restraint and growth policy of this kind and others only did so much later on — the West Midlands Green Belt was not introduced until the 1960s. Moreover, some cities did not see the relevance of containment or found it impossible to achieve agreement with neighbouring authorities over the siting of New Towns. Among conurbations, West Yorkshire and Greater Manchester have no New Towns — in West Yorkshire because it was possible to secure a considerable peripheral development within the city boundaries, in Manchester because attempts to find suitable locations were consistently thwarted by Cheshire County Council.

Central government's interest in regional strategic planning waned during the 1950s and 1960s although the Board of Trade's involvement in regional policy remained. The first steps taken to develop regional development plans were unrelated to urban containment. The Labour Government created a new Department of Economic Affairs (DEA) in 1964 to produce a national economic plan and to coordinate an integrated series of plans for ten newly-defined economic planning regions (eight in England, one each in Scotland and Wales). The preparation of plans was the job of the Economic Planning Councils (EPCs) and Boards who were expected to advise on the economic needs and potential of their region and develop long-term strategies. They had no specific interest in the outer areas but their attempts to match regional economic requirements with central government objectives often led them to support policies that directly promoted industrial expansion there. Indeed their role was 'as far as possible, to be disinterestedly in favour of more rapid economic growth'.[7]

Examination of the regional studies published by the EPCs confirms the emphasis given to industrial requirements. The West Midlands EPC sought substantial employment (and population) decentralization as a means of promoting economic growth in the region.[8] The Ministry of Housing and Local Government had earlier designated Dawley (1963) and Redditch (1965) as New Towns and the regional studies had to accept these decisions. The strategy produced by the South East EPC in 1967 strongly supported decentralization of population and jobs from London. It thus accepted the principles outlined in the previous plans for Greater London (1944) and the South East (1964) prepared by the Ministry of Housing and Local Government. But it went further than these in advocating that substantial housing and industry should be allowed to develop in sectors running along the principal transport arteries out of London.[9] Additionally, the Council maintained that the M25 should be a national priority, and its views were listened to by both Tory and Labour Ministers of Transport who agreed to implement this project.

Individually, the EPCs seem to have been obsessed with the notion that if expansion was not allowed to take place in outer areas and the inner cities declined, some regions would see a reversal of their economic fortunes. In this they showed little recognition of the inter-regional dimension in industrial policy, or indeed of the environmental and social consequences which might follow from over-stimulation of peripheral urban development. Their attitude to the shire counties demonstrates this lack of concern. The first consultative drafts of structure plans had to go before the EPCs, allowing them to comment on the degree to which counties were responding to the regional or national interest. Given their economic brief, it is perhaps not surprising, that in the South East

> the Council began strongly to assert a policy line in favour of giving sufficient space for economic growth and for the resulting population growth. It was concerned for instance, at the highly restrictive attitude exhibited in some of the plans towards industrial development . . . it was extremely worried about the restrictive attitude to development generally; and it was surprised at the apparent similarity of policies for the 'growth' area of North East Hampshire and the next-door 'restraint' area of Mid Hampshire.[10]

The last point is telling since it expresses the difficulty that central government faces in channelling growth in the outer areas. However, the assumption that overall restraint was undesirable now seems a much more short-sighted opinion. The local authorities disputed these observations and reacted angrily to the South East strategy, claiming it was unnecessary since they were well under way with the preparation of an agreed plan for the region. The DEA responded by announcing that another study would be commissioned jointly by the EPC and the Standing Conference for the South East.

'From this point onwards the council was effectively shifted into the background of policy formation . . . never again would it be allowed to go it alone in producing its own plans'.[11] With hindsight, the regional problems presented by massive growth in the outer South East and, particularly, the difficulties of securing a diversion of investment into London which the Council supported, suggest that the EPC was going too far in its advocacy of an overall higher rate of economic growth. Admittedly demographic and economic circumstances were to change dramatically in the 1970s, and were perhaps insufficiently understood or anticipated by the Planning Council, but one suspects their commitment to economic objectives would anyway have led them towards a growth-orientated strategy.

The South East Economic Planning Council had a more direct influence on containment strategy than other EPCs. The North West Economic Planning Council stopped attempting to influence structure plans when it was clear that Merseyside and Cheshire County Councils would not agree to them; nor did they attempt to make any assessment of the financial implications of the structure plans produced by the five separate county authorities in the economic planning region.[12] In the West Midlands there were tensions between the EPCs and the DoI, the former seeking a relaxation of regional policy in order to secure the outer-area growth programmes. In the North, Scotland and Wales, the EPCs promoted the establishment of New Towns as industrial growth points and thus assisted the intra-regional movement of manufacturing firms. But these regional differences in attitude towards regional development must be seen in the context of the close relationship between the councils and central government. The links between EPCs and local authorities were rather poor and relations were sometimes antagonistic. As Peter Hall comments: 'the South East Economic Planning Council represented some kind of alliance or pressure group for economic progress and for associated development, not at the sacrifice of conservationist or environmental considerations, but certainly in opposition to rooted anti-development forces which so often seemed to gain the upper hand in this region'.[13] Clearly, the alliance with the DoE became a closer one after this department assumed responsibility for the Regional Economic Planning Councils in 1970. Even though relations with the DoI were more strained than with the DoE, one of 'the main political effects of the regional councils was to step up the competition for government favours, and for the first time the southern regions had spokesmen who could argue, occasionally with some success, for a relaxation of industrial and office controls'.[14]

It is surprising, given its commitment to economic development, that the Tory government decided to scrap the Economic Planning Councils (though not the Boards of civil servants) in 1979. But the response of individual EPCs to regional development needs was never checked within a national planning framework. Admittedly DoI regional policy was at times an obstacle to their growth aspirations although not always a strong one. Ironically, the changes to regional policy introduced by the Tory government since 1979 might have been welcomed by the regional EPCs. The DoE's support for economic regeneration, their modifications to development plans, and the relaxation of planning controls might also have been approved by EPCs. Probably they became superfluous just because they were handmaidens of central rather than local government.

The tripartite arrangements

The effect of the regional planning framework initiated in 1965 was to encourage greater coordination at a regional scale between central and local (especially county) government. The local authorities had earlier joined together to form Standing Conferences covering the same economic planning regions but with a direct interest in environmental and land-use planning rather than regional economic development. The tension between them over the question of who should prepare the regional plan and what policy should be adopted towards the management of outer metropolitan growth, encouraged the DoE to develop in 1970 a tripartite system of plan preparation. This involved a professional team of planners drawn from local and central government and steered by representatives of various government departments including the EPC and the Standing Conference. Five regional strategies were produced under this tripartite arrangement.[15] They were mainly completed between 1971 and 1977 and it was always assumed that a continuing monitoring and review process would roll the plans forward afterwards. The strategies were to be advisory documents only, although it was hoped the counties would take account of them when they prepared their structure plans.

Surprisingly little systematic evaluation of the tripartite plans has been undertaken.[16] Their impact on the investment decisions of public and private agencies could have brought about a spatial redistribution of population and employment between restraint and growth locations. But as more strategies were published it became clear that they were not regarded by Whitehall as bids for financial resources, and that their advisory nature reduced their effectiveness as a corporate framework for the expenditure plans of central government agencies. Moreover, the DoI regarded them as essentially exercises in regional physical planning with little significance for economic development.[17] In Scotland the tripartite arrangement was not used. Yet there has been a greater sense of commitment to regional planning in the Scottish Office. The Scottish regional authorities that came into being in 1975 were asked to prepare regional reports which were wide-ranging statements of policy, covering social, economic and physical planning.[18] They were not bids for resources but were assessed in the context of national planning guidelines outlined first in 1977 and updated in 1981. They provided some stimulus for the national coordination of government investment and infrastructure programmes. Moreover, unlike the tripartite strategies in England, the reports offered clear guidance to the regional authorities when they came to prepare their structure plans (although this has not prevented subsequent conflict between regions and districts).[19]

The English tripartite strategies have sought to plan the spatial distribution of population and employment in the outer cities using a variety of techniques and policies. Most tripartite strategies emphasize the importance of concentrating new industry and housing in 'growth points'. Some of these were seen to promote dispersal from the cities, like the New and Expanded Towns, others to consolidate more local patterns of population movement. Other variants include the 'growth area' (in the South East) or the 'growth corridor' (in the North West). In all cases, concentration was seen as an essential mechanism for accommodating future expansion, securing a balance of population and employment, reducing public expenditure, and protecting sensitive environmental areas from dispersal. Despite the downturn in population growth in the 1970s and despite slower rates of dispersal, the government remained committed to the ideal of concentration, as the experience in the South East showed.

The Strategic Plan for the South East proposed five major 'growth areas' and a number of medium-sized and other substantial growth areas. The 1976 Review of the Strategic Plan for the South East recommended much less rapid expansion in growth areas, more emphasis to be given to New and Expanded Town development, and a limitation on planning permissions over a five-year period.[20] The DoE's response was predictably less restraint-orientated. It argued for the retention of the growth areas,[21] although the target size of Milton Keynes and some other New Towns was later cut.

The tripartite strategies might have helped at a regional scale to rationalize the spatial pattern of urban growth between growth and restraint areas. There is also some evidence that the outward flow of population and jobs has been more balanced, thus tending to reduce lengthy journeys to work. Information about social structure in the growth areas is scanty. In the New Towns there is still a preponderance of skilled labour and a low representation of unskilled or professional or managerial groups.[22] Nevertheless, these trends are not without their consequences: as argued in the previous chapter, growth has been pushed into neighbouring towns and villages as land in the growth points ran out. Imbalances in housing supply and labour demand have followed, and the stimulus given to cross-commuting presents problems for integrated land-use and transport planning. Arguably these are sub-regional rather than regional problems, but they are no less significant for the local authorities in the growth areas. Furthermore, there must be reservations about the influence of these strategies on the physical containment of population and employment, especially in the outer-metropolitan areas beyond the Green Belts, mainly because it has proved very difficult to achieve the rate of planned growth or hold back the expansion of smaller settlements in the restraint areas.

The central Berkshire case is instructive.[23] This area had been favoured for major growth in the Strategic Plan for the South East (SPSE), so-called 'Area 8'. Population and employment growth has been and still is very considerable, a reflection of previous central government investment decisions, including the construction of the M3/M4 motorways, Bracknell New Town, and the overspill arrangements concluded between the GLC and the expanded towns of Frimley and Camberley. Between 1971 and 1979 the population grew by 36,000 (11 percent), a massive relative increase bearing in mind that the population of the South East declined by 1 percent over the same period, and of Great Britain as a whole grew by only 1 percent. Despite revised demographic projections, high levels of household formation continue in the area. To implement the regional strategy and coordinate the local authorities in the area, central government commissioned a sub-regional study to assess the feasibility of accommodating a greater scale of growth in central Berkshire (and other parts of north-west Surrey and north-east Hampshire which had been identified).[24] The study team concluded that an additional 64,000 dwellings would be required in central Berkshire alone. But a steering committee composed of local authority members rejected the study and its proposals. They argued that the whole concept of a regional growth area was 'neither relevant nor desirable and should no longer be used'. Berkshire County Council duly submitted its structure plan to the DoE in 1978. It contained no further allocation for housing beyond the rather limited growth implied by past commitments. At the examination-in-public held in 1979 the county was supported by the districts in its view that sufficient land was already available. The House-Builders Federation said that there was an implied shortage of all types of housing land. In his decision on the submitted structure plan, the Secretary of State said that provision must be made by

Berkshire from 1983 onwards for 8,000–10,000 dwellings *in addition* to the 31,000 dwellings already proposed. Predictably the county protested, claiming that the DoE had underestimated the extent of the present land-bank for housing. The Council for the Protection of Rural England also stepped in to voice its opposition to this new scale of development.

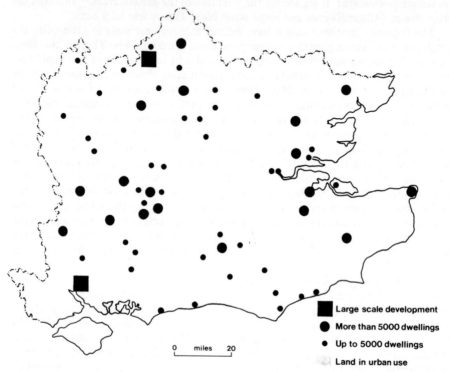

Figure 8.   Structure plan provision for the location of housing growth to the end of the 1980s outside London

The delays in implementation have been considerable in this growth location. Although superficially the outcome of the battle for 'Area 8' appears to be a victory for regional strategy, it is not really clear to what extent the strategy prompted the modifications to the structure plan. The views of the housebuilders appear to have been influential, and it is possible that the DoE seized the opportunity for a greater scale of private-sector investment simply because it fitted in with national economic thinking rather than because it adhered to regional strategy. The variable pattern in the scale of new housing being approved in adjacent restraint counties like Surrey (+ 12,000 dwellings in addition to the structure plan) tends to suggest this. Whatever the real reason, the superimposition of planned growth targets onto the more restraint-orientated local authority plans has introduced uncertainty and political tension into strategy implementation. The reverse side of the coin operates in those countryside areas where the regional plans have proved incapable of controlling the settlement plans of individual counties and the local growth aspirations of the districts.

The protection of the metropolitan Green Belts, Areas of Outstanding Natural Beauty and high-quality agricultural land has normally been conducted by the local authorities. Regional strategies expect only 'limited' or 'normal' growth, and have been remarkably unspecific about the size and distribution of smaller growth points required or the scale of farmland or labour losses which might be associated with improvement in agricultural productivity.[25] The need to focus more closely on these finer-grained spatial differences is important to the management of population and employment growth in the outer areas. A recent evaluation of planning strategy in the outer South East reveals at least four different degrees of growth and restraint: areas where growth is to be promoted; areas where growth is acceptable but needs phasing; areas where the is low growth; and other areas where there is no growth in terms of land-take but not necessarily no development. Clearly, for containment to be effective, the third and the.fourth policies are crucial. Analysis of structure plan provision for housing growth up to the end of the 1980s outside Greater London (Figure 8) shows that a total of 700,000 dwellings will be built between 1976 and 1991, distributed as follows:

15 percent in large-scale development at Milton Keynes and in the South Hampshire area;

50 percent in locations where in the county council's view, 'substantial provision for growth has been made in structure plans' (more than 5000 dwellings);

35 percent in areas where predominately though not exclusively 'small-scale development' can be accomodated to meet some needs of a local nature.

These proposals in aggregate represent a significant shift away from the 'growth point', although possibly not 'growth area' policy. Explaining the change, the Standing Conference on London and South East Regional Planning (SCSERP) points to the inflexibility of the 'major and medium growth' locations shown in the Strategic Plan for the South East, 1970 (Figure 9). In some of these there were sound environmental reasons for restraint, whereas 'the remaining areas into which the region had been divided and which in broad comprised countryside intended for conservation, and which came to be termed "restraint" areas, nevertheless contained towns and villages where a not inconsiderable scale of growth in total was acceptable.... Structure plans have not perpetuated the presentation of development proposals in terms of "growth" areas.'[26]

Some observers detect a weakening commitment by the DoE towards restraint policy. Modifications to draft structure plans are less restrictive, and 'this can be seen as yet another example of government moderating the anti-urban tendencies of the Shire counties'.[27] It is almost certainly true, as the SCSERP argues, that more growth had been built into the structure plans than regional policy implies. However, it has never been really clear what restraint meant in terms of aggregate population and employment change, nor how the figure should be calculated. The sub-area breakdown into past and expected population change used in the Structure Plan for the South East obviously reflects local authority commitments and these can be used to show what restraint will imply in the regional strategy. Any tendency for over-stimulation to growth in these figures or subsequent structure plans is due to county-district strategy itself being influenced by central government. This bottom-up approach to strategic planning has perhaps been inevitable given the local authorities' own desire for 'flexibility' in the light of changing demographic and political circumstances, the government's industrial strategy which supports small-scale

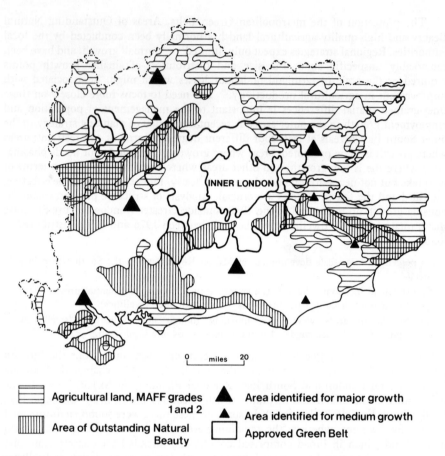

INNER LONDON

0   miles   20

▤ Agricultural land, MAFF grades
    1 and 2

▥ Area of Outstanding Natural
    Beauty

▲ Area identified for major growth

▲ Area identified for medium growth

☐ Approved Green Belt

Figure 9.   Growth and restraint: the strategic plan for the South East

developments in restraint areas, and the DoE's desire to give local authorities
maximum discretion in determining the future scale and form of urban development.
However, a consequence of this approach to restraint policy is that it becomes more
difficult to predict the scale and rate of population or employment dispersal in the
outer areas or to coordinate housing employment transport and social investment
among groups of smaller growth settlements. The solution must surely lie with a
clearer specification of the national policy stance over future housing and industrial
development at the regional scale and a greater commitment by the DoE to support
this stance once it has been agreed with the local authorities. Central government has
been ambivalent about which direction containment should take, seeking to balance
the shire counties' interest in restraint (now changing) with the interests of industrial
and commercial developers who wish to see development take place wherever it can.
The relatively poor performance of the large expansion schemes in relation to the
smaller settlements takes place despite expressed government commitment to the
rationalization of public investment at a regional scale and the desire to reduce overall
public expenditure levels. Sadly it seems that the tripartite strategies, whilst creating

the opportunity for an unequivocal and agreed approach to the outer areas, have proved weak instruments both for planning expansion efficiently in growth locations and for conserving the countryside effectively in restraint areas.

Admittedly, the recent reviews of strategic plans demonstrate a growing awareness of the tensions created by outer-area growth in relation to the needs of the inner cities. Long-range dispersal and large-scale expansion is beginning to lose some currency as a solution for urban growth problems. The reduction in the number of potentially mobile firms, and the slower rate of overspill of population associated with the needs of housing renewal and reclamation in the inner city, have forced upon the regional planners a less expansionist approach. Concern about the energy costs of increased private commuting discourages strategies for indiscriminate dispersal; so does the fear that further outer-city development will lead to under-utilization of infrastructure in the inner cities. Nevertheless, the choice between efficiency (allowing free market forces to continue to promote decentralization) and equity (interpreted as the need to regenerate the inner areas) is more difficult to make at a time of low economic growth and limited public expenditure. The strategies of the late 1970s hold back from the politically unacceptable step of stopping growth in the outer cities; they prefer the middle course of more limited dispersal. Hence, planning is about 'balancing' the needs of protection and development in the outer London region.[28] The strategy for the 'middle ring' of outer Birmingham, for example, involves an 'exceptionally difficult balance' between the restriction of development and the channelling of investment back into the inner-urban areas.[29] Similarly the North West Strategic Plan supports the concentration of investment in the Merseyside/Manchester area as the best compromise between the economic pressures for dispersal and the social needs of the two large conurbations. The problem with this approach is its naive assumption that some form of optimization in the spatial distribution of new investment will occur between outer and inner areas and that increases in the labour supply in the peripheral settlements will be matched by an increase in jobs. Better coordination between housing and industrial policy is required if those uncertainties are to be reduced.

The recent West Midlands regional strategy provides an illustration of this dilemma. The option preferred in the plan is dispersal to the 'middle ring' (broadly speaking, the inner commuting zone) but restraint over long-range dispersal elsewhere. This alternative implies taking some Green Belt land for industrial development. Apart from opposition to close-in development from the county councils, there appear to be technical constraints upon the capacity of the infrastructure systems (especially water supply and sewerage) in the 'middle ring' to support expansion without more public investment. On the other hand, there is, in theory, sufficient housebuilding capacity to accomodate a forecast and substantial overspill of 59,000 households up to 1991, although this figure could prove an underestimate if pressures for additional private housing build up, or land policies are relaxed, or both. The West Midlands regional strategy does not give enough specific advice to district or infrastructure authorities to enable them to plan effectively for these uncertainties.[30]

The difficulties of coordinating the allocation of resources at an intra-regional level may well of course prove greater in the absence of tripartite strategic planning. In South Wales the Welsh Office has been unable to steer decisions on industrial and housing-land release to secure a better balance between growth and decline areas.[31] A number of *ad hoc* decisions have been allowed, and the role of the Welsh Development Agency in encouraging massive factory building in the outer areas is likely to reduce the scope for a coordinated and phased release of both housing and industrial land.[32] Moreover, the risk of increased population dispersal is probably much greater where strategic planning is dominated by the local authorities. In the South West the settlement policies formulated by the South West EPC were little more than an aggregation of county-district plans and seem likely to stimulate considerable commuting, retirement and second-home migration in counties like Avon, Wiltshire and Somerset.[33] In these examples the stronger involvement and intervention of local and central government in the planning process might have encouraged the search for alternative policies, even though the weaknesses of the tripartite approach would probably have remained. An underlying problem with all these regional plans has been the large size of the economic planning regions in relation to the movements of population outlined in Chapter 2. The desire to produce long term frameworks for large regions has obscured the special problems arising in different parts of the outer-metropolitan areas. Forecasts and plans for 'growth' have generally been clearer than those for 'no growth or restraint'.

Conclusion

The regional studies and strategies published during the 1970s confirmed and reflected the post-war history of planned decentralization. Despite the government's official recognition in 1977 of the inner-city issue, no parallel awareness of an outer-city problem is evident in the regional strategies. Indeed, the government's interest in regional planning has retreated at a time when the pressures for economic development are increasing and the need for some coherent policy stance, especially in relation to housing and employment-generating developments, is becoming greater. The tripartite schemes have been replaced by a dual approach to coordination between the economic planning boards (central government ministers) and the local authorities.

Superficially it might seem strange that strategic planning should be out of favour at a time of economic decline. The plans have given considerable indirect succour to development interests in the outer-metropolitan areas. Although there is no call for the encouragement of major expansion schemes, the planned growth areas will continue to increase in size and there is surely a case for coordinating agency programmes more effectively to reduce wasteful public expenditure. There must also be a case for integrating the national and local interest in economic development and environmental planning in the outer areas. The case for separating economic and physical planning may have applied when the counties and districts were essentially custodians of the latter. But the adverse economic situation and current economic philosophy has led the lower-tier authorities into industrial promotion in support of the government's economic strategy, creating a danger of wasteful duplication of investment and, more significantly, increased urban dispersal. The application of the Inner City Partnership principle, particularly to deal with areas of planned growth, might ensure effective implementation of medium-term programmes. Moreover, the dangers of uncoordinated population and employment dispersal in the outer areas suggest the need for a much closer integration of the government's sector and spatial programmes, as argued in the last chapter. The adoption of outer-regional guidelines on the Scottish pattern would be one way of linking national with local planning objectives. Housing, industry, transport, and water 'guidelines' would clearly be priorities. Finally, the definition of sub-regions in those outer areas containing growth and/or restraint locations could be used for interpreting guidelines. That kind of arrangement would involve a move away from regional strategic planning to a more finely grained intra-regional approach with separate plans for outer and inner areas.

Nevertheless, greater commitment to strategic planning for the outer areas would imply a firmer government stance on dispersal than is implied by its official abandonment of the planned programmes. While, superficially, greater commitment would seem easy given the government's inner-city policy, it would be contrary to industrial strategy and to the policies for modifying the national planning system described in the last chapter. Moreover, as several commentators have observed, government has backed away from spatial or long-term strategic planning because it conflicted with its desire to decentralize political control to the local level. The disappointing experience of regional and county structure planning is testimony to the difficulties of operating a planning system in a mixed economy when emphasis is given to *ad hoc* incremental decision making at a local scale.[34] Administrative and organizational weaknesses in strategic plans may have induced a 'certain hopelessness about the power of high level strategic planning to influence events anyway.'[35] Recent experience in the West Midlands tends to bear this out. Regional strategies there have failed to direct development. They have avoided seeking tighter restrictions in the outer areas, partly because restraint was seen to be undesirable as a solution to the problem of urban and economic growth and partly because physical planning had a limited influence on the powerful decentralization forces at work. Moreover, the strategy assumed that any attempt to guide economic development and investment would be counter-productive in the present economic climate. There was also the feeling that the search for a solution acceptable to the different interests of local and central government had weakened the ability of the strategy to resolve conflicts. The political lobbies of the shire counties and the urban areas had both to be accommodated. Hence, in the West Midlands, 'it is not surprising that the discussion surrounding the issue of concentration versus dispersal is never satisfactorily resolved; for to do so would require central government to adopt a much firmer stance on the allocation of the Rate Support Grant and other public expenditure, and clear national direction on the spatial allocation of economic and physical development.'[36]

Undoubtedly, the importance which central government has attached to giving greater discretionary planning powers to local authorities has undermined strategic plans. Central government's commitment to the districts has weakened the strategic influence of the counties. This may work to the government's advantage in so far as it may secure a greater degree of industrial expansion than if county restraint policies were effective. The counties recognize the problem, especially in the Green Belt areas where it is feared that breaches of local policy could lead to bids from the metropolitan counties for boundary extensions. The cooperation of the districts in any new arrangements for regional planning must be essential. But the DoE has encouraged them to take a more active growth-orientated stance in the outer cities through its policies on private housing land and industrial development, which makes it much less likely that the counties will be able to contain growth outside the planned centres. Yet, strange though it may seem, the counties are also changing their attitude towards containment in the outer areas. It is to these we must turn next.

Notes

1.   G. STEELEY, 'Regional planning and regional change in the south east', *The Planner*, vol. 69, no. 4, July/August 1983.

2.   See for instance, P. SELF, 'Whatever happened to regional planning?', *Town and Country Planning*, vol. 49, no. 7, July/August 1980; D. DIAMOND, 'Regional planning — alive and well', *Town and Country Planning*, vol. 50, no. 1, 1981.

3.   G. LOMAS, 'Marching backwards on regional development', *Town and Country Planning*, vol. 48, no. 7, October 1979.

4.   Report in 'Assisted area plan for West Midlands', *The Financial Times*, 1 September 1983.

5.   *Report of the Royal Commission on the Distribution of Industrial Population*, cmnd. 6153 (HMSO, 1940).

6.   The history of regional planning between 1945 and 1972 is fully explored by P. HALL, *Urban and Regional Planning* (Penguin, 1974).

7.   P.HALL, 'The life and death of a quasi quango: the South East Planning council', *London Journal*, vol. 6(2), Winter 1980.

8.   West Midlands Economic Planning Council, *The West Midlands: Patterns of Growth* (HMSO, 1967); *The West Midlands: An Economic Appraisal* (HMSO, 1971).

9.   South East Economic Planning Council, *A Strategy for the South East* (HMSO, 1967).

10.   P. HALL, op. cit.

11.   P. HALL, op. cit.

12.   R. TURTON, 'Lessons from the experience of the North West Economic Planning Council', Paper to Regional Studies Association Conference, 14 November 1980.

13.   P. HALL, op. cit.

14.   P. SELF, *Planning the Urban Region: A Comparative Study of Policies and Organisations* (Allen and Unwin, 1982).

15.The original plans prepared under the 'tripartite' arrangements (excl. reviews) were: *The Strategic Plan for the South East*, DoE/SE Joint Planning Team (HMSO, 1970); *A Developing Strategy for the West Midlands Report of the West Midlands Planning Authorities Conference with Statement by the Secretary of State* (Birmingham, 1974); *A Strategy Plan for the North West*, DoE (HMSO, 1974).

16.   Useful reviews of regional strategic planning are given in A. G. POWELL, 'Strategies for the English Regions: Ten Years of Evolution', *Town Planning Review*, vol. 49, no. 1, January 1978; G. SMART, 'Strategies in decline?', Proceedings of Planning and Transport Research and Computation (International) Co. Ltd., Summer Meeting, July 1980.

17.   G. WEBB, 'A review of the government's regional machinery, 1965–1979', Paper to Regional Studies Association Conference, 14 November 1980.

18.   S. McDONALD, 'The Regional Report in Scotland', *Town Planning Review*, vol. 48, no. 3, 1977.

19.   S. McDONALD, 'How grows the thistle?', *The Planner*, vol. 69, no. 4, July/August 1983.

20.   South East Joint Planning Team, *Strategy for the South East Review* (HMSO, 1976).

21.   Department of Environment, *Strategic Plan for the South East Review — Government Statement* (HMSO, 1978).

22. P. SELF, op. cit.

23. G. J. ASHWORTH, 'Planning policies on land for housing', Department of Town Planning, Oxford Polytechnic, MSc Thesis, 1981.

24. Berkshire, Hampshire and Surrey County Councils, *The Reading, Wokingham, Aldershot, Basingstoke Study*, 1975.

25. J. HERINGTON, 'A Strategic Plan for the South East: review', East Midlands Regional Development Conference, Regional Technical Unit, March 1971.

26. Standing Conference on London and South East Regional Planning, *South East Regional Planning: the 1980s*, SC 1500, February 1981.

27. P. HEALEY, 'Regional Policy in the South East: How far can restraint and local needs be reconciled?', *Town and Country Planning*, vol. 49, no. 11, December 1980.

28. Department of Environment, *SPSE Review — Government Statement*, 1978, op. cit.

29. Joint Monitoring Steering Group, *A Developing Strategy for the West Midlands: Updating and Rolling Forward of the Regional Strategy to 1991* (Birmingham, 1979).

30. C. SKELCHER and J. MAWSON, 'Updating the West Midlands Regional strategy: a review of inter-authority relationships', *Town Planning Review*.

31. See for instance 'The TCPA in the regions: Regional planning in Strathclyde, West Midlands and the industrial South Wales', *Town and Country Planning*, vol. 49, no. 7, July/August 1980.

32. Reported as 'Welsh industry: the hunt for high-technology winners', *Financial Times*, 8 September, 1983.

33. South West Economic Planning Council, *A Strategic Settlement Pattern for the South West* (HMSO, 1974).

34. A. BLOWERS, *The Limits of Power: The Politics of Local Planning Policy* (Pergamon, 1980).

35. P. HALL and M. BREHENY, 'Whither regional planning?', *The Planner*, July/August 1983.

36. C. SKELCHER and J. MAWSON, *op. cit.*

6   The Role of the Counties

Counties are not anti-growth, they're just anti-sprawl.
(D. Lock, 1977).

The power to shape a structure plan and to control its implementation by those responsible for producing it would appear to be very limited.
(A. Blowers, 1980).

County authorities have traditionally been restrictive towards new residential and industrial development. Containment policies were applied by the counties neighbouring the conurbations and attempts were made to restrain the expansion of the smaller cities. Rapid population and economic growth made it sensible for the counties to control development pressures, especially where environmental needs were paramount. Containment kept at bay the territorial and political aspirations of the metropolitan authorities. Moreover, it was generally supported by central government and by other rural districts. Large-scale or overly rapid rates of land release could be prevented — much to the satisfaction of the agricultural and amenity lobby.

However, although many county plans still give the impression of being committed to restraint and conservation, a subtle and significant shift in their orientation has taken place. During the latter part of the 1970s the rising level of unemployment even in prosperous regions forced a less rigid attitude to employment-generating development. In 1977 central government argued that rigid adherence to old-style development plans could damage industrial firms. In 1980 the DoE, through the Local Government Planning and Land Act, took steps to ensure a more responsive approach to housing provision. Subsequent modifications to structure plans and the relaxation of some powers of planning control have combined to weaken local containment policy. It might seem that because the counties were still committed to restraint they could complement the initiatives being taken to promote economic development in the inner cities. But it is not clear that all counties still wish to contain population and employment growth. Even if they do, their plans have been devalued by the operational weaknesses of land planning legislation and local government reorganisation which severed the direct link between policy making and policy implementation. In this chapter we examine the way in which counties are intentionally and unintentionally moving torwards more positive encouragement of housing and industry, and we try to evaluate the influence county plans might have on future economic development and settlement change.

Strategic objectives

The counties' strategic plans — called stucture plans — are the principal vehicle for establishing the direction of broad spatial policy in the future. They are prepared by the 54 English and Welsh counties and the 12 Scottish regional and island councils. A structure plan sets out the principal policies and proposals for the control of development in the area, giving reasons for them, and demonstrating the way in which they interpret national and regional policies. Monitoring is necessary to ensure that the structue plan remains adjusted to changing, demographic, economic and social trends and may lead to periodic review of the policies in the plan. The structure plan provides the framework for more detailed local planning by the district councils. A problem we discuss more fully later is the gap between policy and implementation brought about by the two-tier system of local government.

The structure plan system may be criticised on several grounds.[1] It has taken much longer to produce the plans than originally expected.[2] Before the reorganization of local government in England and Wales only 20 structure plans had been completed. In Scotland no plans were prepared before reorganisation in 1975. By the end of 1981, 67 plans had received full approval, leaving three for approval in 1982. Most counties are now making formal and informal changes to their plans, either making alterations in them or 'rolling-forward' the plan to a new date while making few changes to the original policies. Some are carrying out a full review of their plan, implying major policy changes in the light of newly emerging problems. But there seems to be little consistency in approach. Some counties are examining all aspects of the plan periodically. Others are responding more selectively to *ad hoc* issues. There is rather limited inter-county coordination over the timing, content or subsequent approval of amendments to structure plans. Moreover, the lack of a clear *regional* planning framework has proved a major stumbling-block especially to the counties of England and Wales. Regional strategies have been understandably reluctant to specify the amount, type and location of development that counties should plan for in the outer cities. The structure planners have been left free to interpret terms like 'planned growth' or 'restraint' in any manner they saw fit since the strategies are not legally binding. Indeed, the chance to build the coherent hierarchical framework for planning in Britain suggested by the Planning Advisory Group in 1965 seems to have been lost.[3] In England structure plans are not evidently coordinated at a regional scale.[4] In Scotland the position was rather better, at least until recently, with regional reports having to be prepared by the regional councils[5] (the equivalent of English counties) in advance of the structure plans themselves, and the structure plans being required to take account of national guidelines.[6]

The *modus operandi* of county structure plans is severely constrained by the activities of central government and the many other public and private agencies that impinge on the operation of strategic policy.[7] Counties have little corporate control over other agencies and are hence constantly having to adjust their policies to changing circumstances. For this reason policies for housing and transport, for example, are poorly integrated into the long-term perspectives of the structure plan. Counties are assailed on all sides by central government and district planning agencies; by private developers and their representatives, and by environmental lobbies of one kind or another. The impact of central government is particularly strong. Modifications to structure plans are made by the Secretary of State for the Environment, which results in substantive change to locally formulated scales of future residential and employment growth. For example, the western Wiltshire structure plan originally provided for 10,400 additional dwellings between 1977 and 1991. It was modified to 14,000. Essex was told to modify their allocation of dwellings at Basildon New Town despite warning the DoE that modification would attract migration from London contrary to government policy.[8] Amendments to the Tyne and Wear structure plan have been wide ranging. Tyne and Wear were asked to find an additional 7,000 dwellings, to delete the policy of an upper ceiling for housebuilding in local plans, and to relax retail policy outside existing centres.[9] In the outer South East more housing development has been allowed — in Surrey an additional 12,000 dwellings and in Berkshire an additional 8,000 dwellings. Industrial development is to be encouraged wherever possible. Green Belts have been cut back to around 12 to 15 miles. 'The modified structure plans are in total, then, less restrictive than the draft plans'.[10]

The counties have good grounds for resenting these central government directives. Firstly, there is no apparent consistency in the government's treatment of different structure plans, a point which the Association of County Councils (ACC) has taken up with the government. Very little explanation is given by the DoE for the changes it demands, worsening relations between counties as well as between counties and central government. Why Surrey was asked to find an additional 12,000 dwellings but Hertfordshire none, is difficult to discern, even within the context of the regional strategies for the South East. Secondly, modifications cause delays, especially if they arouse public controversy as in Berkshire. Moreover, government advice on streamlining the planning process appears inconsistent with its recent attitude to structure planning — more central policy direction and more detailed structure plans are likely to prove incompatible.[11]

Behind these issues stands the altered relationship between central government and the counties. This is not simply a matter of the former seeking growth and the latter seeking restraint, although that is often the case. Rather it is a question of the relative autonomy of the counties. The counties are reluctant to accept greater central control; yet they know that in reality they must yield to it. If the counties pursue overly restrictive policies developers will appeal over their heads to central government. If developers get their way, county and district plans are weakened. Of course, counties are sometimes their own worst enemies, inviting central intervention because they cannot agree themselves on policy (as the long running battles between shire and metropolitan counties in the West Midlands illustrate);[12] or arguing with lower-tier authorities about the interpretation of strategic objectives. Disputes between counties and districts are common, and when the DoE intervenes the outcome is often in favour of the districts' plans in preference to the counties'.[13] At stake is the counties' ability to force through developments they consider essential to their strategy or, more often, resist those they feel override it. Central government is of course largely to blame, since it has persistently reduced the power of the counties to control development.[14]

A county's policy stance toward population and employment growth in the outer areas varies according to its political complexion. The reorganisation of local government in 1974 did away with the division between town and country areas, producing large and varied geographic units. The post-1974 counties contain councillors who belonged to the old county boroughs. These councillors tend to be more receptive to growth than their rural counterparts from the old rural districts. Moreover, not all shire counties are Conservative controlled. There have been some recent victories for Labour in the shire counties or situations of no-overall-control after lengthy periods of Tory rule. Although structure planning issues are invariably non-political, shifts in the balance of power can force a total reassessment of policy.[15] Conservative councillors may be expected to favour private-sector investment and well-dispersed small-scale overspill. Labour councillors will prefer greater public-sector housing and more concentrated overspill close in to existing centres. Many Conservative councils have sought solace in 'local needs only' strategies because they imply the defence of local industrial interests, protect communities from urban development, maintain local councillors' power to determine special cases, and check the enthusiasm for too much growth on the part of the districts.[16]

Notwithstanding these local political circumstances, the planning legislation within which counties operate severely constrains the form and direction of structure plan policy. While the limitation on development in rural areas, for example, is clearly a crucial issue, and one which can be addressed largely through land-use control, any attempt to provide a more socially equitable distribution of housing is thwarted by the narrow definition of land-use planning employed by the DoE. Policies to assist particular types of low-income household are not admissible to structure plans. This is unfortunate since the absence of low-cost housing is often a cause of both political tension and social segregation. The DoE may have retreated from its earlier advice,[17] but it seems likely that social considerations in structure plans may be strictly confined to land-use policy.[18] The scope for comprehensive long-term strategic plans embracing social and economic issues now appears hopelessly over-ambitious. Moreover, the link between strategic objectives, sector policies (housing, employment, transport, for instance) and spatial patterns is often unclear. Underlying all these problems is the operational weakness of structure planning and its inability to address itself to the question of the dispersal process and many of the problems that arise from its.

County structure plans must attempt to balance the needs of the economy with the needs of the environment. They must be permissive enough to accommodate the interests of commerce and industry, as the government's industrial strategy requires; yet if too responsive to economic development they jeopardise other desirable policy goals, especially the protection of the environment and the possible long-term regeneration of the inner cities. The task is a complex one. It is not simply a matter of designating areas for growth or restraint but of applying sensitive judgements at a local level that do not prejudice short-term economic needs or long-term social and environmental considerations.[19] Moreover, growth and restraint cannot be interpreted simply in terms of land use. Counties have long realized the need to supplement spatial policies, over which their control is somewhat limited, with wider strategies for economic and employment change, transportation, and urban development. Policies for land use may form only a part of economic strategy. Some counties fear that a 'growth spiral' will result if they continue to encourage the expansion of industry and housing. The resulting 'unfulfilled demand for either housing or jobs, together with deficiencies in roads and other services, may lead to a progressive erosion of the environment'.[20] Even when 'growth' is encouraged the total amount of land required for housing and industry may be less in the 1980s than in the 1970s.

Counties approach their task of formulating strategic objectives in different ways. Some directly or indirectly encourage population and employment growth. Others wish to see both contained more effectively. Most would not wish to see sprawl or unrestricted physical expansion. However, the degree to which strategies encourage market trends varies widely, and there is much ambivalence over whether economic needs or the environment should take precedence. Even within counties avowedly committed to the restriction of population and employment growth — the so-called 'restraint' authorities neighbouring the cities and under the greatest pressure for development — there are different degrees of selective restraint and development promotion. Counties next to each other may interpret development and restraint in widely different ways, as Hertfordshire and Bedfordshire do. There are variations in containment strategy between the more prosperous southern counties and less prosperous counties of the West Midlands and the North of England. The latter seem more willing to adopt an aggressively market-orientated approach to employment-generating development compared with the former who seek stronger protection for the environment.

Some counties seek to exercise strong restraint over new housing and industry. The aim of these authorities is to minimize the physical extent of urban development by relocating new local firms and volume housebuilders outside their areas, preferably in the planned growth locations. Virtually the whole of Hertfordshire and Surrey adopt this type of low-growth strategy, although it is exceptional. In other outer areas it is more common to find counties opting for severe restraint in certain selected sub-divisions like east Berkshire,[21] south-east Dorset[22] or south-west Hampshire.[23] But in such cases severe restraint does not usually apply to all rural settlements. Limited development to meet 'local needs' (usually housing rather than industry) is permitted even within Green Belts. Studies of south-west Hampshire refer to 200 new dwellings per annum, 50 percent of which will be on greenfield sites. An embargo on new building is reluctantly rejected because 'while in theory turnover within the existing stock could provide all locally generated housing needs . . . this situation is unlikely in practice and new houses will continue to be required'.[24]

Although many structure plans claim to restrain development, counties realize that given the broad scale at which their strategic objectives apply they must leave the districts some discretion in individual villages or groups of settlements. If they are unwilling to do so central government will ensure that responsibility for the scale and distribution of housing development remains with the lower-tier authorities. In these circumstances, whether the county favours more or less development in Green Belts, for example, is almost immaterial since the power to implement settlement policy lies with the district councils. Cheshire sought some relaxation of housing and employment development in the Green Belt but the Secretary of State modified the plan by deleting the lists of named vilages where strict control would not apply.[25] Hertfordshire wanted the option of identifying small and large villages for 'local needs' development both within and outside the Green Belt. The DoE's modifications insisted that only smaller villages within the Green Belts and selected villages beyond the Green Belts could be so identified, provided the districts had decided to prepare local plans.[26] Other counties' attempts to achieve restraint by specifying settlements for 'limited development' or 'infill' have been effectively thwarted by DoE modifications to structure plans.[27] The scale of future housing growth will be determined by the districts not the counties. While it cannot be assumed all districts would like more growth, the result of weak strategic control is a less predictable and indicative kind of short-term planning. Almost certainly many counties will adjust their structure plans to accommodate higher levels of population growth than they want.

However, the argument is not as straightforward. It is not a simple matter of counties wanting to restrain urban development and the districts or central government wanting to overrule them. Counties recognise the inherent political difficulties of implementing restraint and at the same time meeting the need for local development. In counties close to the conurbations, the social polarization and restriction of local industry caused by restraint has in any case forced a more permissive attitude towards development. But in counties including or adjacent to growth points a similarly more relaxed policy stance is noticeable in the restraint areas. For instance, despite the presence of the Central Lancashire New Town, many smaller towns and villages in central and north Lancashire will receive limited scales of development.[28] Mid-Hampshire, saddled between the growth points in the north and south of the county, contains quite permissive employment policies favouring local industrial development.[29] In Gloucestershire a more residential development will be encouraged in the north and south Cotswolds to reverse the decline in local services, jobs and housing.[30] These examples of a more permissive attitude, found particularly in the outer commuting areas, clearly present problems for regional strategy and sometimes for county restraint policy. They are county policies and, with the exception of Gloucestershire, represent a failure to relate settlement change to the strategic interest of the authority. The same cannot be said of those counties that have deliberately shifted their policy stance in favour of encouraging economic activity. Cheshire's proposed modification argues that 'the emphasis of the structure plan should be to facilitate development to create jobs whilst maintaining essential enviromental safeguards as far as possible'.[31] In Kent renewed effort must be put into the promotion and encouragement of economic activity in the county.[32] In Bedfordshire 'the county council hold the view . . . that national priorities are such that there is a strong case for structure plan policies assisting economic growth, wherever appropriate, unless there are overiding local considerations that make it undesirable'.[33]

It would be difficult not to agree with the observation that contemporary development plans are now essentially growth-orientated instruments, which require additional financial resources to secure their implementation. Nowhere is this more clearly demonstrated than in regional sector policies, for economic development, employment and housing.

Economic development and employment

A combination of factors draws county councils into the sphere of economic regeneration and employment stimulation. The recession severely restricts industrial development and job prospects; the supply of mobile industry has dried up, implying that new jobs must be sought from the indigenous rather than the regional or national economy; and central government cuts in the rate support grant have encouraged councils to seek local rate income from industry. The present government argues that councils 'have a positive role to play in sustaining and fostering local economies and employment'[34] and previous governments have urged them to give favourable consideration to industrial concerns.[35] However, the Tories want local authorities to limit their initiatives to small firms, a rather narrow approach in view of the growing evidence that small firms create few new jobs.

County councils have powers to promote economic development under a variety of Acts of Parliament including the Local Government Act 1972, which allows loans and grants to be paid to firms. In this way county councils can support private enterprise directly. Counties may allocate capital expenditure to industrial development and estates. In 1976-7 local authorities as a whole spent £529 million. By 1980 this had risen to £1000 million.[36] All councils are now being urged by the government to increase capital spending, especially on infrastructure, roads, water supply, and construction for industry and housing. In practice they will find this difficult since most capital programmes have already been decided two or three years in advance. Industry would like a programme of planned capital investment over a number of years, but the present method whereby local authorities' capital expenditure is adjusted annually by central government means that counties cannot make such long-term plans. It is also contradictory for the government to seek increases in capital spending while wanting revenue expenditure held down since capital projects invariably lead to greater revenue spending on staff and day-to-day administration.[37]

Not all counties attach the same importance to economic strategy. Some counties focus solely upon locally established firms or upon small firms. Others give priority to attracting investment from outside the county, especially high-technology firms with a national or international market, accepting all the implications of the greenfield development. There is also considerable variety in the methods used to achieve economic strategies. Many counties use their powers under the Town and Country Planning Acts to control the provision of land and buildings, providing the necessary infrastructure and coordinating the services provided by statutory undertakers. Planning departments in shire counties play a role in the 'economic development teams' used to overcome the lack of corporate liaison between departments. There is little coordination as yet between counties over the implementation as distinct from the promotion of economic development. Many counties operate outside the structure plan framework altogether entering into partnerships with private businesses or carrying out development themselves. Most find themselves involved in a range of additional activities such as providing industrial information, advice and promotion, employment training, cooperative agencies and job creation projects. The crucial distinction between enterprises which stimulate growth and those which provide jobs however is rarely made. Unlike the metropolitan authorities it would seem that the non-metropolitan counties are putting their money on industrial growth. In doing so they are being supported by central government.

Employment policies also form part of a structure plan. In outer London — in Hertfordshire, east Berkshire, south Buckinghamshire and Surrey — attempts have been made to confine the expansion of industry to those firms which are local and provide local jobs. Containment of employment growth is secured by diverting major employers to planned growth locations elsewhere in the South East or in the Assisted Areas. Warehouse and office developments have to serve a local catchment area. Studies in the Dacorum district of Hertfordshire show these policies were strongly effective between 1974 and 1980. Most approvals were for extensions and redevelopments on existing sites by Dacorum-based firms. However, rising unemployment and firm closures forced Hertfordshire and Dacorum to take a more relaxed stance, removing the condition that local firms should occupy small units and, since 1982, allowing the redevelopment of existing sites by quite substantial non-local firms up to a limit of 3000 jobs. While industrial development in Hemel Hempstead had for long been held back, an electronics firm was granted permission in 1981 to move from central London to a greenfield site, and 2000 new office jobs will be allowed serving, it is argued, a national and a regional need.[38] The Hertfordshire experience demonstrates that a 'local firms only' strategy worked until 1980, and was supported by central government as an acceptable method of containment in the outer cities. Nonetheless there is great pressure in the outer cities from non-local business and commercial developers. The rationale for restricting approvals to local and often small firms is that if little land is taken for development the Green Belt can be upheld and the landscape protected. In this sense a policy of 'local need only' will come closest to upholding the ideal of containment strategy in the same way that 'local need' housing has been used as a means of restricting the total quantity of development.

In contrast, counties located in the Assisted Areas have actively sought enterprises from outside the region, although there has been little effective development of high-technology industry.[39] An exception is in north Cheshire, in the area adjoining the M6 and M52. The Birchwood Science Park in Warrington includes seventeen high-technology firms including British Nuclear Fuels, Data General and Digital Equipment. Cheshire's aim is to encourage the expansion of existing firms since, they argue, fewer new firms will be attracted from outside the county. However the Structure Plan First Alteration makes clear that sufficient land will be allocated for new firms as well as for the expansion or redevelopment of existing ones. There is no presumption against national, regional or research offices.

Avon county has five sites for high-technology developments in outer Bristol. Each will be developed for offices and light industry. The buildings will occupy only 30 percent of site areas, implying a very low density form of development. Avon county face great pressure for new warehousing land and there are doubts as to whether they will be able to prevent land approved for light industry being turned over to warehousing. Although prepared to countenance dispersed industrial sites near the motorways, they hope that enterprises with separate but linked functions (research, manufacturing, administration, for example) will be located just as easily in the city of Bristol. Avon seeks firms which manufacture the products from research, especially those employing semi-skilled and unskilled labour.[40] All five sites are dispersed around the city fringes. One is located on unallocated 'white land' in the green belt yet the structure plan blindly pins its faith on the Green Belt as a tool for diverting employment growth to preferred locations.[41]

Counties still believe the structure plan has an influence on economic development, not so much in containing growth but facilitating it. A pleasant environment can attract entrepreneurs and safeguard local firms. Public investment intentions and priorities can be indicated in the plan.[42] Moreover, there is still widespread adherence to spatially redistributive strategies as a means of promoting or steering employment and economic development. For example, Gloucestershire refer to the critical and overriding importance of their employment policy, and urges dispersal over short distances from Cheltenham and Gloucester across the Green Belt, and 'small-scale' industry in villages where population growth has produced a bulge in the number of school leavers. Other counties like Cheshire and Kent are now taking a more lenient attitude to employment-generating enterprises in Green Belts. One limitation of all these policies is the emphasis given to employment as distinct from economic growth. The counties may be right to emphasize employment since they are marginally more able to control it. Encouraging industrial output, on the other hand, could encourage in areas of rapid population growth, enterprises that are not labour intensive, merely fuelling unemployment. The counties' employment strategies are often unspecific about the quality or type of labour. The tendency for skilled occupational groups to live in the outer city has encouraged the relocation and growth of skilled jobs. It is unlikely that a simple aggregate increase in employment without the introduction of new *kinds* of job will alter the position. Structure plans have not given much thought to matching jobs with local labour skills. A 'local need' policy cannot of itself ensure semi-skilled or unskilled employment for local people, although it is likely to be more successful than a strategy which encourages non-local firms.

Improvements in infrastructure provision, especially water and transport, also offer the counties a prospect of adjusting future economic development. Ideally the structure plan should coordinate the investment decisions made by other agencies, especially the regional water authorities and statutory undertakers, but this does not often take place in a satisfactory way. The role of the regional water authorities is crucial. These bodies block the implementation of schemes by refusing to allocate investment when and where it is needed to secure structure plan policies. They 'have regard to' structure plans but the structure plans are insufficiently detailed to cover the future scale of investment in infrastructure, meaning that its provision must wait until the districts have produced their local plans. It is thus lower-tier authorities who are required to liaise with the regional water authorities over plans for new investment or alterations to sewers and watercourses; and districts who are directly involved in capital expenditure. The link in the structure plan between employment allocation and the expenditure programmes of the regional water authorities is a weak one. An acute problem in areas where development pressures are great is the absence of financial accountability amongst the counties and districts, which encourages them to 'bid up' their infrastructure requirements. Too generous allocation of industrial land will overstretch the water authorities, a point which already concerns regional conferences of county authorities. The arguments in favour of a *regional* approach to infrastructure planning and programming are surely strong at a time of reduced public investment. The tendency for counties to outbid each other for economic development is already leading to wasteful duplication of effort. Water investment is essential to the effective implementation of both regional development and inner city programmes. The compelling pressures for growth in the outer cities mean that investment is directed there before anywhere else.

The counties also see spending on roads as essential to economic growth. Although the need to reduce traffic congestion is often given as a reason for new schemes, a more important one is the prospect of attracting new industry. Hence new access links will be approved only where the county can be assured that industrial development is likely to take place. Reductions in government capital grants seriously eroded county road programmes between 1978 and 1981, although there has been some increase since then. Cheshire for instance will spend £40 million in total on transport between 1981 and 1991, half the figure projected in the structure plan. But it should not be imagined that counties have lagged too far behind in their road projects. The scale of investment has been colossal in the outer London fringe, as mentioned earlier. Furthermore, the government's recently announced revised budget figures for spending changes between 1982/3 and 1983/4 show a national increase in transport spending from £3181 to £3318 million.[43] Much of this will go on new trunk roads and bypasses as the Transport Secretary has made clear.

In general it is too early to judge the success of the counties' economic strategies — many are still being formulated. The inherent conflicts created by a much more permissive attitude to growth are, however, obvious: the threat, real and potential, to long cherished strategic planning goals for the protection of farmland and Green Belts; the further boost it is likely to give to skilled jobs and the effect this will have on the occupational balance in the outer city; and the rising public costs of infrastructure. Counties face real difficulties in controlling the scale and pattern of employment shift at a time of recession unless they own industrial land or enter into more direct forms of partnership.[44] Yet they have to respond to a number of forces and agents beyond their control. The rhetoric of economic growth is strong even though in reality settlement systems may prove difficult to adjust. There is clearly a 'widespread concern amongst politicians, practitioners and the public that planning should become more actively involved in enabling development to occur and creating an attractive environment'.[45] If they are right, the county planners may find that a more lenient approach to industry and commerce has a powerful psychological effect in reinforcing the attractions of the outer city over those of the inner city.

Housing

Structure plans define the total number of dwellings required in the future. They also specify when and where they will be built. There are major problems in evaluating the impact of structure plans on housing. In the first place there are no national housebuilding targets. Counties may claim that they use central government forecasts of population change and household formation, but these have not hitherto been worked into any form of coherent strategy for housing land allocation at the local scale. Second, housing policies in structure plans are often poorly related to general goals for development or restraint. It is not usually clear how much housebuilding is acceptable within a restraint county. Most counties assume it is desirable to meet at least some local housing need (however defined). This means either a low or slower rate of new housebuilding than has been experienced in the past, or the replacement of existing stock with new dwellings thus avoiding the need to take fresh land. What a 'low rate' means in practice varies greatly between authorities; nor is the balance between new and replacement stock clearly defined. The need for *any* new dwellings in settlements under pressure is rarely questioned. A third issue is how the scale and rate of development taking place in the outer city is to be judged in relation to the inner city. Because of the absence of regional planning, and despite the rhetoric employed by some counties to justify their housing strategies, there is little apparent match between the housing policies of metropolitan and non-metropolitan counties. A fourth difficulty is that in the short term recent structure plans can only be judged by their impact on the spatial pattern of housing development since the actual scale and rate of housebuilding will depend on the housing market. A number of broad assumptions must be made before we can forecast the level of population growth likely to arise from proposals in recent plans.

Counties are clearly left to prepare their housing strategies without a national or regional framework. It is therefore difficult to know whether in aggregate terms the counties' structure plans prescribe too little or too much housing, an issue we return to later. Nonetheless an orientation to growth in housing is noticeable, and seems to arise both from the legacy of past commitments to housebuilding and the scale of outstanding planning permissions even in restraint areas, points already mentioned in Chapter 3. Additionally, 'local needs' may turn out to be quite substantial if they refer to an entire county and take account of new household formation. In Bedfordshire, even a 'low-growth' housing strategy meant an additional 29,700 dwellings built over a fifteen-year period. Significantly, at the 'examination in public' some neighbouring counties argued that the figures in Bedfordshire's structure plan were too high. They feared that a growth spiral of demand for more housing and employment-generating activity would result. The county council, for self evident reasons, maintained that the point had not yet been reached at which no further land should be released for development. In the panel's judgement a policy of meeting local housing needs was 'unrealistic, unimplementable and not necessarily compatible with slowing the rate of population growth.' At the same time the panel objected to an overly strong definition of 'infilling'.[46] It is difficult to see how a policy of non-local needs would have been any more compatible with slowing down population growth, but the truth is that the structure plan is not capable of implementing a social goal of that kind given the reluctance of the DoE to countenance 'local housing need'. Of course the real problem was that the scale of housing provision was predicated on the assumption of a (relatively) high level of household formation, making it likely that any spatial readjustment would have a marginal impact. Another dilemma facing counties concerns the acceptability of its housing strategy to the districts — low growth or restraint policies must be sufficiently flexible to accommodate the political interests of the local councils; if they are not, and indeed even if they are, the gap between structure plan targets and the amount of development permitted locally will be wide.

All counties are now being pressed by central government to release more housing land. It is fair to say that most shire counties are still conservative in their attitude to large scale allocations. But they are not afraid to see small-scale incremental growth taking place, especially if they can claim it helps economic recovery. Yet the potential magnitude of change in the housing stock implied by an incremental approach in the outer cities is surely not fully appreciated by decision makers. Apart from the problems of long-term physical, environmental and social change, over-rapid housing release creates tension for the inner-city authorities anxiously striving to regenerate urban communities. At stake is the potential of the planning system to redistribute housing growth in accordance with broad social goals. These very different ideologies and strategies towards housing provision are illustrated by the Cheshire and Strathclyde experiences.

Housing in Cheshire

Cheshire plan for 60,000 new dwellings to be built by 1991, 20,000 of which are to be built in the New Towns of Warrington and Runcorn and 40,000 spread between existing settlements.[47] Translating dwellings into population figures is always hazardous, but if we assume an average occupancy rate of 2.5 persons per dwelling (which will fall over the plan period), then a migration of 150,000 persons could result from the proposed housebuilding targets (and the figure of 150,000 does not account for the fall in occupancy rate as it affects the existing population).

Cheshire have altered the generally restrictive policy which applied outside the New Towns in the approved 1979 structure plan (Figure 10). A new type of housing strategy is proposed that will change the allocation of housing land in each of sixteen urban sub-divisions. The scale of provision will reflect both forecast housing requirements and past rates of housebuild, priorities for employment land, and the need for Cheshire's housing policies to complement those of the adjacent metropolitan counties.[48] It is argued in the recent plan that where past rates have fallen below the rate of building implied by the structure plan any further allocation would be unnecessarily generous. Where the past rate has exceeded the structure plan figure it would be unrealistic not to continue meeting the local demand for housing, unless there were overriding strategic constraints. In other words, the performance of the housing market provides the criterion for future spatial policy. Yet Cheshire argue that (in the case of five sub-divisions) their strategy represents the restraint on housebuilding necessary to support the interests of guiding development pressures towards neighbouring inner cities.

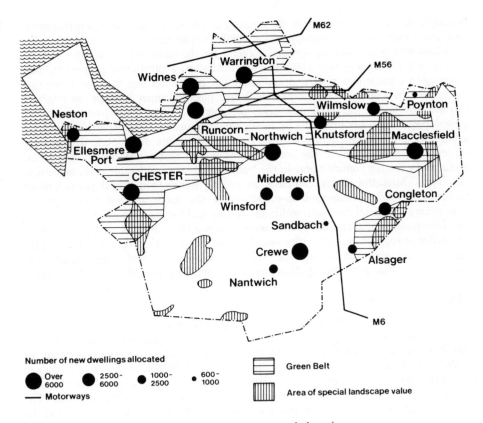

Figure 10.   Cheshire county structure plan: proposed alterations

It is difficult not to be sceptical that these plans will be achieved. The possibility of steering development away from the pressure areas of 'restraint' — notably Macclesfield, Poynton, Alsager, Neston, Wilmslow and Knutsford — must be slight, bearing in mind that this hasn't been achieved under less permissive development plans. Short-distance migration and housing relocation sound like wishful thinking. New housing in these towns has often been sold to out-migrants from the Manchester conurbation. Dropping the term 'local need' and relying on the private sector will tend to encourage that trend. Although the districts could effectively control the size, mix and density of private housing, and hence its price, the DoE's Circular 22/80 discourages this, as mentioned in Chapter 3. A related problem is the scale of growth likely to be generated in the rural areas of the county by Cheshire's more adaptive approach. Here, small-scale conversion of existing building, 'infilling' and small groups of new dwellings will be permitted. The key point is that the *districts* will determine the land allocations and make development decisions on housing applications. The structure plan urges them to ensure a steady rate of housebuilding during the life of a local plan and to guide development into the towns. But if past housebuilding rates prove buoyant in some locations the local plans will need to reflect this fact; if they do not, and there are few physical planning constraints upon development, then the allocations for housing could still be increased. Furthermore, local plans may not even be prepared for smaller settlements.[49]

Cheshire's policies create serious problems for the outer city. First, while not all new housebuilding will take place on greenfield sites, a substantial proportion will, resulting in a major loss of agricultural land. The plan states that 'it is inevitable that the greater part of new development will take place on open land on the edges of towns'.[50] Second, substantial new areas of housing will be permitted outside the growth points, possibly involving up to 40,000 dwellings by 1991. Apart from placing a burden on the infrastructure costs of public and private developers, this strategy represents a further nail in the coffin for the notion that concentration is the best method of effecting containment. In the 'restraint' areas considerable extra housing is required. Third, the strong emphasis on private rather than mixed public/private tenure will further encourage in-migration of the more affluent social groups, dramatizing the social contrasts within the county and between Cheshire, Manchester and Liverpool. A final and important consideration is that Cheshire's claim to support the policy of regenerating the cities sounds rather hollow. If the recent structure plan alterations are approved by the DoE, the implied annual rate of housebuilding will come close to that proposed by Manchester and greatly exceed that for Merseyside.

Housing in Strathclyde

In contrast, Strathclyde Regional Council recognizes the inherent growth potential of a 'local housing need' policy and takes a much more aggressive stance against development in the outer city. Strong controls over residential development will be applied for the sake of urban regeneration as well as for the sake of stabilizing trends in the rural areas.[51] The strategy wants positive discrimination in favour of the Glasgow conurbation at the same time as promoting investment in the central lowlands. The conflicts and tensions created by this stance are illustrated by the controversy over the scale of investment in the New Towns outside Glasgow. The structure plan alteration wants limitations on future dwelling targets in the New Towns but would not resist industrial growth. Without some control it is clear that population increase in East Kilbride, Cumbernauld and Irvine could amount to over 70,000 by 1990. Although the role of these towns in relieving urban congestion is now greatly diminished, the housing requirements of 'second and third generation' households living in these towns remain. Strathclyde has therefore had to modify the hard line of its earlier structure plan under pressure from the Secretary of State for Scotland. The Scottish division of the TCPA, committed as it is to decentralization, voiced its objections at the examination in public, arguing that apart from discriminating against 'second generation' housing requirements in the New Towns, a restriction on the rate of housebuild in line with employment growth was unrealistic and ignored the role of housing availability in future employment generation.[52]

The Strathclyde approach to countryside protection is equally determined in style. Development proposals in the Green Belt will only be justified if they satisfy a 'specific locational need', if there are economic benefits, or if infrastructure is available and environmental impact is minimal. The TCPA argued against this strongly protectionist line on the grounds that it might hold back economic growth in the region. They sought a more positive attitude to development in the 'areas of regional scenic significance' defined in the plan. Given the logic of the strategy, however, it is difficult to see how the planners could have argued in any other way. Somewhat ironically, we find the TCPA, for so long an advocate of urban regional planning, objecting to a comprehensive plan covering the inner and outer city on the grounds that it is too restrictive of growth in the outer areas.

The Strathclyde plan is not without its drawbacks. It is likely to prove difficult to show 'specific locational need', in much the same way that it is difficult to show 'local housing need'. A strong restraint on housing in Green Belt areas will not eliminate the need to list other greenfield locations where additions to the supply of land for private housing will be acceptable. Some non-urban land will have to be taken. As in England, the Strathclyde Regional Council is likely to find controlling the lower-tier authorities a major problem, especially in outlying rural areas attractive to private housing developers. Nor can the strategy reverse the tendency to social polarization between inner and outer urban areas. Although future infrastructure spending in the outer city could be curtailed and redirected, there is always a risk that existing capacity will be under-utilized especially in the New Towns. A further difficulty is the conflict between regional policy and urban strategy. Holding back on growth may have come too late. The in-built pressures for growth in the outer city are enormous and will prove strong encouragement to further industrial investment.[53]

At a time of recession one rationale for extra housing must be the prospect of more jobs. Perhaps the Cheshire approach is more realistic in this respect. By allowing for 'choice' and for market factors, this type of structure plan recognises at least the contemporary realities of change in the outer city. But the idea that further employment might be stimulated is at best doubtful and at worst utopian. More likely is a short term gain in construction jobs. Housing is likely to grow faster than jobs given the scale of growth being planned, hence creating sizeable labour surpluses. If more commuting followed employment dispersal might be encouraged. If out-migration were followed the outer commuting areas would suffer a loss of skilled workers. It is difficult to see how growth-orientated housing strategy will prove beneficial to employment in the long-term, although it is the most likely scenario for many shire counties in the future.

Inherent contradictions underlie the counties' approach to strategy. The bulk of intra-regional migration occurs within the outer city itself, rather than between the inner and outer areas. Hence adjustments to housing totals in the outer city may have only a marginal impact on spatial patterns of growth and decline, at least over the short term. Admittedly, this is less true of those outer cities where decentralization is less advanced and where there is a more immediate trade-off between inner and outer areas. Nonetheless, the development of housing in the outer cities has been a desirable tenet of planning strategy for thirty or forty years. The physical, economic and social restructuring of the urban region has followed a long and positive programme of public and private investment. Any reversal of the impetus to the growth of the outer city will take an equally long period of readjustment in public and private-sector policy. Sadly, we do not know how much housing investment should be allocated in the outer city to secure both social and economic objectives. History shows that counties will not gladly impose a total embargo on housing since population growth is necessary to gain financial support from central government. The political implications of withholding rate support grant to outer shire counties are bound to be unpalatable. Yet this action could prove more effective than attempting to contain housing through development plan procedures. There are arguments for stronger control over the scale, rate, and type of housing development in the outer city but these will only become apparent when the counties recognize that the problems created by further population growth are as much theirs as the inner cities'.

Settlement policies

Counties are as much concerned with the spatial distribution of employment and housing within their areas as with the total volume of growth. By and large their aim is to consolidate or concentrate additional development in larger towns and rural settlements in order to avoid dispersal. Here we see the 'growth point' philosophy favoured at the regional scale emerging at the local level also. Indeed, concentration has become the principal method by which shire counties attempt to contain urban development.[54]

Major difficulties surround the evaluation of concentration strategies. One problem is the relationship between strategic objectives and rural settlements in the outer cities. The general location of future housing land release beyond existing commitments is shown in the structure plan. Although housing 'targets' might be specified by sub-division or district they are rarely disaggregated by settlement or groups of settlements. Indeed, some counties and districts argue that this level of detail is inappropriate in a structure plan, preferring a general presumption that *all* rural settlements should allow for housing and employment provision.[55] Thus the written statement is no more than a very general guide to the scale of concentrated or dispersed development, leaving actual levels to be determined by the districts. A related problem is the strategic significance of housing change in small rather than large settlements. The assumption is all too often made that below a certain unspecified threshold of population size, only modest urban growth will occur in accordance with restraint policy. Even 'key' rural settelements may not be expected to absorb much development relative to urban centres. The danger is that the cumulative impact of housing developments on total population change will be underestimated. Even apparently minor 'infill' development in villages and country towns plays an important role in total housing provision, which, simply because development is dispersed and change is incremental, can easily be missed. Moreover, the scale of development that rural settlements have had to absorb has been affected by failure to achieve desired levels of growth in the major and strategic growth allocations. This appears to have been the unintended consequence of counties putting all their faith in the successful implementation of just one or two growth points. For instance, the south Hampshire structure plan seeks a dispersed type of development, with the bulk of growth to take place in selected allocations on the fringes of Southampton and Portsmouth in places like Toton, Chandlers Ford, and western Fareham.[56] The rate at which these growth areas have expanded has alarmed the county, and much more 'infill' and minor development than expected has occurred in smaller settlements. The chief proposal in Leicestershire's structure plan was the development of Hamilton, a greenfield site north-east of Leicester. Hamilton was to accommodate 19,000 people. Opposition by local pressure groups, opposition within the county council, and difficulties in supplying water and other services, have severely curtailed the project. Other major problems have beset the implementation of Leicestershire's growth allocations. Under pressure from central government and local housebuilders the county was forced to ask the districts to find land for additional housing in 'key' and other settlements forced to take on the task of absorbing strategic levels of housing growth.[57]

These examples demonstrate the practical difficulties counties face in containing urban expansion and growth, in both small and large settlements, in the interests of 'restraint.' Another fundamental issue concerns the separation of urban and rural settlement policy in the outer cities. The smaller settlements can meet a wide range of strategic housing requirements in much the same way as urban settlements do: it is strategic functions not sizes of settlement which should be given more weight in the structure plans. Most residential mobility in the outer cities is exurban rather than either urban or rural in character, a point brought out in the studies discussed in Chapter 2. There is surely a strong case for devising strategic exurban settlement policies that bear some relationship to the complexity of residential, employment and travel patterns in the outer cities. This would allow counties to plan for the amount and location of future housing possibly over groups of smaller settlements. Housing objectives in the structure plans could be translated more effectively into instruments of socio-spatial policy. For example, a planned reduction in overspill could be effected by rigorous control on land release in larger settlements and these centres could in turn accommodate a higher proportion of out-county key workers and managers. Additional housing in non-key villages might permit more affluent commuters to move further out into the countryside. And so on according to the direction of policy sought. It would thus be possible to monitor the rate and scale of overspill, out-county movement and local mobility in a way not done at present, and to adjust housing programmes in step.

The opportunity for a more radical socially-orientated approach to settlement policy is unlikely to be taken because of the limitations of planning legislation.[58] Counties have been notably reluctant to specify social or demographic objectives beyond making bland statements about overall population targets or spatial distributions. The social and redistributional consequences of settlement policies are thus not dealt with. Some structure plans refer to social objectives under housing policies, but there is a wide gulf between the statement of concern contained in a structure plan and the policies proposed or put into action. However, settlement policies can redistribute social and economic resources by channelling growth into some centres and not into others. It is debatable how effective settlement policies have proved as instruments for achieving positive planning of this kind. Key settlements are expected to serve as service centres for a rural hinterland, but service provision depends on development agencies whose decisions are poorly coordinated on a county scale. Indeed county-wide application of a key settlement policy may have little if any strategic significance in terms of the delivery and accessibility of services. Moreover, it must be doubted whether a functional-size hierarchy of settlements based on given scales of service provision is appropriate or even desirable.[59] The most counties can do is liaise with agencies, investigate the feasibility of new types of service provision, and examine the patterns of service use and behaviour more closely. A strong and more effective control over housing in the private and public sectors is possible and has proved to have a much more direct impact on demographic and social patterns.

'Local need' policies have been predicated on the assumption of little change and the existence of latent housing need. Which groups fall within the category of a 'local need' is often not clearly defined, nor is it clear how the policies will be implemented given that powers to control housing development lie with the districts. 'Local need' *could* imply the provision of housing for commuters moving short distances from neighbouring urban centres. 'Local need' is especially difficult to implement wherever the private market dominates, especially in the smallest villages, since the high relative price of houses will ensure that new dwellings will invariably go to non-locals.[60] The policy can do little more than control the overall number of dwellings constructed and the rate and density of building. The environmental character of outer-city settlements has been protected, but the chief beneficiaries have been the better-off social groups who can afford to live in the countryside. 'Local need' policies and 'infill' developments have thus been socially regressive to the extent that local development pressure was denied. Social polarization has been exacerbated.

By themselves, the rural settlement policies operated by the counties must be viewed as negative methods of dealing with the unique circumstances of the outer city. In so far as they have achieved the objectives of the structure plan — namely, to concentrate population growth rather than permit dispersal, and to protect the environmental quality of the smaller villages — they must be regarded as successful, although there are case studies to prove exceptions to this.[61] However, their unintended social consequences give cause for concern, particularly their effects on social polarization and the costs of infrastructure and social provision. Restraint policies have assisted the wealthier groups. The inability of some structure plan to distribute growth between large and small centres, and of rural settlement policies to increase the opportunites for housing different social groups, supports the case for abandoning them forthwith and replacing them with a new kind of flexible strategy that recognizes the desire by more affluent commuters to live in smaller villages and yet avoids creating one-class villages. Sadly, such social objectives have been missing from settlement policy because it has been formulated solely in terms of physical planning problems.

Conclusion

The attitude of the counties to containment has changed rapidly in the last few years and there would now seem to be much less conflict between national economic goals and local planning policies. It is true that restraint policies are still the norm, but the rhetoric and reality of restrant are very different. Furthermore the first round of structure plans is now over. While these had at least the semblance of continuing the generally restrictive approach found in the early development plans, this is no longer true of the reviews, modifications and alterations in progress. We are probably still in a stage of transition away from restraint to growth, but it is happening.

Counties still rely in large measure on spatially redistributive policies and controls whether in employment or in housing. These could be adjusted to the requirements of growth in the future, but for the time being there are limits on their effectiveness stemming partly from poor coordination and partly from over-rigid application of policies in very different spatial contexts. The settlement strategies show little imagination on the subject of local demographic and social trends or about the policies of adjacent counties. Landscape and settlement policy contradict each other. A selective restraint strategy in a Green Belt may soon prove to be a growth orientated strategy since any release of land in the larger settlements will rapidly be taken up. Conversely, in a non-Green Belt area, rural settlement restrictions may present an obstacle to substantial housing release. At issue is the method of achieving strategic objectives. Can major and minor goals be separated? If landscape protection is to gain priority then settlement policy needs adjusting and vice versa. Furthermore the scope that counties have for effecting change through redistributional policies is often severely limited by the legacy of past planning decisions and commitments. For this reason, the presentation of future options in terms of 'urban concentration', 'dispersal', or 'balance', if often no more than window-dressing.

None of this implies that the counties have no important effect on population and employment shifts in the outer city. They still set the general framework for development control. Also, some counties have been very effective. In the London Green Belt physical restraint has been exceptionally strong, with pressures being passed on to the outer-metropolitan areas. In regions without a Green Belt the county's role must be evaluated differently. We still know little about non-Green Belt areas like the West Yorkshire fringes or outer Leicester, but the evidence is that although it is now easier for counties to pursue more growth-oriented policies this has not always proved to be so. The issue in both areas is the relative weakness of the counties in controlling lower-tier authorities.

Nor must we underestimate the impact of counties on those occasions when their policies agree with the wishes of central government and are not flouted by the districts. Counties perform well when there is a high degree of conformity between policy goals, strategies and implementation at all levels of government. Ironically, however, in pursuit of economic development, central government is straining its relationship with the counties and shifting power to the districts. It is to the county-district relationship that we turn next.

Notes

1.   The problems are fully discussed in M. BRUTON, 'The future of development plans — PAG revisited', *Town Planning Review*, vol. 51, no. 2, 1980.

2.   See, for instance, B. MORRISON, 'The progress of structure plans in England and Wales', *Built Environment*, vol. 4, no. 4, 1978; I. BRACKEN, 'Structure Plans — submissions and alterations', *The Planner*, September 1980.

3.   Planning Advisory Group, *The Future of Development Plans* (HMSO, 1965).

4.   G. SHAW and A. WILLIAMS, 'The regional structure of Structure Plans', *Planning Outlook*, vol. 23, no. 1, 1980.

5.   Scottish Development Department, *The New Scottish Local Authorities: Organisation and Management Structures* (HMSO, 1973).

6.   Scottish Development Department, *National Planning Guidelines*, Circular 19/77 (HMSO, 1977).

7.   The weaknesses of the structure plan process are comprehensively analysed in A. BLOWERS, *The Limits of Power: the Politics of Local Planning Policy*, (Pergamon, 1980).

8.   Reported as 'Overspill row brews again', *Planning*, vol. 402, 23 January 1981.

9.   Reported as 'Outrage on Tyneside over modifications', *Planning*, vol. 405, 13 February 1981.

10.   P. HEALEY, 'Regional policy in the South East', *Town and Country Planning*, vol. 49(11), 1980.

11. County Planning Officer's Society, *The Development Plans System — The Needs of the 1980s*.

12. See for instance A. JOHNSTON, 'Metropolitan housing and strategic planning in the West Midlands', *Town Planning Review*, April 1982; also 'Labour county backs peripheral development', *Planning*, vol. 466, 30 April 1982.

13. Local challenges to structure plan policies are reported in 'Bristol City objections to mark II Avon Structure Plan', *Planning*, 10 December 1982; also 'Avon surrenders in belt battle', *Planning*, vol. 503, 28 January 1983.

14. The need for counties to exercise greater control over significant departures from structure plan policies has been argued by the Association of County Councils and the Metropolitan Counties. See 'Counties demand DoE intervention', *Planning*, vol. 497, 3 December 1982; 'Metropolitan counties demand call-in', *Planning*, vol. 505, 11 February 1983.

15. The Avon structure plan was withdrawn after the Labour Party took power in May 1981. The revised county structure plan was published in November 1981. Reported in *Planning*, vol. 419, 22 May 1981.

16. P. HEALEY *et al.*, 'The implementation of selective restraint policies: approaches to land release for local needs', Oxford Polytechnic Department of Town Planning, 1980.

17. See for instance Department of Environment, Structure Plans Note 7, 'Social Aspects of Development Plans' (HMSO, 1973); and 'Structure Plans', Circular 4 (HMSO, 1979).

18. J. JOWELL and D. NOBLE, 'Structure Plans as instruments of social and economic policy', *Journal of Planning and Environmental Law*, July 1981.

19. A. BLOWERS, 'Industry versus the environment in the metropolitan fringe' in Planning and the Quality of Life: Proceedings of the 3rd Anglo-German Symposium on Applied Geography, 1982.

20. Hertfordshire County Council, *County Structure Plan* (Herts. CC 1975).

21. Berkshire County Council, *East Berkshire County Structure Plan: Approved Written Statement* (Berkshire CC, 1980).

22. Dorset County Council, *South East Dorset Structure Plan: Submitted Written Statement* (Dorset CC, 1978).

23. Hampshire County Council, *South West Hampshire Structure Plan: Approved Written Statement* (Hants CC, 1980).

24. Ibid, topic reports, April, 1980.

25. Cheshire County Council, *County Structure Plan: Approved Written Statement* (Cheshire CC, 1979).

26. Hertfordshire County Council, *County Structure Plan: Alterations* (Herts. CC, 1980).

27. See, for instance, Hampshire County Council, *Mid Hampshire Structure Plan: Approved Written Statement* (Hants. CC, 1980); also, *North East Hampshire Structure Plan: Approved Written Statement*, (Hants. CC, 1980); Kent County Council, *County Structure Plan: Approved Written Statement* (Kent CC, 1980).

28. Lancashire County Council, *Central and North Lancashire Structure Plan: Submitted Written Statement* (Lancs. CC, 1980).

29. Hampshire County Council, *Mid Hampshire Structure Plan: Approved Written Statement* (Hants CC, 1980).

30. Gloucestershire County Council, *County Structure Plan: Submitted Written Statement* (Glos. CC, 1979).

31. Cheshire County Council, *County Structure Plan: First Alteration Consultation Report*, (Cheshire CC, March 1982).

32. Kent County Council, *Schedule of Proposed Alternatives to the Written Statement*, April 1981.

33. Bedfordshire County Council, *County Structure Plan* (Beds. CC, 1980).

34. Statement by T. KING, Local Government Minister, 11 February 1982.

35. Department of Environment, *Local Government and the Industrial Strategy* (HMSO, 1977).

36. C. MILLER and D. MILLER, 'Local authorities and the local economy', *Town and Country Planning*, vol. 5, no. 6 June 1982.

37. J. CARVEL, 'Build or bust', *Guardian*, 5 November 1982.

38. See for instance M. ELSON, 'Fringe development', *Local Government News*, October 1982.

39. The need for more flexible planning attitudes to high technology industry is argued by Herring Son and Daw, *Property and Technology — The Needs of Modern Industry* (London, 1982).

40. Avon County Council, *A Draft Strategy for Economic Development* (Avon CC, 1982).

41. Avon County Council, *County Structure Plan Revised Written Statement* (Avon CC, 1981).

42. County Planning Officers' Society, *County Planning and the Local Economy*, March 1981.

43. The Treasury, Public Expenditure White Paper 1983/4, Circular 8494 (HMSO). The budget modifications were announced by Geoffrey Howe, *Hansard*, Sixth Series, vol. 31, 8 November 1982.

44. See for instance 'Work in the Shires', *Planning*, vol. 425, 3, July 1981.

45. County Planning Officers' Society, op. cit.

46. A. BLOWERS, op. cit. p. 176.

47. Cheshire County Council, op. cit., para. 8.2.2.

48. An account of the methodology is given in 'Past rates set the pace in Cheshire alteration', *Planning*, vol. 464, 16 April 1982.

49. Department of Environment, Draft Memorandum on Structure and Local Plans.

50. Cheshire County Council, op. cit., para. 3.2.

51. Strathclyde Regional Council, *Strathclyde Structure Plan: First Review and Alteration* (Strathclyde RC, 1981).

52. See the account given in 'Strathclyde Structure Plan: Examination in Public', *Town and Country Planning*, July/August 1980.

53. The conflicts between regeneration and outer city growth are examined by K. CLAYTON, 'Pulling the plug out of Strathclyde', *Planning*, vol. 402, 23 January 1981; the counter-argument is presented by G. DAVIES, D. HICKLING, M. WRIGLEY, 'Going beyond the problem areas of Strathclyde region', *Planning*, vol. 413, 10 April 1981. The Town & Country Planning Association's views are outlined in 'Strathclyde Structure Plan:

examination in public', *Town and Country Planning*, July/August 1980, and by D. HALL, 'Assessment of Secretary of State's response to the Strathclyde structure plan', *Town and Country Planning*, vol. 49, no. 11, December, 1980, pp. 399–400.

54.   P. J. CLOKE and D. P. SHAW, 'Rural settlement policies in structure planning', *Town Planning Review*, vol. 54, no. 3, July 1983.

55.   Nottinghamshire County Council, *County Structure Plan: Approved Written Statement* (Notts. CC, 1980).

56.   Hampshire County Council, *South Hampshire Structure Plan: Approved Written Statement* (Hants CC, 1977).

57.   Leicestershire County Council, *County Structure Plan: Approved Written Statement* (Leics. CC, 1976).

58.   Settlement policy is evaluated by Martin and Voorhees Associates, *Review of Rural Settlement Policies, 1945-1980*, Report for the Department of Environment, (HMSO, October 1980).

59. See for instance B. McLAUGHIN, 'Rural settlement planning: a new approach', *Town and Country Planning*, vol. 44, no. 3, March 1976. A more recent review of the theoretical arguments for and against settlement policy is given by P. J. CLOKE, J. AYTON and I. GILDER, *The Planner*, July/August 1980.

60.   J. HERINGTON and D. EVANS, 'The social characteristics of household movement in "key" and "non-key" settlements', Department of Geography, Loughborough University, Research Paper 4, 1980.

61.   See for instance G. JACK and J. OAKES, 'The effects of differing planning policies on three Cambridgeshire villages', Studies in contemporary rural settlement, Goldsmith College, University of London, 1978.

7   County District Relations

The political differences between County and District on the interpretation of the Structure Plan are not so much ideological but rather arise out of, on the one hand the County, which sees matters in a strategic light, and on the other the District which is concerned with local issues.
(C. Caddy, 1981)

The county structure plans contain only general policy guidance which must be translated by the districts into more detailed planning proposals. Strategic objectives for containing urban expansion are easily challenged by districts wishing to take a laissez-faire attitude to development. Central government has given the districts a wide measure of discretion in small-area planning under the Local Government Planning and Land Act 1980, and urged them to adopt a more positive attitude to the release of new land. The districts' response varies greatly. Some growth is assured by sensible local solutions to development problems — the rationalisation of housing into larger settlements, for example, or building restrictions that force a more efficient use of existing infrastructure. But the cumulative impact of these developments is significant since over-provision of housing and employment in restraint areas throws into disarray the county's structure plan and its principal policies for the spatial redistribution of new development.

Recent trends in the relationship between non-metropolitan counties and districts in the outer areas must be seen in historical perspective. The question of the scale and location of future urban growth has long been a source of contention between cities and their neighbouring shire counties. One of the root causes of this has been the spatial organisation of local government units. The effect of the 1974 reorganisation of local government was to create a smaller number of large districts within each county. The powers of the old county boroughs were reduced and transferred to newly created metropolitan and non-metropolitan counties. Large cities like Liverpool, Newcastle, Leeds, and Sheffield were incorporated in metropolitan counties, while smaller free-standing cities like Bristol, Kingston-upon-Hull, Derby, and Nottingham joined with non-metropolitan counties. In these readjustments lay the seeds of the uncooperative relationship between shire counties and districts ever since.[1]

The way in which planning responsibilities were divided up under the Local Government Planning Act 1972 has been a major cause of poor inter-authority relations.[2] Although counties were to set the framework for district planning and remain nominally in charge of local plans, responsibility for development control was divided. The county was to deal with 'matters of county significance' (defined under a Development Control Agreement which had no legal basis) and the districts were left to process most other applications for planning permission. Various administrative arrangements were devised to secure consistency and coordination in plan formulation and development control[3] but these have been rendered increasingly academic as the balance of planning power has been tilted in favour of the districts. The Local Government Planning and Land Act 1980, transferred all planning control powers (other than minerals and waste disposal) to the lower-tier authorities and the power of the counties to direct the refusal of certain applications which were contrary to the structure plan was done away with. The counties have rather more influence over development plans, since decisions about which are to be prepared is governed by the development plans scheme drawn up by the counties in consultation with the districts.[4] Even so, some districts have ignored this arrangement by producing their own internal development plans which, once they have received the blessing of local planning committees, have been used to guide development control decisions. The counties can refuse to 'certify' any local plan which does not confirm to the provisions of the structure plan. But this is virtually the only weapon they now possess for achieving some kind of strategic control over local urban change. Yet even certification is not without its problems. The DoE argues that when counties refuse to approve a local plan and cannot reach agreement with the districts, the conflict is to be resolved by a local public inquiry.[5] But if the DoE rules in favour of the districts, as seems increasingly to be the case, the counties' strategic position may be eroded further.

Relations between counties and districts have a geographical and a political dimension. In some cases there is little disagreement over the policy of the structure plan or over its local interpretation. In others, tension may be caused by political differences between those in control of the county and those in control of the district. Also, it is common to find a divergence of opinion between professional planning officers and elected representatives, whatever political circumstances obtain, with the former upholding the virtues of long-term comprehensive decision making and the latter articulating short-term public opinion. Moreover, conflict is not always the result of the counties seeking restraint and the districts growth. Both argue for and against restraint in different areas and on different occasions. Moreover, some outer districts may be as opposed to the growth aspirations of city districts as shire counties are to the development interests of outer or city districts.[6]

Local plans

Local plans have become a widely recognised approach to planning on a small scale in Britain. Their purpose is to interpret the structure plan in some detail and provide a framework for development control. Local plans are slimmer and more explicit about objectives than structure plans. Their horizons are short. There is a feeling among some observers that local plans should concentrate entirely on short-term problems of implementation, a view which the DoE might support. Implementation rests almost entirely with the private sector because of the steady decline in central funding for public projects.

There are three main types of local plan.[7] District plans for the whole local authority area are widely used in the 1980s as a method of linking the strategic framework in the structure plan with the more detailed design briefs and other types of local plan guidance. Some counties, like Hertfordshire, have urged districts to prepare district plans, seeing them as the best way to coordinate strategic restraint policy and secure a joint commitment to a lower rate of physical change. Action area plans are less often used in the outer areas. Their purpose is to provide a spatial framework for areas where substantial physical development, including the improvement or redevelopment of the housing stock, is intended over a short time, often no more than ten years from the approval of the structure plan. Subject plans allow detailed treatment of particular policies in the structure plan, the plan taking the name of the subject it deals with, for example, a Green Belt subject plan. Although the development of statutory local plans is quite recent,[8] shire counties have for many years been producing informal local plans. The original development plans were slow to be produced and approved. In the absence of approved development plans many counties devised their own policies and informal guidelines for development control. Hertfordshire, for example, enjoyed an approved development plan for a total of only six years since 1948.

The necessity for the existence of a local plan is open to question. The development plan scheme, drawn up by the county in consultation with the districts, specifies which authority will be responsible for the local plans, their title, the areas covered by the plans, and the programme for preparing them. In drawing up the list, counties have given priority to settlements under greatest pressure for urban change. It is not surprising that the many inner and outer commuting areas are included in the development plan schemes. Indeed, coverage is much more comprehensive in these locations than for the inner cities. By March 1982, 95 plans had been adopted while a further 153 were on deposit. Of the 95, 61 related to outer city locations.[9] The remaining 34 referred to districts in metropolitan counties, or, in non-metropolitan counties, free-standing cities like Leicester, Portsmouth, Nottingham. Among these, priority was given to plans for rapidly changing urban fringe locations, for example, the Solihull Green Belt Subject Plan covering an area of intense development pressure. Although the spatial pattern of local plan coverage reflects the different and joint decisions of counties and districts, the criteria laid down by the DoE have in practice encouraged the emphasis on outer cities. The main types of local plan clearly reflect this bias. They include:

(a) *Plans for substantial satellite growth:* e.g. Chandlers Ford, Totton, and Fareham Western Wards in outer Southampton/Portsmouth; Hamilton, Groby, Markfield in outer Leicester; Wilford, Clifton, and Ruddington on the Nottingham urban fringe;
(b) *Plans for New and Expanded Towns:* e.g. Milton Keynes, Warrington, Bracknell, Crawley, Stevenage, Swindon, Tamworth, Banbury, Winsford;
(c) *Plans for country towns:* e.g. Southam (Strafford DC), Eynsham (West Oxon DC), Newbury, Atherstone (N. Warwickshire), Macclesfield, Malmesbury, Farringdon, Towcester, Sherburn-in-Elmet (Selby), Sandy/Biggleswade;
(d) *Plans for commuter villages:* e.g. Quorn, Sileby, Wreake Valley, Rothley/Mountsorrel in outer Leicester; south and north-west Staffordshire; Horsham area, West Berkshire, Alton area; East Hertfordshire;
(e) *Green Belt Subject Plans:* for Manchester, Nottinghamshire, Warwickshire, and Avon.

Although it is difficult to make firm generalizations until more plans are published, there must surely be concern about the resource implications implicit in a programme of local plans of this kind. The counties' structure plans indicate the scale of current and capital expenditure necessary to achieve broad sector policies, but rarely are the sums disaggregated to the local scale. Many local plans in the outer cities imply some increase in the amount of housing and employment. While some infrastructure expenditure, such as transport costs, will fall on the county, most of the financial burden will fall on the districts — unless they persuade the private sector to bear public costs. Districts can bargain with developers about the provision of 'social uses'. In the cities, where delays on planning permission are costly, private developers appear to have reluctantly accepted the principle of 'planning gain'[10] but in the outer areas it is not yet clear whether they will. Several authorities now seek a financial contribution towards the infrastructure costs needed to open up greenfield sites, especially the building of new roads and junctions. Larger developers appear to be sympathetic to the principle. Higher expenditure by developers might prove inflationary if the extra costs were passed on to households through higher house prices. It might also have the unintended effect of encouraging socially exclusive residential development in commuter areas where there are local housing needs. Notwithstanding these comments, however, it must be remembered that there are equally strong financial advantages to local authorities in attracting some local development — either extra investment, rateable value or possible 'planning gain'. At a time of recession such factors weigh heavily with local councillors, making it likely that the long-term financial implications will be forgotten.[11].

The development plans scheme has proved a major source of conflict between counties and districts. The issue turns on which authority should prepare which type of local plan. Behind this choice lie the financial interests of each authority. As Circular 7/49 pointed out, consultation alone will seldom ensure adequate liaison between county and district authorities.[12] The prospect of considerable pressure for development and the need to provide for comprehensive and cost-effective infrastructure, may force the districts to adopt a more conservative approach to the outer cities than the counties. The dispute between Avon County Council and Northavon District Council over the future method of planning the northern fringes of Bristol is a case in point.[13] The county argues that it should prepare an action area plan for one specific area where residential development is proposed. The district wants a comprehensive Bristol North Fringe district plan prepared and adopted by the district council. The district insists that this will provide a framework for structure plan policies. But the county, clearly with its sights set on the financial benefits of drawing national and regional firms into the Bristol area, has taken a high-handed approach, claiming that a local plan would inhibit the rate at which the district could release land for economic development, and refusing to amend the development plans scheme to include the district plan. Admittedly the district had previously acquiesced in the county's growth-oriented strategy by granting permission for a number of industrial developments in the area bounded by the M4, M5 and M32. But the district, even if rather late in the day, clearly takes a more serious and cautious approach to peripheral expansion than does the county. Moreover, the DoE supports the district's view and has asked the county to provide for a district plan in its second review of the development plan scheme.[14]

Which authority should prepare local plans for the Green Belts is a further source of political tension. The counties' strategic interest in restraint lies behind their desire to establish Green Belts within their structure plans. The Green Belt represents a county's policy towards urban containment and the location of new peripheral development. But the structure plan is intended to show general principles only. It cannot show the precise boundary of the Green Belt on a map. Many counties are seeking a way round this problem by themselves preparing a subject plan, although this type of plan was strictly intended for sector or topic rather than spatial policies.[15] The DoE is ambivalent,[16] but in general it seems that the boundaries of Green Belts can only be set in association with policies for new housing and industrial land, which is the responsibility of the districts. The preparation of a detailed subject plan on these matters by the county would be seen as pre-empting the freedom of districts to determine their own local planning policies. The counties are caught in a dilemma:

they want stricter development control in Green Belts and argue in their structure plans for an extension of the Green Belt principle, but they must defer to the districts on their precise boundaries and hence on the degree of restraint which the districts will operate.[17]

The weaknesses of the split introduced in 1974 in local authority planning responsibilities are exposed by the conflicts over the Green Belt which have arisen between non-metropolitan counties and districts. The districts claim they know best where there is potential for further development or restraint, that they have the powers to control change, and that they should therefore determine the boundaries of the Green Belts in any subject or district plan. Districts in outer Bristol have complained to the DoE about the county's decision to prepare the statutory plan themselves despite the fact that no reference is made to it in the development plan scheme. The result is deadlocked negotiation over the line of the boundary.[18] Some counties avoid a fight by agreeing not to prepare the subject plans, as Essex and Bedfordshire have done. Some prefer to wait until the districts have prepared their own local plans, as the West Yorkshire Metropolitan Council has done. Dispute focusses sharply on the amount of growth which can take place between the inner boundary of the Green Belt and the continuously built-up conurbation. Some counties argue that if the Green Belt is to prevent urban sprawl (its primary function) then the boundaries should be tightly drawn. Districts tend to regard Green Belts less rigidly, arguing, as do the housebuilders, that the inner edges of Green Belts contain some land of little amenity use which could better be developed. In practice the subject plans produced by the counties are often more flexibile than some of the earlier non-statutory Green Belt policies[19] — by, for example, excluding settlements where previous expansion has occurred or where there is further potential for development[20] — and making it clear that where the subject Green Belt plan has been prepared in advance of other local plans, later plans can change the boundaries of the Green Belt defined in the subject plan.[21]

Whether a local plan conforms with the strategic guidelines in the structure plan is a further source of conflict in both Green Belt and non-Green Belt areas. If a county regards the local plan produced by a district as unacceptable it may refuse to 'certify' it. If the district subsequently refuses to change its plan, the Secretary of State resolves the issue, either by directing the county to issue a certificate, getting the district to revise the plan, or urging a local public inquiry, the results of which often go against the county's strategic interest.[22]

The dispute between Bromsgrove District Council and Hereford and Worcestershire County Council illustrates some of the problems. The county refused to issue a certificate of conformity for the Wythall and Bromsgrove district plans.[23] The Green Belt surrounding the Birmingham conurbation has been the scene of many classic planning battles in the post-war period. In the case of Wythall, the county objected to the inclusion of an industrial site in the Green Belt and the failure of the district to show how a housing development would meet local housing needs. But Bromsgrove argued that conflict with the Green Belt would inevitably arise since there was limited vacant land available for residential and industrial development. The district suggests a dispersed pattern of new development in a north-south direction along the line of the A38, including two larger releases of land, 23 ha to the south-west of Bromsgrove and 8.5 ha in the village of Stoke Prior. The county opposed this form of development. They saw it as tantamount to sprawl and counter to the philosophy of compact settlements in Green Belts. The issue chiefly turned on whether the local plan was a 'strategic' departure from the structure plan. The DoE ruled that the local plan did conform and asked the county to issue a certificate in favour of Bromsgrove.

Central government often complains that progress with local plan preparation is too slow, damaging the prospects for private sector investment. Yet by dealing with appeals separately from local plans, central government itself holds up plan preparation. Moreover, it has failed to clarify the procedure for settling disputes. Counties may vainly justify their Green Belt proposals in terms of the need to regenerate the urban cores or direct investment towards existing centres, but the power to implement such policies lies with the districts. The counties could of course play a more purposeful strategic role if central government gave them additional means to define which issues were strategic and which were not.[24] In Scotland, the regional councils 'call in' planning applications from the districts which they consider are strategically significant. Scale of development, infrastructure implications, and degree of conformity with regional policies, are all criteria of significance.[25] Such approaches have much to commend them.

The preparation of a local plan invariably implies some degree of development. Local plans must be regarded as capable of stimulating the growth spiral taking place in the outer cities. It is difficult to argue that change should not be planned for in a comprehensive way by the districts. The problem is that the principles behind the local plans produced so far represent something of a pot-pourri. Additionally, central government has been singularly unhelpful in making clear its views about the necessity for local plans. It argues that plans should not be prepared where only minor change occurs, where there is little need for policies of restraint in addition to those of the structure plan, or where development plans have proved 'effective'. But what level of restraint represents 'effective' containment of urban growth? And how will future pressures for change be met? These questions are surely of more than passing interest to districts in counties where the DoE has just modified structure plans in favour of much greater growth! The interpretation of restraint in local plans is already variable enough. Faringdon draft local plan, for instance, seeks to restrain development in accordance with the Oxfordshire structure plan, interpreting restraint to mean providing an additional 200 houses and 2.2 ha of restraint land. The plan for Norton-Radstock in Somerset, a commuter pressure area beyond the Bristol/Bath Green Belt, seeks to 'restrain' development to 800 dwellings in Norton/Radstock and 300 houses in surrounding villages, with 31 ha of industrial land. The case for local plans in both settlements would appear strong.[26]

The DoE hopes to speed up the planning process by reducing the number of local plans. But speed up may not occur if developers feel they can challenge the provisions of the structure plan more easily. A more probable scenario is an increasing number of *ad hoc* development decisions in the outer areas most attractive to industrial developers. This might not matter within a strategic framework at national or regional level. This is missing at present. Firmer and clearer structure plans would undoubtedly help. Present policies are ambivalent and far from being restraint oriented. The presentation of policies is too general for local planners, a problem that remains to be tackled by the DoE.[27] Giving strategic planning powers back to the counties is unlikely to gain much political support at present, although this is surely one solution to the impasse over local plans. The counties could be in a marginally more powerful position if districts were told to produce fewer local plans. But the counties would still be unable to exert much authority over development control, an issue we turn to next.

Policy Implementation

Obviously the test of any development plan is the degree to which it can be translated into action. The difficulty of implementating the sector policies of structure plans has been mentioned already. Local plans present similar technical difficulties and, moreover, provide an unsatisfactory framework for the day-by-day development control decisions made by district authorities. Research by the Building Research Establishment in 1979 revealed that a high proportion of planning application decisions were not covered by any specific policy in the written statement or in the proposals map; the proportion was highest in the case of applications to undertake 'physical development' rather than to change the use of land. This suggests that local authorities neglect to have policies on the physical form of development and that the local plans, rather like the earlier (old-style) development plans, give little indication to private developers of the planning authorities' likely response. The strategic implications of this mismatch between policy and implementation have not passed unnoticed. 'A succession of control decisions can incrementally, yet substantially, alter the character of the plan area'.[28] The political implications are no less significant. If developers feel local plans are inadequate they may seek to obtain permission for development on land not covered by the plan or try to breach the policies stated in it. Either way there is an increasing number of planning appeals and more conflicts with central government are likely. Indeed, these weaknesses of the development planning system have been compounded by the fact that most structure plans now show demand for additional housing — and the DoE's advice to make more land available for housing makes it more difficult for districts to refuse permission for developments in the outer areas.

The content of development plans could certainly be specified more clearly. Many authorities supplement policy advice in the form of informal reports or development briefs which do not have the status of local plans. County planning authorities prepare non-statutory plans and other forms of guidance to show how structure plan policies apply in particular areas which may or may not be covered by local plans.[29] But the scope for county-district conflict arising from the lack of clarity, irrelevance, or wide discretion allowed in the wording of policies, remains considerable. Area and plan-wide policies are not always indicated on the proposals map in the way recommended by the DoE.[30] Furthermore, the problem of securing consistency goes beyond the inadequacy of the districts' own development plans to the wider interpretation of structure plan policy by development control officers. As argued earlier, district authorities often abuse the discretion available to them and some local plans might barely accord with the structure plan. But 'development control decisions may subsequently undermine the policies of both plans. In other words, local plan and development control decisions can distort or override policies defined in a strategic framework, thus redefining policies'.[31]

The political tensions between county and district are found up and down the country because all authorities face common problems in handling the development plan system. But the task of marrying the strategic goal of urban containment with demands for local development is becoming greater as the commitment of central government and the counties to the containment principle weakens. Indeed, there would appear to be a growing contradiction between strategic objectives, sector policies and settlement policies.

Restraint Areas

Strong restraint has long been accepted by districts as the counties' policy stance in Green Belt and other areas of the outer city. It was an objective easily formalized in the old development plans. It has been carried through to some of the structure plans. Past support of central government for urban containment meant that containment philosophy permeated all levels of the planning hierarchy. There was a great deal of agreement between county and district over Green Belts. In non-Green Belt areas like Leicestershire there was a fair measure of conformity in the 1970s between settlement approvals and new dwelling construction.[32] Even where lower-tier authorities granted development permission without apparent regard for settlement policy, the scale of additional housing or employment growth was generally limited. The counties' traditional, rather than conservative approach to settlement rationalization appears to have been carried forward from the old development plan to the structure plan era.[33] Structure plans generally reject greater dispersal in favour of urban concentration. However, there is much ambivalence. Some counties claim they still do not support dispersed development even though their structure plans seem to have moved in this direction.[34] Counties may argue that greater dispersal is not a sound proposition, but their own sector policies for housing and economic development, discussed in the last chapter, are difficult to square with concentration. The districts find structure plan restraint policies increasingly vague and ambivalent. Terms like 'concentration' and 'dispersal' are open to wide interpretation. There are also subtle shifts in the counties' policy stance towards restraint which the districts have not been slow to seize upon in their justification for additional development. These tensions grew when districts were given more power under the Local Government Planning Act 1980 to determine most development decisions without reference to the counties and when the DoE made it clear in Circular 22/80 that districts should normally grant permission for housing and small industrial developments when there are clear planning objections.

In this changing political climate districts have more readily challenged restraint policy, especially where it limits new development to that which meets a 'local need'. 'Local need' is often the main loophole. Effective challenges have not been confined to housing developments. For instance, the potential impact of large supermarkets on employment in central Oxfordshire proved an insufficiently strong argument with the DoE when Vale of White Horse District Council stressed the 'local need' for new shopping facilities in Abingdon.[35] It would, however, be misleading to place all districts in the same camp. The strategic context varies greatly in different metropolitan regions as do political circumstances. It is not uncommon for districts to take a tough line against the growth-oriented strategies of the counties. In the West Midlands, Solihull Metropolitan Borough Council opposed a road freight 'port' in the Birmingham Green Belt adjacent to the National Exhibition Centre, against the views of the Labour-controlled West Midland County Council who favoured close-in development.[36] In the North West, Cheshire's attempts to relax Green Belt employment policies met with little enthusiasm from some districts.[37] The prospect of a major threat to the strategic interests of both counties and the districts may evoke united opposition to proposed development in the Green Belts especially if they fear creating a precedent for further development in the future.[38] Hence the situation is changing and uncertain. The absence of approved Green Belt subject plans, the traditionally strong line taken against Green Belt development in structure plans, and the ambivalence in attitude to new employment generating developments, all means that county-district relations are likely to remain tense and ambiguous in restraint areas.[39]

The essence of the problem with local housing needs policies is that land allocation and development control procedures cannot by themselves ensure that 'local needs' are met. All counties can do is to bargain with developers and districts about housing needs in their area. They are powerless to control housing strategy directly. This is well illustrated by the case of the Little Bramingham Farm Development on the fringe of Luton.[40] Bedfordshire County Council and Luton Borough Council agreed on the development of the site, which could accommodate 7,000 people. But should the housing be public or private? The county wanted the land (purchased under the Community Land Act) to be used for major public housing in line with the structure plan goal of checking in-migration from outside the county, especially from London. Luton Borough Council, after a change in political control from Labour to Conservative in 1976, wanted greater private housing and the phased release of sites so that local people could buy their own properties. The county pointed out that it was predominantly non-locals who could afford private housing and that the needs of those unable to purchase would still have to be met on other sites around Luton. The district granted approval for a phased release. There was little the county could do to intervene, despite the likelihood that it will have to find the land for future public housing.

Similar difficulties face the operation of 'local need' policies in exurban settlements. Although counties have gone to great lengths to define the meaning of 'local need'[41] their efforts are largely academic. The power to control the amount and type of housing lies with the districts. The DoE will not countenance 'local need' policies in some structure plans. The districts can justifiably say to the counties that 'local need' policies have done nothing to promote housing for local people — indeed the reverse has occurred, with a steady influx of professional and managerial groups into the smaller 'local need' villages. But districts have been rather slow to enter into flexible partnerships with private developers, happy to approve small 'infill' developments which cumulatively add to growth pressures in the outer areas. Central government policies have in any case made it difficult for them to achieve positive forms of intervention in the private housing market. Housing investment strategies have been savagely curtailed in recent years and public housing provision has proved rather easier to provide in larger settlements. Moreover, the districts have been consistently encouraged to provide for a higher level of home ownership[42] at a time when the sale of council houses has become enshrined in housing legislation.[43]

Growth Areas

Urban containment always implied an element of growth in order to avoid more widespread dispersal in the countryside. The counties have tried to work jointly with the districts to manage the scale, form and phasing of large-scale growth areas or centres. Some of these were 'superimposed' on county structure plans by earlier regional strategies, as in the case of Central Berkshire; or represent the more detailed formulation of ideas presented in previous sub-regional planning studies as in the case of Hamilton on the north-east of Leicester. Other areas, such as Banbury in Oxfordshire or Swindon in Wiltshire, were selected for expansion under the town Development Act 1952. The growth locations have a varied planning history and various administrative arrangements have been devised for them. The Expanded Towns have had the benefit of joint local authority working for some time, often in tandem with the 'exporting' authorities. Elsewhere, new sorts of management, negotiation, and agency arrangements, have been necessary, and in all cases the nature of county-district relationships has been closely bound up with the role played by separate agencies involved in housing, employment, services, water, electricity, and transport.

Conflicts over large-scale growth management turn on the policy stance of the counties. In Berkshire the county council was unable to adopt a negative stance to the extension and consolidation of urban development patterns in the area lying between Reading and Wokingham, despite local opposition to growth. This area is under enormous pressure for housing, industrial, office and warehouse development, which, if not contained in central Berkshire, might threaten Green Belt areas to the east and good farmland to the west. County-district relations have been good, both authorities putting emphasis on the need for partnership with the private sector as a way of reducing public costs. The county negotiated development plans jointly with Wokingham district. It proved possible for both county and district to work closely with other development agencies to satisfy the objectives of growth in the structure plans. The county officers monitored the rate of progress of development, coordinated agencies, and advised the district, which dealt with detailed development control and design and drew up management agreements with developers. County councillors sought to balance growth against restraint, while the district sometimes argued against growth. 'The stability of local authority planning policy stances has not been threatened by county-district conflicts, still less by problems of coordinating the policy and development control sections within planning departments . . . councillor decisions which in effect overrode policy were few'.[44] One of the reasons for good relations between the district and the county was the shared fear of more dispersed development if growth could not be effectively channelled and the support given by the county in the implementation of proposals. The political tensions which have surfaced since 1980 in central Berkshire, discussed later, have been associated rather with the DoE's modifications to the county's structure plan, which are tending to unite county and districts against central government.

At Swindon the district favours much more growth than implied by Wiltshire's structure plan. It has challenged jointly with local and national developers the county's overly restrictive population and housing targets.[45] The issue has been complicated by the reorganisation of local government in 1974, which led to a significant shift in the policy stance of the county, and by the pre-emptive actions of central government in granting permission on appeal for substantial greenfield development in advance of the structure plan. Swindon was designated an Expanded Town in 1952. Several policy studies suggested to the then Swindon Borough Council how development could be directed westward to embrace a comprehensively planned scheme for several urban villages, including Westlea Down. In 1970, the Greater London Council, Wiltshire County Council and Swindon Borough Council agreed a figure of 200,000 as an acceptable population target for 1986. After 1974 Wiltshire questioned the continued validity of this figure, and forecast, in its North East Wiltshire Structure Plan, a figure of 140,000 for the Swindon area, considerably lower than previously agreed with the district, who duly contested the lower figure.

The district challenged Wiltshire County Council directly by applying for planning permission from Wiltshire for two very substantial sites (374 ha and 221 ha respectively). Both these applications, if approved, would make it necessary for Wiltshire to substantially modify its structure plan, which allocates land for relatively little additional housing beyond existing commitments. The conflict is complicated by central government's past intervention. Decisions by Mr Peter Shore, Labour's Environment Secretary, went in favour of the developers on appeal, although Shore did argue that future target figures for Swindon should be determined by the structure plan. Unfortunately Wiltshire County Council and Swindon District Council have not been able to agree on these figures. The county argues that too high a rate of housing could lead to a labour surplus, bearing in mind that there is insufficient employment now for young school leavers. It also emphasizes the considerable public infrastructure costs it would need to bear if growth on this scale occurred. In raising both issues they appear to be doing nothing more than drawing attention to the problems of growth which arise in many outer cities. The districts point to their successful partnership with the private sector, which has reduced public costs, especially through joint financing of land acquisition and road building, although they cannot claim that long term community costs have been reduced or that the private sector will always continue to fund infrastructure. Clearly a factor in the district's attitude has been the financial advantage to be gained by close cooperation with the private sector in promoting large-scale growth. The considerable market pressures in this area, the absence of an approved development plan, and central government's previous encouragement to development, have all encouraged Swindon to challenge the county on its plans for the future of the area.

By contrast, the Leicestershire structure plan seeks substantial housing and employment-generating development in central Leicestershire, a broad policy ring around Leicester.[46] The county argues that 40,000 dwellings should be provided there between 1976 and 1991. They favour major expansion at Hamilton, a greenfield site north-east of the city straddling the administrative boundary between two districts, Leicester City and Charnwood. The population was expected to grow to 19,500 as a result of building 7,000 new dwellings. Because substantial infrastructure in roads and water was needed the county decided to prepare the local plan itself. Local opposition was mounted. Charnwood district opposed growth on environmental grounds. The county suspended the preparation of the plan during 1977 and 1978. Hamilton was crucial to the achievement of strategic housing totals in the structure plan. By the late 1970s Leicestershire realized that the progress of implementation was proving too slow. The rate of construction at other strategic allocations had also been slow. Major public opposition led to a scaling down of the original targets. The district members had been forced to oppose the structure plan even though the officers were broadly in agreement with the principle of growth. In June 1979 the county urged the districts to find land for a further 2,000 dwellings in central Leicestershire to redress the likely shortfall. It said it would support developers on appeal if the land was not found. By 1982 the districts had learnt the hard way — that unless land is released in a planned way in an area of great housing pressure, central government will step in and take the initiative, which is precisely what it did. But opposition to large-scale growth management appeared to remain. In 1981 the county produced a revised plan for Hamilton, with a target of 13,000 people (perhaps 4,500 dwellings) mainly within Leicester City. Charnwood District Council still wanted the plan deferred because of its potential long-term impact on farmland. It has now been given the go ahead. The delays have been so severe that it seems unlikely that even the reduced housing targets will be met by 1991.

Underlying these conflicts lies a rather naive faith among the counties that housing growth can be kept within fairly strict bounds. Apart from their interest in reducing the scale of farmland loss to a minimum and avoiding urban sprawl, their fear is that the financial burden will be too great, especially when no special arrangements are available. Counties have too often assumed that implementation will be comparatively straightforward whereas, as the Berkshire case illustrates, prior public investment is necessary and partnership arrangements between local authorities and developers must be established if the investment plans of different agencies are to be coordinated. Furthermore, changing economic and political circumstances have been underestimated by the counties. When the pressure for housing is strong, as at Swindon, the demand for further development requires a carefully integrated and agreed programme of investment before approval is granted for new land release. Delay in providing infrastructure in the Wokingham area meant that by the time development land was assembled the market had flagged. The same thing happened in Hamilton. Moreover, developers have begun to express dissatisfaction with estate development in large blocks, favouring smaller-scale expansion. Hence the districts can point with some justification to the inflexibility of the large-growth schemes, which because of their public investment requirements, require high initial capital expenditure and a long lead time before they satisfy housing shortfalls. The districts have of course not been slow to turn these difficulties to their advantage, welcoming the prospect of smaller-scale dispersed development, and challenging the tenets of the structure plan when it suited them.

Central government initiatives

Although the relationship between local authorities is having a critical effect on the operation of containment policy in the outer cities, we must not overlook the way in which local government relationships are subsumed within the wider conflict between central and local government. The introduction of the Local Government Planning and Land Bill and of Circular 22/80 represent moves towards much stronger central control, although possibly less intervention at the local level in the interest of stimulating private investment.[47] The spatial impact of recent central government decisions is already apparent in the outer cities.[48]

The development plan is no longer regarded as an adequate basis for securing a short-term supply of housing land. Circular 9/80 therefore asked local authorities to work closely with developers to agree a schedule of sites to be released *in accordance with* approved structure and local plans. But the circular also makes it clear that the absence of these plans is not a reason for failing to produce a schedule. Circular 22/80 outlines the government's new approach to development control. Weight is given to traditional planning arguments: urban sprawl should be avoided, towns and villages should be kept separate, good quality farmland should not be released for housing development; national landscape designations should take priority unless 'there is an exceptional need for housing'. On the other hand some 'modest expansion' and 'infilling' may be allowed in villages. Infrastructure objections should not alone determine whether planning permission is refused, unless specific evidence of overload is available or a developer does not offer to reach agreement on the costs and provision of facilities (as under Section 52, Town and Country Planning Act 1971).

The growing intervention of central government exposes the extent to which counties and districts have a common interest. Both authorities are required to produce development plans that will guide future change in an orderly manner, taking into account alternative sites, the balance between housing and other local policies for infrastructure and services, and local public opinion. The ambiguous and random pattern of recent central government decisions, however, introduces a new element of uncertainty into this development plan process. Developers, sensing a more relaxed policy stance, are more prepared to press home their case for more housing growth, even in locations that are not shown on the development plans. Delays in the structure plan process make matters worse. It is easier for the housebuilders to argue for greater flexibility on the part of both counties and districts. The experience in Leicestershire demonstrates vividly that the developers turned the failings of the structure plan to good advantage, using Circular 22/80 (and its predecessor 9/80) to support their argument against delay in land release. One developer applied for residential permission on 17 sites in central Leicestershire, most of them outside areas allocated for growth. Other developers applied for locations where there was no likely presumption that development would be forthcoming.[49]

Ordinary and conventional planning criteria get swept aside in this process. If the counties follow central government's lead in supporting planning applications, seeking to show that they conform to broad structure plan objectives, county-district conflict may surface quickly. In some respects the districts would appear to lose more than the counties. Their local plans are delayed by the appeal process. If appeals are approved they pre-empt the logical development of sites. Political opposition to further growth may become strident, with the district rather than the DoE at the receiving end. But counties also stand to lose from central initiatives of this kind. Although structure plans are sufficiently vague to permit considerable flexibility, incremental change of this kind can undermine the long-term strategy, especially when expressed in terms of sub-area or zonal targets for future numbers of dwellings. It has been suggested that we are moving into a period where country-district conflicts are, if not replaced, at least toned down by increasing central-local conflicts.[50] Whether this is so remains to be seen.

There is a growing feeling among some observers that the development plans are too restrictive in practice. Containment often implied prevention of development and this is no longer appropriate under conditions of little or no growth when economic expansion is required.[51] But professional planners and members of local authorities may not wish to move too far towards growth-oriented strategy for the outer cities. If they do so, the consequences for physical, economic and social change will be enormous. The political implications are no less daunting: 'It is easier for district councils to tempt developers and the rising middle classes to cover Britain's green fields with bricks and concrete than to settle down to deal with the problem of redeveloping our cities. The Secretary of State should legislate to limit the massive powers local authorities now have to choose the easy option. But would the regenerated cities vote Tory, and would his Tory district councillors still love him?'[52]

Notes

1. For a full examination see N. MOORE and S. LEACH, 'An interaction approach to county/district relationships', *Policy and Politics*, vol. 7(3), 1979; N. MOORE and S. LEACH, 'County/district relations in Shire and Metropolitan Counties in the field of town and country planning', *Policy and Politics*, vol. 7, no. 2, 1979.

2. S. BRAZIER and R. J. P. HARRIS, 'Inter-authority planning: appreciation and resolution of conflict in the new local authority system', *Town Planning Review*, vol. 46, no. 3, July 1975.

3. These are outlined in Department of Environment, Local Government Act 1972: *Town and Country Planning Cooperation between authorities, Circular 74/73* (HMSO, 1973). See also, M. BICHARD, 'Inter-authority collaboration', *Municipal Journal*, vol. 28, June 1974.

4. 'The development plan' scheme is outlined in Department of Environment Circular 4/79: *Memorandum on Structure and Local Plans*, paras. 3.16-3,28 (HMSO, 1979). Certification procedure is also outlined

5. See for instance M. J. BRUTON, G. CRISPIN, P. M. FIDLER, Local Plans, public local inquiries', *Journal of Planning and Environment Law*, June 1980; also, 'Planning comment: certification and Local Plan inquiries', *Planning*, vol. 480, 6 August 1982.

6. Reported as 'Havant plan prejudiced by Pompey science park scheme', *Planning*, vol. 485, 10 September 1982.

7. Some slight amendments were introduced in the Department of Environment, *Town and Country Planning (Structure and Local Plans) Regulations* 1982, 26 May 1982.

8. P. HEALEY *Statutory Local Plans — their evolution in Legislation — administrative intrepretation*, Oxford Papers in Planning, Education and Research, vol. 36, 1979.

9. Department of Environment, *Local Plans progress to 31 March, 1982* (HMSO, 1982).

10. See for instance Department of Environment, Property Advisory Group *Planning Gain*, (HMSO, 1980); P. WEATHERHEAD, '"Reasonable" tests for gain circular', *Local Government News*, June 1983.

11. C. CADDY, 'Local planning in an area of restraint' in C. FUDGE (ed.) *Approaches to Local Planning*, University of Bristol School of Advanced Urban Studies, Working Paper 17 1981.

12. Department of Environment, *Memorandum on Structure and Local Plans*. Circular 4/79 (HMSO, 1979).

13. Reported as 'Row over Avon plan scheme', *Planning*, vol. 472, 11 June 1982.

14. Reported as 'Avon considers DoE Local Plan request', *Planning*, vol. 484, 3 September 1982.

15. See, for instance, R. WILLIAMS, 'Development plans and the definition of green belts', *Planning Outlook*, vol. 23(1), 1980; and the report 'Districts belted by subject plans', *Planning*, vol. 48, 17 September 1982.

16. M. ELSON, 'Perspectives on green belt local plans', Department of Town Planning Oxford Polytechnic, Working Paper 38, 1979.

17. M. ELSON, 'Structure plan policies for pressured rural areas', *Countryside Planning Yearbook*, vol. 2, 1981.

18. Reported in 'Withdrawal decision due', *Planning*, vol. 221, 5 June 1981.

19. Nottinghamshire Environment Committee, *Draft Green Belt Subject Plan*, (Notts. CC, 1981).

20. See for instance, West Midlands County Council, *Green Belt Subject Plan — Draft Written Statement* (WMCC., 1981); Merseyside County Council, *Merseyside Draft Green Belt Subject Plan: Written Statement* (Merseyside CC, 1980).

21. Warwickshire County Council, *Green Belt (Subject) Plan for Warwickshire: Draft Written Statement* (War. CC, 1980).

22. For recent examples see the following reports: 'Settle at public local inquiry counties told', *Planning*, vol. 483, 27 August 1982; 'Oxford bags a certificate in just a year', *Planning*, vol, 530, 5 August 1983; and 'Latest certificate resolved in district's favour', *Planning*, vol. 533, 26 August 1983.

23. P. SWANN, 'Green Belt threat: is it strategic?', *Planning*, vol. 480, 6 August 1982.

24. S. LEACH, 'Battle of the two tiers', *Planning*, vol. 487, 24 September 1982.

25. E. YOUNG, 'Call-in of planning applications by regional planning authorities', *Journal of Planning and Environmental Law*, June 1979.

26. C. RAND, 'Rural planning on the block', *Planning*, vol. 221, 5 June 1981.

27. County Planning Officers' Society, *Development Plans: the needs of the 1980s*.

28. P. W. KINGSBURY, 'Local plans: increasing their usefulness for development control', Building Research Establishment Information Paper, February, 1982.

29. Department of Environment, *Non-Statutory Plans, Circular 58(1)* (HMSO, 1974).

30. Department of Environment, *Form and Content of Local Plans: Local Plans Note 1/78* (HMSO, 1978).

31. P. HEALEY, 'On implementation: some thoughts on the issues raised by planners current interest in implementation' in C. MINAY (ed.), *Implementation, Views from an Ivory Tower*, Oxford Polytechnic Department of Town Planning, 1979.

32. J. HERINGTON, 'A statistical profile of key and non-key settlements in Charnwood', Research Paper 2, Department of Geography, Loughborough University, 1979.

33. J. DEROUNIAN, 'The impact of structure plans on rural communities', *The Planner*, vol. 66, 1980.

34. P. J. CLOKE and D. P. SHAW, 'Rural settlement policies in structure planning'. *Town Planning Review*, vol. 54, no. 3, July 1983.

35. G. H. CADDY, ' A Superstore for Oxfordshire', *District Councils Review*, May 1981.

36. Reported in 'Port scheme tests green belt policy', *Planning*, vol. 419, 22 May 1981.

37. See the report 'Cheshire set to tone down green belt relaxation', *Planning*, vol. 474, 25 June 1982.

38. See the report, 'Green Belt in inquiry test', *Planning*, vol. 424, 26 June 1981.

39. See the report, 'Business eyes on Green Belt', *Planning Bulletin*, 19 November 1982.

40. A. BLOWERS, 'The politics of land development', in *Urban change and conflict: an interdisciplinary reader* (Harper & Row, 1981).

41.   See for instance D. CHIDDICK, 'Hertfordshire's housing study identifies "need" areas', *Surveyor*, vol. 153, no. 4532, 19 April 1978. For a general discussion of the problem see S. C. EVANS, 'Planning for local needs in an area of growth restraint', Department of Town Planning, Oxford Polytechnic, MSc thesis, 1980.

42.   See the report 'Authorities to promote home ownership', *Architects Journal*, vol. 171, no. 18, 30 April 1980.

43.   See for instance B. BARKER, 'The sale of council houses: A housing policy and political issue', Department of Town Planning, Oxford Polytechnic, MSc thesis, 1980.

44.   P. HEALEY *et al.*, *The Implementation of Development Plans*, Report of an exploratory study for the Department of Environment, Department of Town Planning, Oxford Polytechnic, February 1982.

45.   For a fuller account see 'Going West', *Planning*, vol. 402, 23 January 1981.

46.   Leicestershire County Council, *County Structure Plan: Approved Written Statement* (Leics. CC, 1976).

47.   S. BARRETT and J .UNDERWOOD, 'Planning at the crossroads — a review of 1980', *Planner News*, vol. 67, no. 3, 1981.

48.   M. ELSON, 'Farmland loss and the erosion of planning', *Town and Country Planning*, vol. 50, 1981.

49.   The problems are examined by J. HERINGTON, 'Circular 22/80 — the demise of settlement planning', *Area*, vol. 14, no. 2, 1982.

50.   S. LEACH, 'County-district relations in town planning' in S. LEACH and J. STEWART, *Approaches in Public Policy*, Institute of Local Government Studies (George Allen and Unwin, 1982).

51.   The point is implied in the report by the Association of District Councils, *Economic Development by District Councils*, Paper five: 'The effect of planning controls on economic development' (ADC, 1982).

52.   R. WILSON, 'Ominous developments', Letter to *The Times*, 20 April 1982.

8   The Role of the Housebuilders

The close interpenetration of the idea of containment with a concern for the activities of speculative house-builders has been a consistent theme in much recent planning literature.
(A. Hooper, 1980)

The house builders, together with their friends in Marsham Street, are planning to unbuckle the country's green belts and unleash a torrent of peripheral development.
(Jack Graham, Association of Metropolitan Authorities, 1983).

Central government has always tended to use the construction industry as a convenient tool for regulating the economy. Fiscal and monetary policy may work for or against the confidence of the industry, but land policy may be used to help support the speculative land holding aspirations of the development companies and thereby indirectly finance housing production. It is no accident that as speculation in land has become more lucrative, the DoE has encouraged greater release of land for private housing. This strategy is a far cry from the early intentions of the post-1945 public planning system, which implied strong control over private development and a dominant role for local authorities in the provision and building of new houses.[1] In reality the opposite has happened. The development industry has become a more potent force in land acquisition than the local authorities. Private housebuilders have been able to purchase considerable land-banks in the expectation of obtaining outline planning permission for their future developments. Moreover, local councils are beginning to dispose of their surplus land to private bidders as fast as possible.

The speculative builder has long been a *bête noire* for the shire counties, a threat to rural preservation, someone to be kept at bay at all costs. Housing developers regard planning constraints as a barrier to be overcome before their own plans can be brought to fruition. If it were not for these restrictions housebuilders could build wherever they liked. They see planning as restrictive and negative. It also makes it difficult for them to anticipate when land will be available, and it creates uncertainties during the interval between land purchase and construction. Developers thus started to press for a greater total quantity of housing construction, aggravating further the conflicts between economic growth and environmental values, between the investment needs of the inner cities and the developers' interest in the outer city, between housebuilders and other agents in the development process. Nowhere are these better dramatized than in battles over the release of Green Belt land. A more aggressive, growth-oriented strategy already governs land development decisions at a local scale. It cannot be doubted that more freedom for speculative housebuilders will encourage rather than diminish dispersal and aggravate rather than lessen environmental social and political conflict.

The housing land issue

Housebuilders and planners disagree fundamentally about what scale of housing land release in the outer cities is appropriate. The purpose of the planning system is to ensure the orderly release of sites within an approved policy framework. In arriving at a preferred housing allocation structure plans take account of a wide range of demographic, economic, social and environmental factors. Estimates of future demand for housing are based on national and regional forecasts of population change, local studies of household formation, calculations about the changing balance between new and existing stock, vacancy rates, housing improvement, redevelopment programmes, and many other issues. An attempt is also made to match the scale of new housing with the number of jobs at a county and sometimes local scale. The distribution of housing land will demonstrate the relative weight given to restraint or growth in different sub-areas. The capacity of infrastructure networks and the costs of improving them must be taken into account too, as must the need to protect agricultural land and high quality landscapes and conserve historic settlement patterns. Inevitably the concerns of the planners are long term and broad ranging.

Housebuilders have none of these public interests in mind. Their aim is simply to bring land forward for development and realize a profit from the sales of houses. To do this they must acquire, assemble, finance, obtain planning permission and construct dwellings over a relatively short period of time, perhaps two or three years at most. Developers have to acquire land to secure continuity of production. The majority of firms are small and have small land-banks.[2] Containment policies impinge severely on the smaller firms, who may find it hard to purchase sites highly priced as a result of the planned shortage of housing land. In Green Belts and non-key settlements where small 'infill' developments have occurred, planning policies have tended to increase the price of housing. Large firms are likely to be less adversely affected by rising land prices, because their more extensive land holdings free them from the need to buy land at high prices from other owners, and because the larger the sites the longer is the period of completion during which any general increase in land prices may be realized.

Housebuilders have found difficulty in finding enough land for building in recent years. Although much of the land with outline planning permission is obviously in the hands of private builders, 60 percent of land covered by planning permission but where building has not begun, is in the hands of other owners, either non-builder developers, private owners or government bodies.[3] Moreover, the builders claim there is not always a market for land in public ownership. Thus land ownership has become an increasingly important question for the large housebuilding companies, which may account for the recent interest shown by the House-Builders Federation in planning and land issues and their attempts to consolidate political influence at national and local level.[4]

Housing demand has been highly volatile since the war. For the housebuilders, periodic change in the fiscal and monetary policies of central government and their effects on interest rates and hence mortgage finance, create uncertainty about the adequacy of land supply in the future.[5] The need to improve long-range planning within the industry and to cut the costs of housing production lie behind the housebuilders' pressure on national and local government to increase the supply of land. A general increase in the supply of land would help to reduce the price which builders have to pay for land, taking into account the costs of construction and the selling prices of houses. Land prices vary greatly according to the availability of land with planning permission: where this is very limited, as in restraint settlements, land prices represent a high proportion of the selling price of a house. The builders argue that an increase in land will help meet the rising demand for houses by adding to the stock of dwellings completed. In practice, of course, granting permission for more building land does not ensure this. Indeed, the relationship between the aggregate amount of land available and the number of buildings constructed (though not necessarily sold) is highly variable.[6] As the builders see it, the most marketable sites lie in the most scenic parts of the outer-metropolitan areas. This is where many people would like to buy a house if they could, but where planning authorities wish to restrict supply in the interests of protecting the countryside.[7] Not surprisingly, political pressure is brought to bear on local authorities, particularly in the inner commuting areas, many of which are designated Green Belt, to release more new land for housebuilding. The situation in the outer commuting areas is no less troublesome. Here previously high rates of house building and household formation combined with local containment strategies imply the existence of high pent-up demand for housing, encouraged further by the past expansion of employment opportunities in the growth centres. Housing pressures in these areas are an outcome of the dispersal processes discussed in Chapter 2. The shift in population beyond the Green Belts has effectively shifted the market for medium-priced housing further out. It is hardly surprising that housebuilders wish to argue for greater land release in shire counties like Wiltshire, Northamptonshire, Buckinghamshire and Bedfordshire.[8]

The dynamics of urban change in the outer cities, particularly the cumulative growth of smaller towns and settlements in association with the expansion schemes, undoubtedly underlie the tension we now see between builders and planners. The point is illustrated by the case of Cheshire where 'it seemed to the Housebuilders' Federation that Greater Manchester, in its policy of largely meeting needs within its own area or in Warrington New Town, was now trying to prove (mistakenly) that it could reduce the outflow of residents into north east Cheshire, where there was now a restricted supply of housing land'.[9] The housebuilders' objections to planners' attempts to redirect housing development to the inner areas, are based on social and economic arguments: the restrictive policies of planning authorities in areas where population redistribution takes place has the effect of raising land prices, limiting the opportunity for first-home buyers, and threatens the livelihood of small builders. Moreover, argue the housebuilders, it is impossible to increase the supply of housing land in the inner cities to match the demand.

Empirical studies carried out at regional or county level suggest that the housebuilders have a slender case for claiming that there is an overall shortage of housing land in the rapidly growing outer-metropolitan areas of central and southern England, although we still need more detailed surveys at a district scale to prove the point. The research carried out by the Department of Environment and published in a series of land availability studies between 1973 and 1976 shows that an absolute aggregate shortage of land for residential development does not exist and, moreover, that fluctuations in housing demand may be related to structural conditions in the housing market rather than to land supply factors. The studies produced by the Standing Conference on London and South East Regional Planning and the HBF in 1981 show that land is available during the next five years for around 270,000 dwellings, compared with the structure plan provisions for about 243,000 in the same period. Large private sites will provide 60 percent of the total, small sites 16 percent and public sites 24 percent. There is some doubt about the true figure on small sites — this is difficult to estimate — but public sector housing land may be sold off to private developers, and there are not likely to be major ownership or other difficulties with the large sites.[11]

Such surveys are hardly representative of Britain's outer cities in general, particularly those in the less prosperous regions in Scotland and Wales where we still know little about the situation despite the evident political tension between central government, builders and local authorities, discussed earlier. However, the DoE in England now accepts that generalised impressions about land supply can be misleading and that land supply can only be assessed by detailed local investigation. The DoE's conversion to this view was based on the findings of a housebuilders' survey of ten district councils in Greater Manchester which showed that much of the land for which permission was obtained was in the wrong position or was of the wrong type to meet housing demand. Out of an estimated 27,500 plots the joint HBF-DoE surveys suggested that only 17,000 could be built on.[12]

The Manchester survey highlighted the point that the total amount of land available for housing is less important than its distribution (marketability factor), ownership, and immediate availability. In the West Midlands 50 percent of land ready for development lies in the inner commuting band around the conurbation, only 25 percent in Birmingham itself. Moreover, while 47 percent of the residential land in the Metropolitan County is in private hands, the figure for the shire counties is 79 percent.[13] The nub of the problem is that most of the urban sites are less capable of development in the short term because they require some initial public sector investment before they can be marketed. The metropolitan counties thus face immense difficulty in countering market trends, which favour private housing in the outer shire counties. This does not imply that there is a shortage of land in aggregate terms in these areas: the surveys of metropolitan authorities clearly dispel that idea.[14] But even if all land available on sites in cities and towns was developed, the total number of dwellings would be unlikely to exceed 6,000 annually, less that 3 percent of the HBF's desired annual output for England of 215,000–222,000 houses (250,000 for Great Britain). Its own analysis of 63 land registers shows that on average 11 percent only may be available for the private housebuilder — a total area of perhaps 100,000 acres.[15]

It must be admitted that housebuilders face some difficulty in achieving a desirable rate of production even in the outer areas. There is a maximum number of dwellings that a single development company can build and sell each year, regardless of how large the site is. Thus the rate of completion in an area of high demand will depend on the total number of sites available rather than the total number of dwellings for which permission exists.[16] Furthermore, the existence of a planning system designed to safeguard public and private rights, implies some delay for developers in obtaining permission. With land costing an average of £40,000 an acre and interest rates as high as 15 percent, every month's delay caused by having to appeal costs the housebuilder £500 per acre per month.[17] Delays of up to twelve months may occur in some planning appeals. But lags within the housebuilding industry are at least as important as delays created by the development control process. A study of the average time taken for sites in Worcestershire to pass through various sub-stages in the development process showed that it took an average of four months to gain outline approval and a further nine months before housebuilders and developers submitted detailed proposals. It took on average three months to process the detailed planning application, but a further six months elapsed before housebuilding started. The 'planning' stages thus accounted for only one-third of the total time taken from submission to construction. Blockages within the housebuilding sector are greatest when demand is slack and least when bouyant. The converse applies to the planning system. In addition, the more land available for residential development the more delays there are in the development process because of the additional number of planning applications.[18] Hence the housebuilders' desire for both greater land release *and* speedier planning decisions is rather self-defeating — at least without a strengthened local planning administration, a prospect hardly likely to endear itself to the present government.

Nevertheless it is difficult to be enthusiastic about the housebuilders' diagnosis of the housing land problem. The Manchester study led to a number of important recommendations which appear to have the tacit acceptance of central government — that housing land should be made available where people choose to live; that provision should be made for all sub-categories of the housing market; and that planners should ensure a constant flow of land in excess of current and forecast rates of construction. Yet a growth-oriented strategy directly challenges the containment principle which still underpins some county development plans. It seriously undermines attempts to redirect housing investment towards the inner city. The introduction of marketing criteria in structure and local planning must be problematic. Furthermore, a wider range of markets in any one location will favour the large development companies, and applications for housing permission cannot be refused on the grounds of monopoly. Finally, excessive new housing land provision in the outer areas must add to the problems planners already face over the provision and phasing of services, the financing of public expenditure, and the other environmental conflicts mentioned earlier. Greater population dispersal would inevitably result. In claiming that scarcity should be overcome in the short term, housebuilders are effectively challenging the long period of consensus in favour of restraint, when *underprovision* of residential development was a mark of successful local and to a considerable degree national planning.

Agency initiatives

The Department of Environment has traditionally taken a sympathetic attitude to the housebuilders' argument that shortage of land was restricting housing output. Under Conservative governments private developers have usually benefited, although the consequences of a freer market in housing land, namely excess profits from land speculation and higher land prices, are not strictly Tory policy. The Labour party has also favoured making land more available for private housebuilding.[19] Significant differences between the two parties emerge over the methods of doing this. Conservatives favour a relaxation of planning controls. Labour prefer a stronger land policy in which profits from private speculation are returned to the community. The latest DoE circular 9/80 appears to have accepted some of the housebuilders' arguments — in particular that allocation of land in structure and local plans should guarantee its availability and that housing land should be allocated in areas where people want to live.[20] The government responded to the Manchester Study by asking county and district authorities to carry out residential land availability studies to ensure adequate supplies of available land over a five-year period. The housebuilders were able to say that 'for the first time in many years they find themselves entirely in step with the objectives of the Government of the day'; a less partial view would be that circular 9/80 'established an unprecedentedly close relationship in the field of planning between local authorities and organisations representing pressure groups'.[21]

A general prescription in favour of housing anywhere (unless there are outstanding planning objections) is the basis of 9/80 and reminds us of the initiatives on housing land taken when Mr Geoffrey Ripon was Secretary of State in 1973. Many areas thought to be 'available' then for development turned out to have no prospect of water supply, drainage, or roads, or the social infrastructure of schools, shops, and jobs.[22] The same concern must be aroused by circular 9/80. But an even more worrying issue is the ability of the counties and districts to approach land-use planning within a coherent framework, and the political consequences of not doing so. There are also several technical objections to the methodology for assessing 'available' land supply. In counties which still seek to restrain the overall total of development and where low rates of housing construction prevail, the DoE argues that there is a case for increasing the five-year supply of housing. In other areas the reverse applies, suggesting a relative reduction in housing provision. Hence the effect of the circular is to simply equalize out the amount of new housing land provision according to housing policies in structure and local plans and the market-determined rate of building construction.[23]

The position appears little changed by the draft circular 'Land for Housing' published in July 1983. This replaces 9/80. It contains tighter specifications for land availability, and local authorities must ensure an immediate two-year supply of land, based on current building rates, in addition to the five-year supply. Land should not be defined as 'available' if infrastructure is not present or in prospect, it advises, but sites should also be capable of development without due cost. Most new housing will have to be on new sites; structure plans and local authorities must make provision for them. In some areas it may be preferable to develop new settlements rather than expand existing communities. The circular also states its belief, surely totally misguided, that no significant public expenditure implications are likely to arise.[24].

The spatial effects of these DoE initiatives may of course not be as dramatic as suggested by some spokepersons for the conservation lobby. The circulars still make protection of good quality agricultural land and areas of special restraint a priority. Quality of land and the planning factors surrounding the development of particular sites may be given as much weight by planning inspectors on appeal as the notional quantity of land available in two or five-year schedules; in other words, whether there is or is not sufficient land in structure and local plans, building permission might still be refused. However, there are equally strong grounds for believing current building rates will put pressure on local authorities to release land even in restraint areas. The Green Belts are not mentioned in the circulars. Structure plans, they suggest, offer the prospect of some strategic framework but will need to be altered by the pressure of events. In short, the emphasis given to providing enough land to sustain a rising rate of housebuilding is likely to make it more difficult for planners to manage the containment of population growth. It must also be noted that the latest draft circular follows a recent round of modifications to county structure plans which has significantly increased the total allocation of new housing land in many shire counties in the outer-metropolitan areas, particularly in the so-called restraint counties in the outer South East. The approved structure plan provides the starting point for calculating the five or seven-year supply, and these modifications must have an inflationary effect on the scale of future provision in the land availability schedules.

Local authorities

Local authorities have presented their own assessment of the housing available in structure and local plans which challenges the housebuilders' estimates, creating a good deal of heated argument about the national situation. Less discussed but at least as problematical is the question of which authority should carry out land availability surveys. Previous DoE circulars have suggested that both counties and districts should strive for a five-year supply. In practice, progress with drawing up schedules has been varied and led to political tension over the case for releasing sites — counties arguing that land is available when the districts are not aware of a surplus and vice versa. Some duplication seems inevitable but agreement on the aggregate amount of land available must be reached if developers are not to further exploit disagreements between the officers of county and district authorities.

Additionally, the stance of the counties to the housing land question has been non-committal and somewhat ambivalent. The Association of Metropolitan Authorities (AMA) argues that a national housing shortage is created by lack of government investment in housing and construction; that there is no overall shortage of land in the metropolitan authorities; and that it is the shire counties upon whom the greatest pressure will fall. In saying this they are simply pointing out that this is where the private builders see more attractive and profitable opportunities. Furthermore, in claiming that metropolitan authorities can make up only a proportion of land requirements for future housing, the AMA comes close to accepting the HBF's argument about the limitations of land supply in the inner areas. The link between lack of demand in the inner cities and pressure on the outer cities is recognized by the AMA, but perhaps understandably it does not see its task as proffering solutions. Nor, it must be said, has the Association of County Councils (ACC) faced up to the strategic implication of greatly increased housing provision, preferring to say that more land is available in structure plans than the HBF claims, and to express satisfaction with the commitment to 'overriding planning objections' in the latest draft circular. It has been left to the regional forums of county council representatives to take a less equivocal position. In the West Midlands there may be no total shortage of building land but the inflationary pressure on the outer areas is worrying:

Accommodation of development pressures, by allowing continuous expansion in attractive areas will be counterproductive. It will result in the erosion of the very attractions which created the pressure in the first place and do little to satisfy local needs. Environment and land use controls, such as the green belt and policies on land release, are essential mechanisms for guiding private investment in accordance with strategic policy.[25]

Undoubtedly the low level of public investment in housing has affected the scope of metropolitan housing programmes, although extra spending will not by itself create the conditions for a great increase of private market activity in the inner areas. This is more likely to come from a change of heart among the private builders and an associated reduction in land values which would encourage redevelopment. New policies and stronger development controls in the outer shire counties and districts is nearer the mark. For strategic planning of this kind to operate effectively requires a clear political consensus on the direction of policy, firm leadership in carrying it out, and, underlying both, central government support. This is patently lacking and provides the HBF with a good opportunity to exploit local authority ambivalence towards overall policy. Significantly, the builders have shifted their attack from the shire counties to the metropolitan authorities. Thus in the North West, builders profess support for the redistribution of housing into Greater Manchester but only if adequate supplies of land are available in the metropolitan authority backed up by restraint in Cheshire. They claim housing allocations provide at best for three to four, not five-years' supply of land, that too much land is located in the north and north-west of the city where demand is slack, and too little in the 'better parts' of Greater Manchester, Cheshire and Lancashire, where demand is buoyant. The only way round these local conflicts of opinion would seem to be a greater understanding of the problems which face builders and planners in the outer city and elsewhere.

The Joint Lands Requirement Committee

The Joint Lands Requirement Committee (JLRC) was brought into being to provide a national forum for exchange of views between planners and housebuilders. The failure to achieve minimal levels of housing target or to coordinate national with local housing policy has been a source of frustration for the housebuilders. In 1980 Cheshire's County Planning Officer, who was then President of the Royal Town Planning Institute (RTPI), initiated the JLRC, which was 'designed to provide for the first time, an impartial and authoritative view as a firm basis for future planning and house-building policies'.[26] The first report updated national forecasts of housing and argued that, given the economic recession, the present land currently allocated in English structure plans would be adequate; but that if recovery occurred, it would not be.[27] The report called for a firmer national framework within which local authorities could make decisions about the scale and location of new housing land. The County Planning Officers' Society (CPOS) quickly challenged this view. In its reaction can be read both fear of stronger central control over local housing provision and, possibly, some concern that control will involve a more generous allocation in the outer areas. The second draft report of the JLRC[28] started from the assumption that it would be prudent to provide for a likely annual rate of housing production for Great Britain of between 160,000 and 250,000 houses a year in 1981-86. There was a case for increasing both the national scale of housing allocation and remedying deficiencies in local supply. Long-term planning was advocated to overcome problems of land shortage. Stronger national and regional frameworks were necessary. The standing conference might play a firmer role in establishing jointly with the HBF appropriate regional scales of growth. Counties could do more to implement their own housing policies, perhaps by appointing special housing development officers to promote housing, as already done for industry. The districts could pay more attention to those in housing 'need' than to the views of local residents seeking to oppose growth: 'We deplore decisions having to be taken on appeal so frequently just because local political difficulties inhibit the authority from forthrightly pursuing a clear and logically argued case for land development where this seems to be called for'.[29] In 1982 about 196,000 houses were started in Great Britain. The housebuilders argue that a revised realistic rate would be an annual production of 250,000 houses equivalent to 215,000-220,000 a year in England on cleared, redevelopment and 'infill' sites. This contrasts with a figure of about 180,000-190,000 dwellings calculated by the builders to be available in structure plans. The county planning officers challenge this figure, claiming that if smaller sites are taken into account then between 219,000 and 221,000 houses are available.[30]

In many respects the national argument over housing land provision is a sterile one. Firstly, there is little agreement on the aggregate target. The 1977 Housing Green Paper, after considering past trends, projected an annual rate of 300,000 dwellings in Great Britain up to 1986. Clearly these forecasts have proved of little value. Secondly, the regional land availability studies mentioned earlier point to a different evaluation of land supply, showing in general no overall shortage of residential land. Thirdly, the actual figures do not matter much except to assess the degree to which planning policies are, or are not, inhibiting the achievement of a notional national housing output. The housebuilders are right to seek to adjust national and local policies within a coherent national and regional framework, although this would imply the existence of national planning policy for *all* types of land use, plus a form of indicative target planning which post-war governments in Britain, unlike other European countries, have been reluctant to adopt. National planning for housing land release would also require a political consensus about the conservation or development of rural land, which is clearly absent at present. Fourthly, the existence of a national housing problem is less important than the excessive rate of speculative private housebuilding in suburban and village communities which has exacerbated urban dispersal and threatened the inner city — if this is accepted, then the uniform application of nationally derived housing requirements, as in Circular 9/80, is likely to have a damaging effect, since it will further encourage the inflationary land spiral and reduce the ability of local authorities to redistribute growth. Neither would more effective regional planning, as proposed by the JLRC, have much impact on the dispersal process if the overriding desideratum is an increase in aggregate housing output. Fifthly, trying to meet national targets for housing has proved hopelessly unrealistic in the past, simply because requirements have changed as macro-economic conditions have changed. In 1969, Mr Kenneth Robinson, then Minister of Planning and Land, claimed there would be a housing surplus by 1973, and an end to spiralling land and house prices! Sixthly, the implementation of any national programme would be difficult since central government has no control over the many separate housing agencies, and there is much variation in the way regional and local building firms respond to the market. A related point is that local authority discretion over housing land release can only be called to account by central government at the time of development plan approval and when permission is refused for development. There is the final and related difficulty of ensuring that land with planning permission is actually built on within a reasonable period of time — delay for speculative purposes has contributed in no small way to rising house prices.

Thus central government attempts to control the aggregate amount of new housing seem doomed to fail. It may try to influence and encourage more flexible local approaches to housing land, but stronger indicative planning of the type being advanced by the JLRC will be very difficult. It could also work against the interests of the builders who may be forced to renegotiate targets whenever housing market factors changed. A more fundamental objection concerns the manner by which national policy should be formulated. The HBF represents the volume sector of the industry. Why should they alone be party to national decision making on housing. policy? Owner-occupation will not solve the national housing problem; the public agencies need to be involved too. And why should housing policy be formulated without the consultation of the other pressure groups having an interest in rural land, especially the Council for the Protection of Rural England (CPRE) and the National

Farmers Union (NFU). The issue at stake is strategic land use planning. Without that there is no basis for evaluating the scale of provision in the outer cities. The link between housing and other aspects of urban policy has not been considered by JLRC and could be a reason why the RTPI decided to reject the recommendations contained in the second draft report.

Excessive emphasis on the total amounts of land available, however, diverts attention from the crucial issue of the distribution of housing land as between inner and outer cities, and between growth and restraint areas within the outer cities themselves. It has been difficult to channel housing to growth areas because private housebuilders are sometimes reluctant to invest there. Given stronger central and regional guidance and more effective public policy those conditions need not apply in the future. But who gains from a spatially selective housing land policy? The housebuilders claim that 'growth' locations are associated with down-market housing, whereas more environmentally attractive areas will be up-market. In arguing as they did in the Manchester study that planners should provide for both types of market in the same location, housebuilders have come very close to accepting the long-established planning goal of social mix. Planners too must be criticized for failing to tackle social issues in structure and local plans. The relationship between size of site, type of dwelling produced and type of housing developer is rarely discussed. Yet the size of site made available is crucial in determining the local character of the housebuilding industry: larger sites will be favoured by non-local development companies will lead to a much more standardized type of housing market. The implication is that if planners could make available a greater range of different size sites a more varied housing market might result in the outer cities. This approach to housing land would require a fundamental rethink of existing settlement policies.[31] The housebuilding industry might accept this, if only to avoid the infrastructure blockages which surround the development of larger sites. But their excessive concern with overall dwelling allocations and the total quantity of housing available has so far obscured the importance of these questions. Furthermore, they have been reluctant until recently to question conventional wisdom about the type of housing being constructed in the outer cities.[32] To do so would again imply a less important role for large national and regional development companies which have mainly specialized in three- or four-bedroomed housing. An overall increase in dwellings would again seem less important than selective growth in smaller dwellings for single and two-person families,[33] though the land-take and socio-demographic impact of such a policy should not be underestimated.

The battle for land release — who is winning?

Too ready an acceptance by the DoE of the argument that land scarcity inhibits housing output might make it seem that private housebuilders are getting it all their own way over how much housebuilding should take place and where. Few would deny the HBF's role as an effective pressure group at the national scale. The Local Government Planning and Land Act 1980 gave powers to the Secretary of State to determine that local authorities carry out residential land availability surveys in which explicit weight is given to market criteria. But what role do housebuilding interests play in the local development process? The conclusions of the DoE-sponsored research carried out by Oxford Polytechnic[34] are somewhat equivocal, but in general terms volume housebuilders and property companies have fallen in line with county and district development plans, deflected by strong restraint policy and the particular characteristics of the housing land market. Private speculative housing interests thus modify containment policy at the margins only. The role of central government in supporting local restraint policy through refusing appeals had been effective between 1974 and 1978. The report acknowledged some important breaches in policy at the time of buoyant demand in the late 1960s and early 1970s and in response to more recent shifts in economic and political attitudes since 1978.

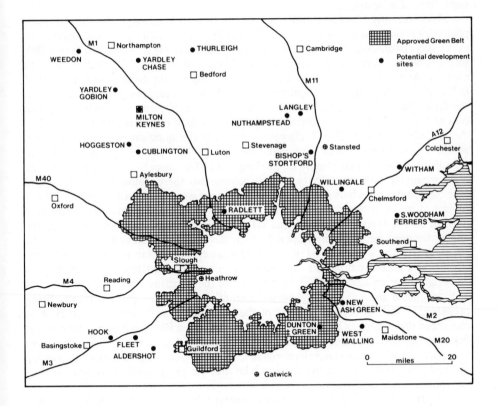

Figure 11.   The possible location of London's new 'villages'

The difficulties which the private housebuilding industry faces at the local scale should not be underestimated. Political opposition to growth is a paramount concern. The actions of national and local pressure groups reduce both the scale of plans put forward by planners and some development applications proposed by the housebuilders. The JLRC, to which housebuilders were party, insist that districts will have to make some very unpopular decisions to get housebuilding underway. The agricultural lobby is another obstacle. The well-documented history of battles for housing land in the outer cities is sprinkled with accounts of the role played by the MAFF in opposing development, although admittedly its concern was then public housing as much as private housing. The legacy of 'white land' exclusions from Green Belts, which provided the development industry with a loophole for securing land release, is largely spent, which explains why the HBF has turned its attention to alternative sites, particularly those lying between inner edges of the Green Belts and the cities. Even derelict sites within the Green Belts are capable of improvement by some form of development.[35]

More recently, builders have sought to directly challenge the fundamental principles behind the concept of Green Belts (Figure 11). In doing this they have been partly successful. County-district relations have been severely strained over Green Belt subject plans, as mentioned earlier. The weaknesses of the two-tier system have been exposed. At the Greater Manchester Green Belt inquiry the county were accused of failing to determine housing requirements in advance of preparing the boundaries of the Green Belt. They replied somewhat thinly that local plans were being prepared concurrently and that all the districts had agreed the land requirement which could be met outside the Green Belt.[36] However, this begs the question of how land policy within the Green Belt can be formulated, bearing in mind that some districts have not yet identified a five-year supply of housing land. The inspector disagreed with the HBF argument without really tackling it, saying that there would be sufficient land over the county as a whole and, moreover, that there were other areas of open land not subject to major policy constraints. In rejecting the idea of a permanent 15-20 year lifespan on the Green Belt which the HBF sought, the Inspector acknowledged the imperative need for flexibility imposed by the development plan system: 'it would be wrong to establish a plan period of say 15-20 years on a local plan which has a strategic effect over a substantial part of . . . one of the major conurbations in this country, as this might have an adverse effect on a review of the structure plan'. To do so would be to prejudice and pre-empt the preparation of all the district plans currently being prepared, as well as reviewing parts of the structure plan.[37] Although the HBF is concerned that sufficient land is excluded from the Green Belt it can take some comfort from the fact that although the DoE may argue, as it did in Circular 22/80, that there was a presumption against development in Green Belts, the responsibility for drawing up local plans remains with the districts who may yet prove much more flexible than the counties over land release.

The speculative housebuilders play a central role in containment strategy. Their impact has been greatest in the sphere of development planning and it is estimated that in 18 out of 25 percent examinations-in-public of structure plans the housebuilders have made successful representations.[38] The cumulative impact of modifications to the structure plans may prove far more damaging to the long-term interests of outer and inner city communities than the temporary reverberations of the planning appeals which favour developers and were outlined in the last chapter. An increase in national housing output is desirable but it would be misguided and short-sighted to devise a national housing strategy before a land use planning strategy. Such a policy must take into account the considerable scale of housing already being allocated and permitted in so-called restraint counties and the long run social and economic consequences of a freer market in housing land. It must also recognise the mounting opposition to urban growth in the countryside.

Notes

1. For an explanation of the interaction between government and housebuilders see A. MURIE et al., Housing Policy and the Housing System (Allen and Unwin, 1976).

2. For a review of the role of speculative housebuilders in the planning process see K. BASSETT and J. SHORT, Housing and Residential Structure; Alternative Approaches (Routledge & Kegan Paul, 1980).

3. Department of Environment and Economist Intelligence Unit Land Availability — a study of land with residential planning permission (DoE. 1978).

4. A. HOOPER 'Land for private housebuilding', Journal of Planning and Environmental Law, December 1980.

5. B. R. DAVIDSON, 'The effects of land speculation on the supply of housing in England and Wales', Urban Studies, vol. 12, 1975.

6. Joint Land Requirements Committee, Is there sufficient housing land for the 1980s? Paper II: How many houses have we planned for — is there a problem? (Housing Research Foundation, February 1983).

7. R. COWAN, 'Land supply for housing', Roof, vol. 6 (3), May/June 1981.

8. T. STEVENS, 'Land for housing', RIBA Journal, vol. 88, no. 9, 1981.

9. House-Builders Federation, Where Should the Houses Go? (HBF and Cheshire County Council Planning Department, February 1981).

10. For a fuller discussion see A. HOOPER, 'Land availability', Journal of Planning and Environmental Law, November 1979.

11. House-Builders Federation, Housing land in the South East: a Joint Report, (Standing Conference for London and South East Regional Planning and Housebuilders Federation, November 1981).

12. Department of Environment, Land Availability: A Study of Land with Residential Planning Permission (DoE, 1978).

13. West Midlands Forum of County Councils, The State of Housing in the West Midlands Region (WMFCC, 1982).

14. The Association of Municipal Authorities, Land for Private House Building (AMA, 1982).

15. Joint Land Requirements Committee, op. cit.

16. See the report on housing problems, 'The friction factor', Planning, vol. 413, 10 April 1981.

17. T. BARON, 'Planning's biggest and least satisfied customer: Housing', Paper to the Town and Country Planning Summer School: Report of Proceedings, RTPI, September 1980.

18. G. R. PEARCE and M .J. TRICKER, 'Land availability for residential development' in F. JOYCE (ed.), *Metropolitan Development and Change; the West Midlands — a Policy Review* (Teakfield, 1977).

19. For a review see D. H. McKAY and A. W. COX, *The Politics of Urban Change* (Croom Helm, 1979).

20. Department of Environment, 'Land for Private Housebuilding', Circular 9/80, paras. 6 and 3 (HMSO, 1980).

21. quoted by A. HOOPER, op. cit. 1980.

22. D. LOCK, 'Land for houses', *Town and Country Planning*, vol. 46(6), 1978.

23. For a criticism of the method see J. W. MACKIE, *Goodbye Rural Berkshire? Development Pressures in Central Berkshire and South East England*; Report for Binfield and Warfield Parish Councils, 1982.

24. Reported as 'Housing draft gets split vote?, *Planning*, vol. 528, 22 July 1983.

25. See P. SWANN, 'Playing the land game', *Planning*, vol. 472, 11 June 1982.

26. The problems are discussed in 'The numbers game', *Planning*, vol. 497, 3 December 1982.

27. Joint Land Requirements Committee, *Is there Sufficient Housing Land for the 1980s? Paper 1: How Many Houses Should We Plan For?* (Housing Research Foundation, February 1982).

28. Joint Land Requirements Committee, *Housing Allocation in Structure and Local Plans* (House Builders Federation, February 1982).

29. Reported in 'On the trail of housing land', *Planning*, vol. 496, 26 November 1982.

30. Joint Lands Requirement Committee, Paper II, February, 1983, op. cit.

31. Some local districts are approaching the formulation of housing strategy in these terms. See for instance Charnwood Borough Council, *A Strategy for Private Housebuilding* (Charnwood BC, 1981).

32. Smaller homes discussed in *Planning Bulletin*, 26 July 1982.

33. Standing Conference on London and South East Regional Planning, *Smaller Households*, Report by the Housing Issues Working Party of the regional monitoring group, SCLSERP, SC 1617R, January 1982.

34. P. HEALEY, *et al.*, *The Implementation of Development Plans*, Report for the Department of Environment, Oxford Polytechnic Department of Town Planning, 1982.

35. M. DOBSON, 'Green Belts: planners play canute', *Planning*, vol. 482, 20 August 1982.

36. Report on 'Green Belts: Manchester planner puts his case', *Planning*, vol. 484, 3 September 1982.

37. The results of Manchester's Green Belt inquiry are summarised in 'Builders told to belt up', *Planning*, vol. 495, 19 November 1982.

38. Report by Jane Morton, *Local Government News*, 12 June 1981.

9   The Anti-Growth Lobby

If I knew the Latin for 'I'm all right Jack, pull up the drawbridge', I'd offer it to the Council for Protection of Rural England and the other conservationist organisations for their respective coat of arms.
(Roger Humber, Director of the House-Builders Federation, 1982).

In this chapter we turn to the attempts made by national and local amenity groups to protect the countryside from urban developments.[1] Pressure groups are not planners or developers. They are ordinary citizens who band together to fight the planners and developers. They influence the political process by mobilizing public opinion, gaining the support of elected representatives and bargaining at public meetings and inquiries. Their activities create political tension at various levels.[2] Local residents may resist any expansion which threatens them, whereas county structure planners want some selective development in the interests of overall restraint. Effective resistance to growth in one locality may have the effect of diminishing opposition in another, bringing about shifts in the spatial pattern of social segregation. Which people and groups are involved? How have they gone about opposing housing development? And what does their action imply for the future of the outer cities? First we must mention something of the background.

The rationale for conflict

The history of the environmental movement is well documented.[3] National pressure groups like the Council for the Protection of Rural England have a pedigree that goes back to 1926. They have long promoted the cause of countryside protection in upland and lowland England, in Wales and in Scotland. They feel particularly strongly about the loss of good quality farmland and attractive countryside, especially needless exploitation of rural land. Other amenity groups have been formed in particular localities to fight specific proposals for change. They seek to protect the peace, quiet, or visual appeal of a place, and its accessibility to good quality services. Locality-based groups are most vocal in their opposition to development in Green Belts, although it cannot be assumed their influence has been more substantial there than in non-Green Belt areas. Sadly there is no hard documentation about the rise and fall of amenity bodies in the outer city and we have to rely on anecdotal accounts of particular conflicts. These may be only the more dramatic instances of anti-growth; we cannot tell.

Public interest in the appearance of the rural environment is a long-standing one and it would be wrong to argue that today's battles signify an explosive growth of feeling against urban dispersal.[4] Nonetheless, there are differences between past and present conflicts over land development. The classic disputes in the 1960s arose from concerned proposals for large-scale overspill from the conurbations.[5] Conflict was most intense where development land, either for physical reasons or for reasons of local planning policy was in short supply. Poor inter-authority relationships clearly played an important part especially in the West Midlands. In those controversies it was difficult to separate the objections of local authorities from those of organised amenity groups — both seemed equally opposed to urban development. Around smaller free-standing cities like Leicester and Southampton, where land scarcity was less acute, there were not the same battles on questions of public overspill.[6] The point remains relevant today, although we must add that squabbles about the location of private housing have become much more intense in Leicestershire and are no longer confined to the local authorities.

But trends are changing. Speculative housebuilders are now a major target of the anti-growth lobby. House prices have risen steeply under the combined effects of rising income, rising housing demand and shortage of supply.[7] This might account for vociferous opposition to further land for housing in landscapes of little scenic value. Overspill has been drastically reduced, particularly in England, although the momentum for growth remains strong among the Expanded Towns like Swindon, and this is still a source of environmental conflict. But small-scale incremental additions to the urban area in suburbs and villages provoke protest wherever they occur.

The causes of concern have changed in other ways too. Firstly, the focus of environmental interest has shifted from a narrow concern about protecting countryside resources to a much wider debate about the land use 'crisis.' It seems to make no sense to take more greenfield sites in the outer city when there are extensive areas of vacant and derelict land in the inner cities. This argument has a popular appeal, but of course environmental lobbies will use every available argument to keep urban growth in the cities. Bodies like the CPRE and the Land Decade Council are playing up to public opinion here. Secondly, even if national amenity bodies have developed a healthier perspective on urban and regional change, the same cannot be said of locality-based interests defending their territories against urban growth: indeed, 'few groups appear loath to regard the deflection of an unwanted development elsewhere as anything but a complete victory'.[8] Hence, despite the recession we find widespread obstruction to development proposals in the inner and outer commuting areas. Recession has not diminished the force of the environmental lobby; indeed, recession may have had the reverse effect by throwing into relief those areas where growth is still booming.

Undoubtedly, the in-migration of better-off social groups, analyzed in chapter 3, must be taken into account when explaining increasingly widespread protest. Those who place a premium on their environment and enjoy a high standard of privacy and social exclusivity naturally seek to defend their life-style against the advancing urban tide. They may have been living in the outer cities for a long time, or they may have arrived recently. They see themselves as 'locals', those who haven't yet arrived as 'newcomers'. The dividing line in occupational or social status between locals and newcomers may be a thin one, but this doesn't matter to them: the first groups who move out of the city feel their security threatened by later newcomers. Hence the so-called 'drawbridge' effect whereby the migration of higher status groups is followed by strong opposition to further growth. The pioneers express opposition outside and inside the formal political process. The more articulate middle class secure places on the local council and fight for conservation or low growth planning strategies, helping to reinforce social segregation.[9] In describing the social antagonisms which underpin the politics of local exclusion in the leafy suburbs south of London, Kramer and Young argue that 'the failure of a powerful metropolitan authority to bring about a substantial reallocation of suburban space is rooted in the imperatives of suburban territorial defence'.[10] Suburban separatism is a plausible explanation for much anti-growth feeling, although it may not always lead to the same kind of social exclusion as

Kramer and Young refer to, and it does not always challenge successfully the power base of the central or local planning bureaucracies.

The introduction by central government of public participation procedures cannot be ignored as a factor in the rise of opposition since 1968. The case for giving people a greater say in planning matters had been made earlier by the Skeffington Committee.[11] Skeffington argued that passive majorities as well as active minorities ought to be involved more widely in decision making. Under the Town and Country Planning Act 1971 (following the 1968 Act) local authorities were asked to consult the public during the formulation of policy goals. They were told to ensure adequate publicity for the plan and inform individuals of their right to make their views heard. The experience of popular participation has been a mixed one.[12] Rarely do passive majorities or working class groups become genuinely involved. Some groups show more interest in structure plan examinations in public. Which groups attend meetings may depend more on the way planners set about the participation exercise, although planning proposals affect the interest of all local residents directly or indirectly. The experience of participation shows that local protest can affect the smooth implementation of planning policy and bring political tension to relations between county and district and between local and central government. For this reason participation may be indulged in more confidently by planners when the results are unlikely to challenge the substantive values of the structure plan.[13]

The groups involved

The recent dramatic growth in the number of pressure groups is not well documented. We know that the total combined membership of such national bodies is about three million. Perhaps one million people belong to various local societies; these rose in number from 710 to 1250 between 1969 and 1975.[14] Their social composition, their goals and their strategies differ somewhat. Local pressure groups regard strategy as simply the mobilization of political support; the idea of a coherent policy for urban change is rarely uppermost in their minds. National amenity organisations take a longer-term interest in land use conservation and the environmental conflicts which urban development presents. The protection of the quality of rural landscapes and the safeguarding of designated tracts of countryside like Areas of Outstanding Natural Beauty are common aims. Some national organizations seek to maintain productive agriculture, securing the interests of landowners and farmers, and are not primarily concerned for the appearance of the landscape. Others are concerned with countryside recreation or the conservation of wildlife and agricultural resources. The emergence of all these environmental lobbies must be viewed in the context of public concern over countryside change.

National amenity lobbies

The main role of centrally organized pressure groups is to lobby ministers, educate the public about threats to the countryside, and cooperate with other national and local organizations. In this way they help frame central government policy, shape public opinion, and stimulate local debate. Their direct involvement in mounting national campaigns is confined to major issues such as the Third London Airport, the Vale of Belvoir coalfield, or the M40 Oxford-Birmingham proposal. Much of the bread-and-butter work of the CPRE is the monitoring of local change carried out by its 43 county branches and 200 or more local district committees.

National groups have a vested interest in the planning system — understandably so since they had a formative role in its establishment. Indeed, the maintenance and protection of the countryside is regarded by the CPRE as one of the key priorities for the public planning system. Relaxation of controls in favour of speculative housing and industrial development has been promptly condemned as a reversal of all that planning stands for. It is government and the developers on whom political pressure must be brought to bear: 'The Housebuilders Federation has successfully persuaded the Environment Secretary to increase housing land allocations in the Central Berkshire and West Wiltshire Structure Plans (+8,000 and +3,800 dwellings respectively) over and above the requirements of the local authorities.'[15]

The CPRE says that it has not been so worried about the direction in which planning is moving since the period before World War II, when it was fiercely campaigning against the consequences of urban sprawl in the countryside. The CPRE's position on containment has differed somewhat from that of the Town and Country Planning Association. The TCPA maintains that agricultural land is not necessarily inviolate and that the interests of industry as well as agriculture should be met through carefully planned decentralization. The CPRE, on the other hand has always been firmly protectionist, although some of its members have in the past questioned the merits of containment orthodoxy, including the value of Green Belts, on the basis that they threatened tracts of countryside beyond.[16] This echoes the discussion of a 'two-tier' system of protected countryside — that is to say, areas recognised by central government as worthy of protection and areas which may be written off. The latter, argues the CPRE, constitute all those rural and semi-rural landscapes within which the majority of Britain's population happen to live. Containment cannot be spatially selective, favouring the special areas and not the others. Of course it has been just that, but the CPRE's point is that the land use planning system has formerly been operated more consistently and strictly than it is being now.

Although the CPRE criticises the present Conservative administration for its relaxed approach to land planning, the fault lies as much with previous administrations. Giving more discretion to county and district councils effectively sanctioned a higher scale and rate of change beyond the Green Belts which Circular 22/80 now gives tacit acceptance to. Furthermore, central government is not alone in changing its policy in favour of growth. The counties have undoubtedly connived in the development spiral. Although their recent press announcements make reference to structure plan proposals, the CPRE persist by and large in putting pressure on central government. The counties are clearly not autonomous agents, yet neither are they passive recipients of DoE advice. The political interests of the councils no longer accord with those of the amenity lobby. More are seeking to increase economic development even if it means the sacrifice of containment values. Even rural councillors with interests in land are under fire to facilitate rather than hinder development projects.

National amenity lobbies have always sought to conserve the countryside and protect good agricultural land. These goals no longer command the automatic support they once did; and it is interesting therefore that some groups are now seeking legitimacy for a modified form of containment strategy which implies a less rigid attitude towards the loss of agricultural land and the virtues of state planning. The same appeal to consensus is sought but that consensus has perceptibly shifted in favour of greater expansion within the urban envelope. The organizers of the Land Decade Council 1980–1990 (LDC), which was formed in 1977, want stronger measures to stop the loss of high quality farmland; in return, it will agree to the relaxation of planning controls within the urban fringe.[17] This strategy avoids needless exploitation of good quality greenfield sites and encourages better use of vacant or derelict wasteland within urban areas, as well as securing a rationalization of buffer land (the fragmented farming zone on the edge of the continuously built up area).[18]

Several reservations must be expressed about this kind of strategy, which bears some resemblance to the housebuilders' proposals to develop housing on sites of 'little amenity value' in the Green Belt. Although concerned at the rate of agricultural land conversion, the Land Decade Council ignores the possibility that even if carefully controlled (and the LDC's case implies some relaxation of planning power) the urban development of certain sites could push the zone of fragmentation further out. Moreover, there is evidence to show that farmers wish to remain in farming rather than sell-out to developers.[19] Some of them derive financial benefit from recreation planning either on their land or in association with cooperative management schemes like Country Parks.[20] All of which suggests that the LDC may have underrated the advantages of farming close to the cities.[21] Their claim to represent a new national consensus among professional land using interests must be doubted. They may have the backing of the County Landowners Association (CLA) but their approach to land policy would seem to differ somewhat from that of the CPRE as well as many organisations wanting more rather than less provision for recreation on run-down sites in the urban fringe. It must seriously be doubted whether local residents would support the LDC's argument for more urban development.[22]

Landowning and farming interests

Landowning and farming interests have mounted powerful opposition to urban-industrial developments in the countryside. The County Landowners Association and the National Farmers Union (NFU) have been particularly vociferous in protecting the interests of their members. They comment on national environmental issues, and their local branches frequently make respresentation on development proposals. The power enjoyed by the farming lobbies varies according to regional and local differences in the structure of agriculture, above all in the size and productivity of farms. Larger farming interests seek a tightening or restriction on the geographical spread of development. Smaller farmers may, ironically, want a more relaxed policy for the provision of new agricultural dwellings. The better-off farmers are more likely to belong to national amenity societies, branches of the CPRE, or other local groups, and they may be county councillors. Smaller farming interests are more likely to be represented on the parish council. Their different viewpoints and objectives create political tension at an inter-authority level between county and district.[23]

The question of the relative influence of the agricultural lobby over local planning decisions remains an open one. It is difficult to make general assertions. In the first place, the elected membership of county and district councils is changing. The old rural squirearchy is seldom evident in the inner commuting areas. Agricultural interests may be represented on the shire county councils, but elected members are drawn from a much broader social back-ground than they used to be.[24] In 1976, over 69 percent of non-metropolitan district councillors in England described their occupations as administrative, managerial, technical or clerical. Only seven percent worked in farming and the figure was only 10 percent in the shire counties.[25] Additionally, the reduction in the number of small rural authorities following the reorganisation of local government in 1974 has been followed by the displacement of 'amateur' councillors by middle-class professionals more closely involved in party politics.[26] It is not obvious that these councillors share the same values or have a shared commitment to rural conservation.

Observations about the impact of the farming lobby in different areas must be speculative. Farmers owning the better quality land appear to be in a stronger position to mount resistance to urban growth. Such farms are found in the lowland areas of the outer-community zone. In contrast, farmers owning or renting small farmholdings are less likely to organise themselves as effectively in defence of agricultural land. The smaller, fragmented farms are found especially in the urban fringe. In any case, such small farmers may choose to defer to pressures for urban expansion, either selling up or waiting for the value of their land to rise. It cannot be presumed that they accept their situation passively since many experience the indirect consequences of urban development through trespass, vandalism and fragmentation; but they may be less committed to defence of the status quo than their counterparts living further out. The same may not apply to part-time or hobby farmers. However, these comprise a significant proportion of farms in the urban fringe and Green Belt zones. They depend less directly on farming and might be expected to seek, in common with other local pressure groups, the protection of countryside landscapes and amenities. A further consideration is that the pattern of land ownership is changing rapidly in the outer-metropolitan area as city institutions and foreign interests buy up large estates from private landowners — as in areas of north Hampshire for instance. They are not in general seeking speculative gain from urban development but rather to create more productive agri-business involving the replacement of small with large holdings or the exchange of poorer with better quality farmland.[27] There is no special reason why city institutions should not be just as vociferous in their defence of good quality farmland as the traditional guardians of the countryside such as the Country Landowners Association. They have a strong interest in maintaining high land values and protecting the most productive farm units from fragmentation.

Locality-based pressure groups

Locality-based pressure groups usually emerge when specific development proposals threaten the property values of local residents. These groups often seek to restrict the amount of new housing land, but they may object to other kinds of commercial or industrial proposals as well. Where the pressure for housing land release is most intense, local action groups have proved able to organize efficiently and mobilize public opposition to change. Since these areas are already covered by statutory planning policies like Green Belts or AONBs, the effect of their actions is to uphold county restraint policy.[28] However, regional restraint invariably requires a measure of local development, which is a district matter. Local pressure groups are hence likely to challenge local district plans even in Green Belts. Furthermore, we must consider the role played by pressure groups in outer areas where growth and development strategies are important. In Leicestershire, for example, pressure groups have attacked the whole principle of development in the inner commuting areas, effectively challenging the principal points of the structure plan and bringing about a cumulative and complex series of political tensions between county and district. Their actions patently disrupt 'key' settlement policy which the counties regard as essential for overall restraint of growth in the rural areas.[29]

The attention of most local groups is focussed on deflecting housing developments away from their own patch. Opposition to council housing and to the scale and siting of private housing both illustrate the point. At one time, it could have been fairly confidently predicted that where planned schemes were poorly developed local protest would be muted or non-existent. Now it seems that the steady increase in private speculative building and the tendency for councils, under pressure from central government, to release clusters of estate development in larger villages and on the edge of towns, has provoked a growing storm of local protest. Residents are up in arms about the number of houses being proposed, increases in density, the loss of green gaps between settlements, and sometimes the price of the new houses which locals will not be able to afford. Protest about the type of housing proposed is less common since most proposals involve detached or semi-detached housing rather than terraces or flats which might be associated with social downgrading. The geographical spread of protest is also growing. It is by no means confined to large-scale growth areas like central Berkshire. The defence of social space has indeed become a pervasive element of British experience in the outer cities.

Some local societies have grouped themselves together to form loose coalitions of environmental interest. They draw members from a wider catchment area and take a rather less parochial view of urban change. The Green Belt Society for Greater London, established in 1954, attempts to protect the openness of the metropolitan Green Belt and strongly objects to selective housing on sites of 'little amenity value' arguing that they could be improved for recreational or visual enjoyment.[30] Similarly, the Surrey Amenity Council, founded in 1951 and consisting of 53 separate organizations, aims to maintain and enhance the beauty of the Surrey countryside. As it covers the whole county it cannot obviously respond effectively to particular local problems which do not have a country-wide impact. Its decisions 'tend towards well meaning platitudes; its main role is mediation and guidance.'[31] Other groupings of individual amenity societies face the same political impotence although their views could find some public support. A complete standstill on growth is seldom entertained as a legitimate goal. Other aims are familiar to planners: reducing energy costs by concentrating development, maintaining open countryside, protecting good farmland, redirecting resources to the inner city, reducing interregional disparities, and so on.

The mechanics of opposition

Although all these groups take part in the political process, how effective has their opposition been in changing the direction of growth strategies in favour of restraint and conservation? It may be that settlement changes result less from the influence of the amenity lobby than from the selective way in which planning controls have been operated. Planning officers have considerable power to make decisions on their own. Even if they want public opinion, they need not canvass it from elected members until late in the participation process. The planning officers may set the terms of debate. The role played by individuals and pressure groups may simply be a form of 'tokenism' which leaves the planners free to pay lip service to environmental values without making any substantive change in their policy in favour of restraint.[32]

Evaluating the role played by protest groups in the planning process is a complex matter. The reorganisation of responsiblity for planning policy and implementation which followed the Town and Country Planning Act 1968 artificially compartmentalized the public participation process between county and district. Local pressure groups have invariably been more active though not always effective when specific local interests are threatened. National amenity interests like the CPRE, on the other hand, have spent many hours at structure plan examinations in public directing their fire more at the principle of development or challenging the current development-orientated planning policies which central government and some county councils now pursue.[33] As the economic recession draws central government more closely into decisions concerning industrial and housing development, new political tensions, pressures and alliances are resulting in those areas of the outer city bearing the brunt of development, and it is probably too soon to judge the likely outcome of the combined national and local response which these policies have prompted.

In the case of local pressure groups, there are some empirical studies from which we can draw a number of rather general conclusions about the effectiveness of protest in the outer city. First, well mobilised local opposition can prevent the allocation of new housing land, entirely or in part. Second, the excitement of successful opposition may be short-lived and followed by counter-proposals or reversals of local policy. Some lobbying may simply achieve a reprieve, and the longer the conflict remains unresolved, the more likely it is that circumstances will change attitudes towards conservation and development. Third, there is no a priori reason why local pressure groups should win the argument more often in Green Belt areas — more critical factors may be the history of earlier urban development and the existence or otherwise of 'unspoilt' countryside. Fourth, a chronicle of dispute between local authorities, for example between counties and districts or between metropolitan and non-metropolitan counties, will greatly assist the cause of a pressure group. In this case, the views of the planning officers are less important. Fifth, opposition is likely to fail when elected members give little support to conservation or change their views during the course of the dispute. Failure may occur also when decisions are taken out of the hands of the local authorities — as when developers gain the support of central government for housing land release in small villages where local people oppose further growth.

Protest directed at central government

Protest directed at central government has resulted from the recent round of DoE modifications to county structure plans. In central Berkshire the CPRE has effectively mobilized grass roots opinion in the parish councils by drawing attention to the environmental conflicts which would arise from an extra 8,000 houses being added to the 31,700 dwellings that the county council had already allowed for in the structure plan, 'a staggering 25 percent increase in the numbers of houses, and of course the people, that would need to be planned for.'[34] Such growth was misplaced in view of the changing demographic context in Greater London. Moreover, once the M25 was built, pressure for *even more* new housing and industry in Berkshire would grow intense. These objections persuaded the CPRE to urge local councillors to support the county council's structure plan against the dictates of central government and the developers. The parishes commissioned their own study, appropriately entitled 'Goodbye to Rural Berkshire?' in which the consequences of a much higher rate of residential land release are set out in the context of the history of strategic planning in the South East. The main report makes four recommendations:

(a) the DoE should recognize that there was no need to identify additional land in 1983;

(b) that there was no need to release more land on major sites before the structure plan review was underway; this review would permit proper public consultation on the appropriate scale of future housing;

(c) that there should be a review of Circular 9/80 procedures especially insofar as they require districts to achieve an adequate supply of land over a five-year period;

(d) the removal of the 'growth area' label from central Berkshire and a recognition that the county council would be justified in broad strategic planning terms, as well as on environmental grounds, in pursuing a more restrictive policy to regulate growth in Central Berkshire.[35]

The last comment is undoubtedly the most telling since it draws attention to some of the fundamental conflicts between strategies for growth and conservation. Growth on the scale proposed would appear to be in neither the national nor local interest.

The government's basic argument seemed sound enough. Being just outside the London Green Belt, Berkshire could relieve pressure for housebuilding in Greater London. The high rate of household formation in Berkshire appeared to require much more housing provision. Some rationalization of the existing pattern of development in Berkshire would be desirable. Moreover, the accessibility of Berkshire suggested that there was potential for industrial development. The local social and environmental consequencies arising from a growth strategy were barely considered. If they had been, a rather more cautious regional stance might have been adopted. However, the amenity lobbies have taken a rather narrow view by focussing solely on the modifications to the structure plan rather than examining the rationale behind them. Berkshire seeks to channel growth away from sensitive landscapes east and west of the county into central Berkshire. A concentration strategy of this kind protects the environment for some but clearly damages it for others. The local parishes could usefully have questioned the implication of a concentrated rather than a dispersed settlement policy. But issues of this kind in structure plans have not normally moved the general public because they are rather abstract and their implications difficult to understand. Modifications to development plans can more easily be seized upon by local residents because they refer to *specific* scales of future growth or specific sites for additional housing development.[36] The irony is that if central government were not so involved in the detail of local planning, this opposition to structure plans might not manifest itself at all. But then would central government trust the counties to provide enough land for housing and industry in the outer cities?

Protest directed at the counties

Protest directed at the counties has arisen when relatively extensive areas of land are allocated for development, either as additions to the suburbs or separated from the built-up area in the open countryside. County development plans have been the main focus of public criticism. Sadly, the response of local pressure groups has been largely parochial, but when they have halted a particular development, the housebuilders have invariably appealed to central government. In this way, local pressure groups may have a strong influence.

In the short term, county plans for allocating new housing and industrial land may be overturned by politicians who capitulate in the face of the anti-growth lobby. This was illustrated by two recent cases in Leicestershire[37] and Bedfordshire[38]. Both counties sought substantial yet compact urban expansion close to Leicester and Luton as a way of containing population and employment growth and reducing the pressure on countryside further out. Nothing less than the effective implementation of containment strategy was at stake in both counties. Projections of population growth in Luton showed the need to find land for an additional 3,600 dwellings over that already committed up to 1991. One of the options put forward by Bedfordshire was expansion at Hyde, a site just south-east of Luton on the Hertfordshire border in open countryside. The structure plan for Leicestershire defined a Central Leicester sub-area which was expected to grow by 116,000 people between 1971and 1991. Seven places for major development were indicated including Hamilton, north-east of the city, which would absorb a massive 19,500 people (18 percent of forecast growth in the central sub-area). Hamilton took its name from a deserted medieval village, and the designated area included three small villages and open farmland.

The protests which were mounted in both areas had a number of similarities: First, the anti-growth lobby was essentially a local one. The Hyde development was opposed by the Harpenden Society representing the interests of commuters just across the border from Bedfordshire. The local residents group which sprang into action at Hamilton was composed of farmers and commuters from the three villages closest to the proposed development. Second, both groups claimed they had not been given enough opportunity to debate the proposals. This was not strictly true since each development formed part of the structure plan policies discussed by the county planning officers at a series of public meetings. The way protest developed emphasized the weaknesses of the two-stage approach to public participation: only when policies were formulated in detail, for instance in the local plan for Hamilton, did major resistance emerge. Third, the counties' response to local pressure groups depended on the stage which statutory planning procedures had reached. At Hyde opposition was mounted before the structure plan was submitted to the Department of Environment for approval. At Hamilton, unfortunately for the county, the structure plan had already been approved before protest made itself felt, making it more difficult for the county to back down. To have done so would have required development at less sensitive sites and thus a formal alteration to the structure plan — a lengthy process. The longer public protest went on the more difficult it became for them to drop the scheme. Fourth, the effectiveness of the local pressure groups depended on political circumstances. Following the Hyde protest the county council elections in Bedfordshire resulted in a Conservative administration which was more sympathetic than Labour had been to the protestors. The structure plan was quickly amended to exclude all reference to specific sites. Public protest and political opposition from its own members led Leicestershire County Council in January 1977 to abandon preparation of the Hamilton local plan. County council elections in May 1982 reduced the effective control of both main parties, and in January 1983 the Environment Committee approved a revised scaled-down plan for Hamilton six years after the decision to delay the local plan, but the newly designated area was drawn up to exclude the contentious locations in the rural district.

The strategic interests of both local authorities were exposed by the anti-growth lobby. Was it economically viable, the Hamilton residents asked, at a time of public expenditure cuts and the government's 1977 inner city initiatives, to divert financial resources into greenfield sites? The county planners could argue, as they did, that more land was needed to match future housing demand. But the residents questioned future population estimates. With zero national population growth, why take more farm land? 'Halt Hamilton, not harvests' was their emotive plea. The planners' argument about new household formation was lost, and when migration was mentioned it was taken to mean ethnic ghettoes in outer Leicester! Similarly, the Harpenden society argued for a reassessment of existing land commitments closer to Luton than Hyde, believing that higher density development and the dispersion of growth to Milton Keynes would obviate the need for development at Hyde.

Protest against the districts

Protest against districts is aggravated by the political tension surrounding the implementation of large scale county structure plans. The Hamilton development represented nearly 20 percent of planned future population growth in central Leicestershire. Abandoning it or delaying it can mean that pressure for new housing land release is put upon smaller settlements further out. District local plans for smaller settlements in the commuting areas are the source of public criticism and protest in much the same way that the county structure plans are. Districts face the addititional difficulty, however, of being responsible for the actual implementation of their plans. Nor will it always be the case that the quite modest relative scales of land being suggested for development in districts would be uncontentious. Effective local resistance to growth will raise doubts in the counties' minds about the commitment of the districts to strategic policy. Some districts have of course deliberately provoked the counties by seeking a higher level of growth than the counties wish to see. Effective public opposition against such local plans must be a source of satisfaction for the counties. These conflicts are well illustrated in the case of the Lapworth district plan[39] in Warwickshire and the Quorn Local Plan in Leicestershire.[40] These cases indicate the increasingly local scale of anti-growth feeling. Lapworth is a commuting settlement in the westerly part of Warwickshire, 19 kilometres south east of Birmingham, 11 kilometres north of Warwick. Quorn, a dormitory village, is in central Leicestershire, 14 kilometres north of Leicester, 3 kilometres south of Loughborough. In the case of Lapworth the district's upper and middle range options for growth (90 and 75 dwellings respectively) were rejected in favour of 'infill' only (20 dwellings), a considerable concession to the local pressure groups. At Quorn the district's middle-range option (250 dwellings) was accepted by the local council subject to the findings of a public local inquiry, against the violent opposition of a local pressure group. How do we account for these differences?

The strategic policy context was certainly different in each case. Lapworth was in the Warwickshire Green Belt, defined in 1959 but only approved in July 1975 a few months before the structure plan was approved. The crucial issue was the extent of the 'white land' to be shown in the district's local plan. From the county's point of view only minimal development would be acceptable. Indeed it challenged the district about the scope and purpose of its plan, a classic county-district conflict. At Quorn the county's settlement policy indicated that there was 'potential' for growth. The village was designated a 'key' centre where future development would be best concentrated. There was no Green Belt. County-district disputes were minimal. All the options at Quorn were considered to be free of other planning and land use constraints. This was not so at Lapworth where the Ministry of Agriculture voiced their opposition and lended weight, albeit indirectly, to the protest groups. The role played by the elected representatives on the district council was crucial at Quorn in securing support for the planners' stance, whereas at Lapworth, it was the intervention of county councillors that assisted the cause of the opposition against the district. The experience of anti-growth in neighbouring villages probably influenced the attitude of planners and elected members to the Quorn local plan. Elected members knew that to capitulate might again encourage builders to seek development in other settlements, especially at a time when the county council was urging the district to find more land for housing in central Leicestershire and central government approval of planning appeals was bringing about a more random and less predictable pattern of urban development.[41] At Lapworth the county possibly foresaw that a concession in favour of even 'local housing need' would be likely to prejudice the Green Belt. Additionally, both pressure groups argued on similar lines — no additional development land was needed; any growth at all would destroy the character of the settlements. The Lapworth Preservation Society wanted *extensions* to the Green Belt, no excluded land. This was essentially a 'no growth' strategy.

A final point is that the role of the developers differed somewhat. At Lapworth, although two speculative builders wanted growth, they put no pressure on the district council or the residents, whereas at Quorn the larger building companies took a more aggressive stance, claiming that the planners were proposing far too little land. In both cases the planners sought participation as a means of achieving consensus around their policies. Yet conflict rather than consensus was perhaps inevitable given the social geography of the two communities.

The outcome of opposition — who wins? who loses?

It would be misleading to suggest that the anti-growth lobby has had a substantive impact on the outer city in the last decade. The foundations of containment were laid long before the advent of contemporary political protest. Public participation has if anything simply endorsed those broad goals accepted for so long by the founders of the planning movement: protection of farmland and preservation of the countryside landscape. Where opposition has apparently been more effective in stopping large-scale expansion, or at least in diverting it to other locations, amenity interests have simply played into the hands of the counties who never whole-heartedly supported planned growth in the countryside, being pushed in that direction by the twin arms of central government and the housebuilders. Local authorities have thus been able to use the views of amenity groups to support their arguments on appeal.[42]

There are sound reasons for the ineffectiveness of the anti-growth lobby. Opposition is usually triggered by planners and developers who determine the ground rules for the dispute and the timetable for participation. The timescale over which conflicts persist is often lengthy. It is difficult to sustain interest. Changing political allegiance may jeopardize the groups' initial support. Much vociferous protest affects small-scale developments rather than major projects, although well orchestrated lobbying has been known to stop motorways and airports. Victories over single developments have little bearing on the overall sub-regional distribution of population and employment if restraint in one location is followed by housing and industrial development in another. Much anti-growth simply transfers developments somewhere else. Small-scale settlement strategies will not obviate anti-growth lobbying, but the chances of lobbying restricting development in a *group* of settlements are slimmer. Finally, contemporary development plans for the outer city contain much less reference to public housing: rural settlement policies invariably rely on private speculative housebuilders or private/public partnerships. This means that successful opposition to growth merely readjusts the housing market for similar social groups in different locations.

The anti-growth lobby has undoubtedly provoked some response from central government, the district councils and the developers. The CPRE's warnings about the possible environmental effects of dispersed urban growth have not gone unheeded. Mr. Michael Heseltine remarked that 'we have all seen over 30 years the way in which people and capital have moved from inner cities to suburban and rural areas. . . . I am increasingly concerned about it. A lot of things have happened which have heightened my concern. We are thinking in this department about whether our priorities are right'.[43] But there are real limitations to the political influence of national amenity groups. The initiative of the CPRE in central Berkshire led to an alteration to the structure plan. But under present legislation this alteration can still be rejected by the DoE. When backed up by the ministers, local political protest is likely to be a more potent force for effective change. It remains to be seen when and where government will capitulate to local political opposition against more substantial growth in the outer city. It may have to trade off Green Belt areas in exchange for development further out, an even more contentious issue. Alternatively, where it supports tightening of the Green Belt as well, it may be faced with renewed pressure for more dispersed peripheral development.[44]

The district' housing strategies have been put at risk by resistance to growth, although the demise of Housing Investment Programmes and other policies can be placed at the door of central government. The DoE's insistence on a five-year supply of residential land in each district has forced local councils to take a more flexible stance to new speculative housing, and it is private housing that so often brings local opposition. The Association of District Councils urges elected members to judge each proposal on its planning merits and not to be swayed by articulate pressure groups and to bear in mind the economic and employment benefits of new development.[45] Significantly, the house builders make a related point — it is often Conservative councillors who believe in a market economy, who believe in home ownership, and who subscribe to more private housing, except when it lands in their back yard![46] The districts can do little but grin and bear the consequences of failure, but the developers can and do exploit the divisions between residents groups and planners, especially over the release of specific sites, by appealing over the heads of both to central government.

And they appear to be increasingly successful. Ironically, it was central government which initiated and encouraged participation. It now appears to be in favour of dismantling it for the sake of faster economic growth. Professional planners too have begun to attack the process of participation; it is too lengthy and delays decision making.[47] Opposition to growth provokes mistrust and counter-accusations of sectional interest. Unless policy makers are convinced of its value, participation may just wither away together with the anti-growth lobby.

In substantiating their case against urbanization in the countryside the anti-growth movement has been drawn into the defence of inner city regeneration. 'The present Conservative government's commitment to inner city regeneration is commendable but while Mr Heseltine runs the taps, he has pulled out the plug. Manufacturers and industrialists want the ease and cheapness of greenfield sites. And they are being allowed to get them. . . . We all want to see economic revival. But on present trends, if we get it, the consequences for the countryside could be disastrous. For planning policies are increasingly favouring development in places where formerly there was none!'[48] The case for consistency in national and regional policies could not be stated more clearly. Yet amenity bodies are ambivalent about how *much* further growth they would countenance in the outer city, or indeed how much restraint would satisfy them. Nor are they agreed upon spatial strategies. The CPRE is concerned about urban sprawl beyond the Green Belt. It certainly presents a well argued case. But would it wish to see the inner fringe of the Green Belt violated in the way the Land Decade Council implies may be necessary to satisfy development pressures and safeguard the areas further out? Furthermore, a no growth strategy for the outer city would redistribute income in favour of the wealthy and hence increase social disparities between inner and outer communities. The pressure groups are already open to the charge that they have distributed resources in favour of the middle classes and away from the working class. Public participation does not reflect a representative cross-section of the community, and protest based on middle class support is notably more successful than protest by working class people, wherever it occurs. For all these reasons the socially regressive consequences of the anti-growth movements are likely to be felt most in the outer city where higher status groups are disproportionately represented.

Notes

1.   Useful accounts of the political process are given in J. M. SIMMIE, *Citizens in Conflict: the Sociology of Town Planning* (Hutchinson, 1974); G. KIRK, *Urban Planning in a Capitalist Society* (Croom Helm, 1980).

2.   L. K. STEPHENSON, 'Toward a spatial understanding of environmentally-based voluntary groups', *Geoforum*, vol. 10(2), 1979.

3.   P. D. LOWE, 'Amenity and equity: a review of local environmental pressure groups in Britain', *Environment and Planning A*, vol. 9(1), 1977.

4.   S. K. BROOKES et al., 'The growth of the environment as a political issue in Britain', *British Journal of Political Science*, vol. 6, 1976.

5.   P. HALL et al, *The Containment of Urban England, Vol. I, Urban and Metropolitan Growth Processes* (Allen and Unwin, 1973). Part Three, 'Five Case Studies: A History', contains interesting descriptions of these events.

6.   P. HALL *ibid*. See part four, p. 625.

7.   J. A. AGNEW, 'Market relations and locational conflict in cross-national perspective' in K. COX (ed.) *Urbanization and Conflict in Market Societies* (Methuen, 1978).

8.   A. BLOWERS, 'Much ado about nothing? A case study of planning and power', Paper for conference on planning theory in the 1980s, Oxford Polytechnic, 1981.

9.   H. NEWBY, *Green and Pleasant Land? Social Change in Rural England* (Pelican, 1980).

10.   J. KRAMER and K. YOUNG, 'Local exclusionary policies in Britain: the case of suburban defence in a metropolitan system' in K. COX (ed.), *Urbanization and Conflict in Market Societies* (Methuen, 1978).

11.   Committee on Public Participation in Planning, *People and Planning* (HMSO, 1969).

12.   See for instance N. BOADEN, *Public Participation and Planning in Practice* (Pergamon, 1980); R. DARKE and R. WALKER, *Local Government and the Public* (Leonard Hill, 1974).

13.   N. BOADEN, 'Public participation in planning within a representative local democracy', *Policy and Politics*, vol. 7, 1979.

14.   P. LOWE *et al.*, 'The mass movement of the decade — environmental pressure groups', *Vole*, vol. 3, no. 4, 1980.

15.   Council for Protection of Rural England, 'Where's the planning bath-plug? Conservationists' plea to the Minister', press release, 12 July 1981.

16.   P. HALL *et al.*, op. cit. Vol 11. p. 49.

17.   Land Decade Educational Council, *Land Use Perspectives* (LDEC, 1979).

18.   G. MOSS, 'Land Council and its Objectives', *Town and Country Planning*, vol. 50(1), January 1981.

19.   S. RETTIG, 'An investigation into the problems of urban fringe agriculture in a Green Belt situation', *Planning Outlook*, vol. 19, 1976.

20.   A. M. BLAIR, 'Farming in Metroland', *Countryman*, vol. 85(4), 1980.

21.   A. M. BLAIR, 'Urban influences on farming in Essex', *Geoforum*, vol. 11(4), 1980.

22.   P. LOWE and J. GOYDER, 'The land lobby: a political analysis', *Town and Country Planning*, vol. 50(1), 1981.

23.   H. NEWBY, C. BELL, P. SAUNDERS and D. ROSE, 'Farmers attitudes to conservation', *Countryside Recreation Review*, vol. 2, 1977.

24.   See for instance, C. A. COLLINS, 'Consideration of the social background and motivation of councillors', *Policy and Politics*, vol. 6, no. 4, 1978; I. GORDON, 'The recruitment of local politicians' *Policy and Politics*, vol. 7, no. 1, 1979.

25.   Department of Environment, *Committee of Inquiry into the system of remuneration of members of local authorities* (HMSO, 1977).

26.   S. L. BRISTOW, 'Local politics after reorganization: the homogenization of local government in England and Wales', *Public Administration Bulletin*, no. 28, December 1978.

27.   See report 'City institutions slow growth down on the farm', *Times*, 3 July 1979.

28.   J. CONNELL, 'Amenity Societies: The preservation of central Surrey', *Town and Country Planning*, vol. 40, 1972.

29. D. M. EVANS, 'Anti-growth movements on the urban fringe: a cross-national perspective', PhD. Thesis in preparation, Department of Geography, Loughborough University, 1983.

30. 'Implications of green belt guidance', letter from the Chairman of the London Green Belt Council, *The Times*, 15 August 1983.

31. J. H. CONNELL, op. cit.

32. N. BOADEN, op. cit.

33. See for instance CPRE warnings about industrial and housing developments in Warwickshire and north Oxfordshire following construction of the M40 and the criticisms of the West Midlands County Council for shifting its policy stance in favour of prestige industrial development in neighbouring Shire counties. CPRE press release, 13 May 1982; reported as 'protests over rural land take', *Planning*, May 1982.

34. Council for the Protection of Rural England, 'Grass roots revolt, dozens of parishes to unite' CPRE, 1 June 1981.

35. J. W. MACKIE, 'Goodbye Rural Berkshire? Development pressures in Central Berkshire and South East England', Report for the Binfield and Warfield Parish Councils, 1982.

36. See the report 'Row over suburban housing modification', *Planning*, vol. 444, 13 November 1981.

37. P. SMITH, 'Structure Planning: participation and its results', *Town and Country Planning*, vol. 46, no. 1, 1978.

38. A. BLOWERS, *The Limits of Power: The Politics of Local Planning Policy* (Pergamon, 1981).

39. M. J. BRUTON, 'Public participation, local planning and conflict of interest', *Policy and Politics*, vol. 8, no. 4, October 1980.

40. D. EVANS, op. cit.

41. J. HERINGTON, 'Circular 22/80 — The demise of settlement planning?', *Area*, vol. 14, no. 2, 1982.

42. P. HEALEY et al., *The Implementation of Development Plans*, Report of an exploratory study for the Department of Environment, Department of Town Planning, Oxford Polytechnic, February 1982, p. 62.

43. See the report 'Heseltine reassesses rural "takeover"', *Times*, 22 July 1982.

44. See the report 'Structure Plan Change by Fowler', *Planning*, vol. 462, 2 April 1982.

45. Association of District Councils, *Economic Development by District Councils*, ADC 1982.

46. T. BARON, 'Planning's biggest and least satisfied customer: housing', *Town and country Planning Summer School: Report of Proceedings*, 6–17 September (RTPI, 1980).

47. See for instance M. J. BRUTON, 'The cost of public participation in local planning', *Town and Country Planning*, June 1981; J. ASH, 'Public participation: time to bury Skeffington?', *Planner*, vol. 65, no. 5, 1979.

48. Council for Protection of Rural England, op. cit., 12 July 1981.

10   Lessons for the Future

> It may be presumptuous to assume our descendants will long for a little privacy, peace and quiet, but (to put it no higher) it is hardly less presumptuous to assume they will thank us for the bequest of a throbbing Gigantopolis from Lands' End to John O' Groats. (E. Brookes, 1973).

There appears to be a new national consensus favouring growth in Britain's outer cities. Planned dispersal and restraint are no longer sufficiently responsive to economic imperatives. New town programmes have been abandoned. Green Belts, although at the time of writing still largely intact, are under threat from developer-builders. Structure planning is pursued with vigour but is more growth-oriented than ever before. The 1947 system of land-use control is still an accepted instrument for local management of environmental change, but challenges to the exercise of planning powers are more common. Public participation is under attack. Everywhere the frontiers of the state are being rolled back. As the interests of different actors polarize alternately in favour of more growth and restraint, political conflict in the outer cities intensifies. Not all the goals of urban containment have been jettisoned. Nor does the rhetoric of growth always accord with practice. The danger is, however, that practice will change, fuelling a new round of dispersal at a time when the capacity of the state planning system is being weakened.

Our discussion of strategies has revealed much ambivalence about the best way to manage dispersed urban growth. Local government appears half-heartedly to accept the need to facilitate economic development, as far as this is possible without abandoning the tenets of containment. The possible social consequences of growth-oriented policies, especially their effect on food production, landscape resources, and on social capital in the cities, are understood. However, the strategies pursued do not confront these problems directly, nor do they address themselves to the economic problems of long-term public expenditure which may result from accommodating higher levels of decentralization in the outer areas. There is a sense that dispersal cannot be stopped, despite the government's change of heart over planned decentralization, and that the most urgent problems are posed by employment changes and rising unemployment. In the economic and political circumstances of the past decade the role of the containment principles which helped to frame earlier planning legislation is less obvious. 'Central and local government between them progressively declare revisionist policies which undermine the credibility of a negative system of control appropriate to Britain before de-industrialization'.[1]

Planning strategies for decentralization and peripheral land release are, however, based on three mistaken assumptions: that dispersal is an inevitable 'natural' economic process in which the state is powerless to intervene; that industrial and residential development should be facilitated in the outer areas to bring about national economic recovery; and that containment strategies necessarily involve the concentration of urban development. We must look at each of these in turn before examining the scope for a more coherent approach to the outer areas.

Is outer city dispersal an inevitable process?

Is it possible for the state to stem the momentum towards dispersed urban growth? The development industry appears to have the upper hand, and the economic and political climate encourage industrial expansion and relocation in the outer areas in preference to the inner cities. Even if the government could control the movement of industry and labour more directly, it is possible that it would be constrained by a conflicting desire to secure higher levels of economic production and consumption. Yet because the legal framework of the state planning system limits its influence to the realm of physical change, its indirect role in the management of economic and social change can be underestimated.

The dispersal of population and employment into, and within the outer areas obviously reflects pressures for development associated with trends in the national economy. Manufacturing now accounts for almost one third of all jobs. Continuing recession will bring with it further job losses in manufacturing. Some outer-metropolitan areas will not escape unemployment (the West Midlands for example), but the greatest impact will fall on the conurbations. The small country towns and rural settlements in the outer areas are likely to experience the least industrial decline.[2] Indeed, some observers have noted that the 'de-industrialization' process will promote an outward shift in employment because high-technology industry searches for skilled labour.[3] Whether this search is successful will depend on the demographic trends which affect the outer areas, but it seems probable that high rates of household formation will continue to promote the urban-rural shift. Tertiary employment expands as the primary and secondary employment sectors decline. Service jobs grow in association with population increase and, since many outer areas must expect additional migration, an expansion of services will inevitably follow. Less predictable are the locational preferences of services with a national or regional market — the head offices of major companies or central government, major banking or business enterprises. But the evidence discussed earlier strongly suggests that many of these will continue to seek provincial towns or smaller settlements in the inner and outer commuting zones. The expansion or development of international airports will also encourage the expansion of services. These trends in the pattern of industrial and residential development are seen by many commentators as part of the normal process of economic adjustment in industrial societies.[4]

It is important to place these economic trends in historical perspective. The evidence of previous chapters suggests that central and local levels of government are either too weak or unwilling to bring about a major redirection of industrial investment away from the outer areas. But this has never been adopted as the policy of governments. Hence we cannot assume that the state would be incapable of controlling dispersed urban growth if it set itself different planning goals. Indeed, decentralization in the post-war period has been actively promoted by the state. The planned decentralization programmes have possibly been the most important factor in population and employment dispersal.[5] Dispersal was made to look respectable by grafting it onto the anti-urban ideologies fashionable at the turn of the nineteenth century. The rural idyll and the underlying belief in order and rationality which were later associated with centralized planning represented a reaction against industrial capitalism. Ironically, the momentum towards industrial dispersal in the post-war period, far from being the inevitable outcome of economic forces, is the unintended consequence of anti-urban ideology.[6] The state plays a crucial role in the management of economic trends.[7]

National and international economic factors govern the fortunes of industry. But the dramatic growth and economic performance of some outer areas is affected by government policy. Capital expenditure on motorways and trunk roads, water supply and sewerage, regional industrial development and New and Expanded Towns, all these have promoted population decentralization even though the allocation of public investment has never had a specific outer-area dimension. But since the late 1970s, central and local government have actively sought out ways of promoting economic development in the outer areas through a variety of apparently un-coordinated initiatives for regeneration (in much the same way as in the inner cities). Furthermore, the locational preferences of the most powerful companies are being supported to an increasing degree by central government. Modifications to county structure plans and the outcome of recent appeal decisions favour an increase in the scale of housing and industrial development both on the periphery of the conurbations and further out beyond the Green Belts. All this must be seen in the context of the government's primary objective of bringing about national economic recovery.

There are some national economic trends, in part affected by government policy, which will have a major impact on the dispersal trend in the outer areas. Most economic forecasts for the 1980s point to a continuing fall in demand for labour.[8] We cannot forecast change for the smaller areas, but it seems likely that most regions will suffer a decline in employment between 1983 and 1990. By 1990 the West Midlands may lose a further 10 percent of its jobs. The East Midlands, East Anglia and the South West may expect slight change or small increases in employment.[9] In addition, it is expected that by 1991 the working population will have grown by almost 1.3 million or 4.4 percent since 1979 (as against total population growth of only 2.4 percent) and by almost 2 million or 6.8 percent since 1974. In the outer areas of the more depressed regions of the country the growth in demand for labour will greatly exceed the supply of jobs,[10] and industrial expansion is likely to be curtailed in these areas by the cut in financial incentives resulting from changes in regional policy. In these areas the switch in government policy from giving assistance to industry in favour of stimulating demand (through youth training schemes, etc.) may hence be counter-productive, and divert public expenditure from providing infrastructure that might stimulate development. A significant decrease in the rate of outward population migration, which would result from a fall in household income, might affect some of those outer areas suffering most from the rise in unemployment, a trend already evident in parts of Strathclyde. This tendency could have most effect on less skilled and lower-paid groups without affecting the supply of skilled labour in the outer areas; nevertheless it could result in a spatial redistribution of the female labour force which has proved so important in the attraction of new enterprises into the outer areas of cities in the assisted regions.

In central and southern England, on the other hand, the growth of service-based economies is more likely to absorb some of the decrease in demand for manufacturing labour. Services could also continue to absorb some of the rising demand for part-time female employment. The relaxation of regional policy is likely to encourage a greater proportion of the manufacturing expansion which *does* take place to remain in these outer areas. Policies favouring job creation may well prove a greater stimulus to peripheral industrial expansion in the traditionally prosperous regions like the West

Midlands than it has in the depressed areas. The stimulus being given by the government to private housing production is likely to increase the availability of skilled labour and hence encourage the dispersal of high-technology enterprises and other forms of service employment. There are of course many variations within the regions themselves.[11] The New Towns of Milton Keynes, Peterborough, Stevenage and Northampton all had higher unemployment rates than Greater London in 1982. Similarly Cumbernauld's rate of unemployment exceeded that of the Strathclyde region.[12] Nevertheless, national economic trends will continue to favour dispersal in the South East and other prosperous areas.

Certain government policies will work to restrain the dispersal associated with these economic developments. There is, for example, the government's pledge to bring down the level of public expenditure. Recent pessimistic forecasts of a decline in economic growth from 2.3 percent in 1983 to 1.7 percent in 1984 give added urgency to government plans to curtail public spending, as does the evidence for an increase in public spending from 41 percent of Gross Domestic Product in 1979 to 44 percent in 1983.[13] While new curbs on spending will obviously hit the inner areas hardest of all, it is probable that infrastructural investment necessary to implement existing and planned programmes (particularly in the fields of local transport, water supply and sewerage) are likely to be among the first casualties in any sustained national reduction of public spending or reduced financial support to local authorities. However, such constraints may well prove insufficient to prevent substantial future urban growth in the outer areas. Indeed, the cut back in government expenditure programmes may stimulate rather than check development pressures. The urban programme could face a 50 percent cut or more over the next few years, thus diminishing the scope for inner area regeneration.[14] Reduced regional aid will work in favour of growth in the prosperous outer areas. Reduced public expenditure on public transport will encourage the wider use of private cars despite the risk of higher energy costs. By raising the costs of commuting for the most skilled, a cut in government subsidy to British Rail's surburban services might reduce the tendency for residential dispersal; but if rising costs are passed on to central London employers, there is every likelihood of further employment decentralization. The present government's proposals to sell off profitable New Town assets in order to reduce the public debt will divert resources to the private sector, and the growth of the private sector generally must surely result in a substantial increase in population and employment in the outer areas.[15] The government's relaxation of the statutory planning system, combined with a crisis of confidence in the planning world over its ability to stem the processes of decentralization,[16] must also compound the problems facing the outer areas in the future.

However, although state agencies appear to support and give succour to the dispersal process in a variety of ways, there is no evidence that dispersed urban growth cannot be contained effectively given unequivocal political commitment to restraint. Clearly this commitment is absent at all levels of government at the present time in Britain. Yet, even the ambivalent attitudes towards containment revealed in previous chapters should not lead us to conclude that dispersal is inevitable. The state is not a single homogeneous body having a uniform impact on dispersal. Central government, for example, is more growth-oriented than the local authorities. But there is a plurality of interests at all levels of government.[17] The pattern of industrial development in the outer city reflects the exercise of power within the political process,[18] which in turn depends upon the balance of forces. The response to the pressure of commercial interests varies. State planning agencies have not acted independently of speculative housebuilders and lobbies of private citizens' groups, but they have exercised relative degrees of autonomy at different times and in different places. Central government had a direct impact on the New Towns programme. The counties are regulating (with the districts) the spatial pattern of rural settlement change. Housing developers have forced the release of Green Belt land and an increase in the scale of structure plan housing provision. The anti-growth lobby has thwarted the development aspirations of both private and public agents. And so on. The political process is indeed a complex one. The interests of capital need not necessarily prevail over state planning agents or environmental interests.

Is outer city growth in the national interest?

One of the assumptions that underpins the strategies examined in previous chapters is that economic development in the outer areas will aid national recovery. It will increase industrial output and create more employment. Economic development is often interpreted rather narrowly to mean more factories and houses, despite the fact, as we shall show in a moment, that there are other opportunities for economic growth which do not require the same scale of urban development as industry and housing. Development controls inhibit the opportunity for expansion and should hence be relaxed, even to the extent of sacrificing Green Belt land if there is an overriding national case for development. These attitudes are depressing because they ignore the uncertainties surrounding the recovery of the British economy and fail to consider the social implications of a growth-orientated strategy, particularly for other national priorities and commitments.

It is not at all certain that permitting more industrial development in the outer city would improve efficiency. British manufacturing performance fell by 3 percent between 1970 and 1980. Between 1971 and 1980 growth (measured in monetary output) took place in food, drink, and tobacco, chemicals, instrument engineering, electrical engineering and electronics. Decline occurred in coal mining, metal manufacturing, mechanical engineering, shipbuilding, motor vehicles, and woollen textiles.[19] The assumption that provision of extra land will raise production and increase output is untested. There is no close association between manufacturing output and industrial floorspace.[20] Manufacturing has undoubtedly increased its demand for factory floorspace, but this has happened during a period of declining output and reflects changes in the organization of production and changing space requirements. Little or at best marginal increase in manufacturing output can be expected during the 1980s. It must surely be shortsighted of planners to believe that increasing floorspace will increase production. Much of the present floorspace being made available on greenfield sites is in any case not being used for manufacturing but for warehousing and distribution activities. Moreover, new firms sited in the outer city may suffer from lower productivity because of a tendency to over-recruit in the early stages.[21] Even if productivity is high, the development of a limited range of high productivity firms creating a few skilled jobs would not necessarily provide long-term prosperity. An excessively specialized industrial structure would not be proof against changing market conditions, as the experience of concentrating manufacturing industry in the first New Towns demonstrated.

New manufacturing industries located in the outer areas are unlikely to create much net addition to national employment. The experience in the depressed regions is not particularly encouraging.[22] In the 'sun-belt' the contribution which new high-technology enterprises might make to national employment remains uncertain,[23] except where office or business parks are integrated with research establishments.[24] An alternative approach to economic development favoured by some observers is the injection of capital into volume housebuilding and infrastructure. One investigation claims that £500 million invested there might create 120,000 jobs, increase the Gross Domestic Product but add to the Public Sector Borrowing Requirement. Yet the figure of 120,000 represents about 2 percent only of present (1983) national unemployment levels. Moreover there must be some doubt about the multiplier effect on other employment if a sustained programme of investment were undertaken in the outer areas. Boosting construction jobs would have a short term cyclical effect, but it is unlikely to lead to the expansion of employment in the manufacturing sector since recession and restructuring have combined to cut the supply of mobile and labour-intensive firms. There would be some temporary expansion of service-sector employment accompanying the increase in local population. But over-reliance on new housing construction in the outer areas could divert investment away from older housing stock and reduce the options for private and public new housing in the future.[25]

The national interest is unlikely to be served by over-rapid industrial expansion in the outer areas. The question is whether the scale and rate of development can be managed to reduce the disadvantage to the old industrial cities and avoid environmental and political conflict in the outer areas.[26] The present encouragement given to large business and national or regional development companies makes this prospect unlikely. Even if additional employment is generated by peripheral urban release, a strategy which some observers feel might benefit the inner areas,[27] it has yet to be shown that blue-collar workers would benefit without the provision of suitable jobs and better transport links between cities and the suburbs. The volume builders' plans for substantial private housing investment in the outer areas is a lost opportunity for the inner cities. Restricting or phasing the release of sites on the periphery is likely to encourage even the largest private builders to realize the potential for inner city investment.[28] Furthermore, decentralization of jobs may indirectly add to the social unrest which has afflicted the cities in recent years. Economic development will continue to favour the better educated and wealthier groups and will thus tend to widen the spatial gulf between richer and poorer households. Nor is it unlikely that social tension will increase among the residents of the outer areas. The negative social effects of low density living are already felt among a wide range of different social groups; residential segregation and accessibility deprivation would not diminish if major new housing construction took place.[29] The wealthier groups may also prove less able to defend themselves as the 'production classes' intensify their efforts to revive the economy.[30]

There will continue to be a shift in the location of industrial activity in Britain, but the pace of population and employment dispersal must not be allowed to accelerate to a point where the social costs prove unacceptable. There must be a more cautious approach to the release of new land both for industry and for housing, and a greater degree of experimentation with other forms of economic development that might serve the national interest equally well. The net contribution of large enterprises to the national economy is possibly not very great, either in terms of total output, or net employment gain. The tendency for government to seek economic development by encouraging locally-generated firms and the expansion of small businesses in both housing and industry is a more promising approach in the outer areas. Local initiatives provide jobs which would not otherwise occur — hence they do not divert growth from the inner cities.[31] Their land-take requirements are less than those of the large businesses thus obviating environmental conflict in restraint areas. The smaller shire county towns (5,000-25,000 population) have already proved very successful locations for small-business enterprise. The gradual rate of population and employment growth in these towns has helped to create a better balance between labour supply and demand and thus contributed to the stability of industrial relations. Moreover, the slower rate of expansion has helped to avoid the problems of social polarization which have affected the larger expansions.[32]

The de-industrialization process has encouraged the expansion of service economies in Britain.[33] The limited employment opportunities in manufacturing point to an enhanced role for tourism.[34] In 1982, Britain attracted 12 million visitors and earned £8,000 million from tourism. In 1983, it is expected that the industry will yield £4,500 million in foreign currency alone. The Department of Industry's proposals for tourist expansion appear to have no specific spatial dimension, and some of the projects under consideration seem more likely to benefit the inner rather than outer areas.[35] But a general strategy for the extension of tourism in historic towns and villages in the outer-metropolitan areas could ultimately prove economically and socially beneficial. Major releases of rural land are unnecessary and public expenditure minimal. Tourist enterprises tend to be labour intensive and may assist those social groups hardest hit by recession; they also provide alternative sources of female employment.[36] The growth of tourism in the outer areas would undoubtedly require careful management, but it surely presents fewer problems than a strategy oriented simply towards the expansion of manufacturing industry and housing.

The relaxation of planning controls and the drift away from containment would seem to be a short-sighted response to national economic requirements, however those are interpreted. Industrial output has waxed and waned in the post-war period with no obvious relationship to planning. Since 1971 national output rose slowly to a peak in 1979 before falling again. Before 1979 there were considerable annual variations in land release (with a peak in the mid-1970s) and no noticeable association with output trends. Market conditions and movements of capital are almost certainly more important determinants of economic activity than land policy. We can agree with Peter Hall that post-war containment policy, at least up to the early 1970s, achieved strong environmental control and a measure of social stability at the cost of some economic efficiency.[37] It may also be true that certain capital interests have gained while others have lost: the speculative building industry has been given more encouragement than the retail and distribution trade (until recent times), and agriculture has prevailed over manufacturing. Regulative land use planning has also achieved a measure of aesthetic control which may have facilitated, indirectly, the movement of high-technology enterprises and the dispersal of skilled labour in search of attractive environments. The Chairman of the Association of District Councils has aptly remarked that 'the ability of an area to attract new investment will always be largely dependent on the quality of its environment and facilities. I therefore fully believe that development control is essential.'[38] Nor is it certain that the planning system imposes any major delay on the time taken to gain and then implement planning permissions for residential development.[39] The most serious blockages are posed by the time it takes developers to draw up detailed planning applications which have been approved in outline.[40]

A strategy favouring tourism and smaller scale industrial enterprise in the outer areas would reduce the danger to productive farmland and high quality landscape, assist in controlling public expenditure, and divert investment into inner cities. It would restate the social value of urban containment as well as exposing the often forgotten economic advantages of restraint in the outer cities.

Are concentration strategies the best way to control dispersal?

Although the planned dispersal programmes are officially ended, containment lives on in the guise of selective urban growth and countryside protection. Planned concentration is still favoured at the urban-regional scale as a way of avoiding urban sprawl, and 'key' settlement policies sprinkle the pages of even the most recent county structure plans. But any observer of the dispersal trends of the past two decades must have serious reservations about the effectiveness and the desirability of concentration strategy. The advantages of large-scale planned urban growth have almost certainly been overemphasized: economies of scale have not always materialised; the considerable land-take involved has proved damaging to the immediate landscape and land-use pattern; a good social balance between jobs and population has depended less on size than on sensitive adjustment of employment and housing policy; more equitable occupational structures have not in general emerged; and the contribution of growth points to the scale of the dispersal problem has been minimal.[41] Yet the case for concentrating development in more New Towns and planned growth points is still advanced.[42]

The major difficulties with the large schemes favoured in the early 1970s have arisen over implementation. Absence of corporate planning at a country scale, lack of coordination between local and central government, and cuts in public expenditure, all these continue to hinder the prospect of large scale growth in locations such as central Berkshire and central Leicestershire. The failure to foresee the consequences of delay or to relate the large-scale schemes to the mini-growth points in rural settlement strategies, has also presented difficulties. New Towns were planned outside their sub-regional context with no mechanism for stopping the growth of neighbouring towns and smaller villages. An effective planned dispersal programme should have been accompanied by much stronger central government control over local authorities. Instead, the bias of counties and districts in favour of smaller and multiple points of concentration was allowed to go unchecked.

Similar difficulties have faced the counties. The theoretical advantages of 'key' settlement policy have been given too much weight. The rationalization of services like primary schools into larger units is more expensive per head of population than a greater number of smaller ones.[43] A policy of allowing services to expand in a few centres may well prove more costly than dispersal. In the early development plans of most counties, 'key' settlements were selected because they had the widest range of facilities. But planners have had much more control over residential movements than over education and social services. In addition, it now seems uneconomic to hold back housebuilding in settlements where there is some spare capacity in services and infrastructure. Ironically, it is in the larger centres where services have been maintained that population growth has outstripped the capacity of some services and created problems of accessibility.

Too great a release of housing land may also have prompted market resistence among existing and potential house buyers. This may be due less to the proposed scale of development than to the standardized type of housing which is associated with large blocks of new housing. By responding to volume builders' preferences for larger sites, local planners have indirectly discouraged housing mix and encouraged a degree of social polarization. Now that the structure of the housing market is changing in response to demographic and economic factors one must ask whether this kind of solution will be acceptable in the future. Sales of single person dwelling units trebled between 1981 and 1982.[44] The case for large sites may be diminishing.

It might be supposed that where restraint policies exist, the policy against unwanted dispersal into smaller settlements would be maintained. But restraint policies have been increasingly ineffective as we have shown. Local planning decisions undermine regional restraint objectives. Moreover, it is unlikely that Green Belts will provide the permanent defence some of its protagonists would hope for, as more county planners argue that they should be subject to review in the same way as other strategic policies. The boundaries of Green Belts should be drawn more tightly to exclude the maximum amount of land required by the volume housebuilders' interests.[45] A more fundamental objection to Green Belts is that they are still seen to protect the growth of the larger cities rather than shape the form of smaller settlements which have grown much more rapidly in the outer areas beyond them. At a national scale Green Belts could be used to assist urban regeneration only if they were drawn much more widely, as the counties want. There is some sense in this from the point of view of the counties operating beyond the present Green Belts. Although dispersal leaping across the belts from the metropolitan cores has diminished, the most rapid growth occurs within these outer commuting settlements. One problem here is how to manage future urban expansion in a way that minimizes environmental conflict. The existence of a Green Belt might help those in authority limit the total amount of new development permitted, although it is conceded that given the present discretion to district councils, and the DoE's desire to cut back the depth of the Green Belt (at least around London), a tougher policy of this kind will find little immediate political support.

The twin goals of containment strategies — concentration and restraint — have to some extent been mutually defeating in practice. Concentration proved not to fulfil the promise it seemed to offer. A two-tier system of specially designated areas made the spatial concentration of urban growth more difficult because it placed great pressures for development on all settlements in non-designated areas. In theory, these contradictions could have been resolved under stronger regional planning, but it might still have been difficult to channel development to selected growth settlements because the assumption on which concentration was predicated — namely, that a large number of public and private agents would see advantage in coordinating their investment decisions — has proved false. Small housebuilders, local firms, district councils, environmental interests and a host of other agencies have in effect ignored growth point strategy. The difficulties public agencies face in providing infrastructure to support the scale of growth required has been underestimated. Private builders have shown little desire to assemble land and coordinate spending on large sites themselves, and spending programmes of water undertakings, transport agents and other bodies have proved lengthy.

The prospect of a more spatially dispersed pattern of residential development is not necessarily an unwelcome one. The risk of progressive urban sprawl could certainly be prevented if there were overall limits on the scale of growth. If these could be achieved, the loss of farmland or good quality landscape would be no more than under conditions of concentration. Indeed, it is arguable that large urban growth points have spoilt the appearance of the countryside more than several small developments. An increase in the population of some settlements might retard the rate of decline of the social services. Smaller housing development could reduce the fear of 'swamping'. Some slight adjustment in house prices would help younger and poorer groups among established residents and commuters. With unemployment rising among middle and upper management this could be especially important. Dispersal would not of course overcome housing problems, but there are now a variety of ways in which low-cost housing can be provided in small settlements.[46]

The environmental and social consequences of more dispersed growth would depend upon the amount of growth permitted and the balance between population and employment-generating development. Dispersal has advantages, but they would be obviated quickly if growth got out of hand. It is, moreover, doubtful whether any spatial redistribution of housing can be made effective without the guiding hand of central government. The release of green field sites could be reduced if housing requirements were met within urban areas. In practice most structure plans state there are enough urban sites to meet the pressure. This is probably true. But the radical alternative of *not* meeting the demand in the outer areas is rarely taken. Nevertheless, household formation is partly a function of the number of houses built, and it would be perfectly feasible to plan for minimum rather than maximum forecasts of future households. A limiting factor is the risk of political conflict between local and central government over a housing policy which encourages, through tax relief on mortgages and other measures, the spread of owner occupation (and also reduces the non-profit sector). Thus it is national policy that must be held responsible for indirectly financing and supporting outer city growth. Local authorities will redistribute housing development in the best way they see fit, but the scale of housing demand is determined elsewhere.

Planning and political values

This book highlights the need for a national debate about the direction which urban policy should take in Britain. The choice is between continuing to disperse population and employment into the outer areas and regenerating our cities. This dilemma raises fundamental questions about the purposes of planning and the strategies for managing urban change. The present drift to dispersal is facilitated by many agencies working (not always with great conviction) for economic recovery, with planning seeming to serve powerful interests rather than an explicit social purpose.[47] At the same time the case for managing social and economic change is becoming more obvious as dispersal brings increasing environmental conflict, social polarization and political tension, although the problems of growth and affluence are seldom seen as clearly as the problems of decline and deprivation. It seems that society should either continue to plan for the trend, thus encouraging market forces and meeting the needs of potential home owners, or it should plan for redirecting resources to areas of greatest housing need.[48]

The choice is of course not as simple as this. Even if planning were to identify itself solely with urban deprivation and the redirection of resources in favour of the poor, the present and future scale of economic activity and population growth is such that restructuring of the settlement system in the outer areas would be slow. A complete veto on all developments would be undesirable as well as difficult to implement. In any case land-use planning cannot be separated from other state planning systems for transport, housing, airports, and so on.

While programmes for the inner cities have been incorporated into the policies of the political parties, there is little evidence of any counterbalancing policy for dispersal or any understanding of the relationship between national economic strategy and urban policy. The Conservatives adopt strong market-oriented approaches to economic and social policy, while at the same time recognizing the strength of local political opposition to outer area expansion and the fear of social unrest in the cities. Their attitude to the inner cities remains non-commital, despite the attempts by Mr Michael Heseltine to change attitudes and practices. Indeed, he argued that dispersal was not inevitable but could probably not be tackled through a neatly packaged solution: 'you have to start with the people who have the power — those who run the large public authorities and companies'.[49] The Conservative-controlled local government associations have failed to adopt a policy stance on dispersal. Their concern, paralleled in the Labour Party, is with strengthening rural economies as much as with land-use planning. The Association of District Councils has proposed a strategy consisting of the relief of unemployment, the creation of small-scale factories and the promotion of tourism — very much along the lines argued above.[50] However, the ADC has also urged its members to adopt a more aggressive and permissive attitude to economic development, one which seems to reflect the present government's desire for a relaxation of planning controls.

The Labour Party's Alternative Economic Strategy (AES) proposes rapid monetary expansion combined with controls on imports. This, it hopes will bring unemployment down to 1.9 million by 1990. There is no specific urban dimension to the AES but it will probably favour areas of greatest social need. Roy Hattersley's recent speech to the British Association argued for 'a massive shift of resources into the areas of greatest need and towards the disadvantaged. The obvious example is the need to divert more resources into the inner cities — a policy rejected by this government'.[51] The theme is taken up by Paul Harrison: he argues for 'a new consensus on values: on the importance of compassion and a far greater measure of equality . . . the progressive reduction of inequalities in income and wealth should become an explicit policy goal'.[52] The central problem with the Left's approach is the failure to specify how sufficient wealth will be created to bring about a more equal society. Nevertheless, the Left has at least begun to debate national economic and social policy in spatial terms, something which the Right has been keen to avoid. Yet the impact of their policies on the outer areas remains obscure and undeveloped. It is probable that any serious attack on unemployment would encourage peripheral urban expansion as much as inner-area development. Moreover, the Labour Party's programme for reviving rural areas suggests the expansion of high-technology, especially microprocessor industries.[53] There must also be some lingering doubt as to whether the Left's traditional commitment to the trade unions and to local government would work in favour of a spatially redistributive policy, despite the stated intention of the Labour-controlled

Association of Metropolitan Authorities to secure investment in the inner cities.[54]

SDP-Liberal Alliance policies have similarly failed to address themselves to the relationship between economic and urban policy. The main pledge of the Alliance is the decentralization of power from central to local government. Hence, for them, the question of whether urban expansion should be permitted in the Green Belts should be determined locally rather than by central government.[55] There must be some value for the outer areas in counteracting the strength of central government planning agencies which have consistently taken a growth-oriented stance on housing and industrial expansion. However, more local discretion over planning matters could bring greater uncertainty in urban change and encourage a lack of coordination between local authorities. The SDP's idea for a 'social market-economy' could be developed into a more explicit and realistic urban policy to balance the goals of efficiency and equity; and the SDP's Green Paper on devolution[56] offers the best hope yet for the resurgence of regional planning — essential for effective management of growth in the outer cities.

Present political attitudes and economic conditions work in favour of market-led change which in turn legitimates the unequal opportunities for wealth and prosperity in the outer cities. This book argues that social and economic change *should* be managed, not solely from a desire to reduce inequality, but also in the interests of a more efficient use of capital and labour resources. To argue that planning systems should solely concern themselves with the redistribution of wealth is to ignore the potential that planning has to secure economic change through environmental and aesthetic control. The urban crisis cannot be identified solely with deprivation and the redirection of resources in favour of the poor. It is all too easy to forget, given the currently fashionable emphasis on the inner city, that the growth of the outer areas stores up enormous future problems for local planning agencies operating in the areas suffering the effects of 'over-heating'. Prosperity is necessary. But it brings with it problems of its own. There must be a more coherent political commitment to urban policy in Britain and a restatement of the purposes of strategic and local planning.

The outer areas: policies for the future

The national context

More effective containment of population and employment growth in the outer areas requires both a stronger and a more consistent national approach. The introduction of a clearly defined outer-area dimension to public policy must be a prerequisite to adjustments in spatial planning and sectoral programmes. At present there are several ill-thought out and un-coordinated views of national priorities, some of which work in favour of restraint while others will obviously give a massive stimulus to the decentralization process. The existence of urban and rural deprivation implies some redirection of capital investment in both private and public sectors away from the outer-metropolitan areas. Yet the desire for economic recovery drives the government towards peripheral urban expansion and, although it is not admitted, continued support for the planned growth programmes. The confusion is compounded by the existence of a number of place-specific forms of assistance in present urban and regional policies: inner-city designations for the urban aid programme, enterprise zones, special development areas, planned growth areas in regional strategies, Development Commission Special Investment Areas, and so on.

Modifications to regional policy might usefully draw a sharper distinction between the need for industrial assistance and job creation in the outer and the inner areas of the economic planning regions. This could provide a better marriage between present inter-regional policy and inner-city policy. Certainly it would seem to reflect the evidence for marked intra-regional variations in the decline in employment during the sixties and mid 1970s,[57] although the contrasts in employment decline and unemployment within and between counties surrounding the conurbations had become less clear cut in the period 1978-1982.[58] The relevance and scope of such adjustments will vary between regions. The high levels of unemployment experienced in parts of outer Glasgow and the belt between the Tyne and south Teeside would seem to obviate the scope for any 'planned deflection' of industrial activity from outer to inner areas.[59] In the Midlands and south of England inter-regional movement from the outer areas of one city-region to another is likely to sustain rather than check inter-metropolitan employment decentralization. This could be justified at a time of special hardship, but if conditions improved it would possibly assist the outer areas at the expense of the cities.

Attempts to curb the growth of population in the outer areas seem rather more promising and realistic at a time of national recession than attempts to deflect employment change. The two are interrelated. As long as the dispersal and redistribution of population favours the outer shire counties it must help to fuel unemployment. A concerted programme would undoubtedly require a closer adjustment of housing and land use policy within the Department of Environment. On the housing side, the main element requiring adjustment is household formation; the still declining size of the average household and the reduction in the number of shared households accounts for a major proportion of new housing land-take. Adjustments in the rate of new household formation can be made by the government through fiscal policy and direct negotiation with the housebuilding industry. The demand for single-person dwellings could be manipulated upwards through the building of more small houses, or downwards by encouraging more sharing and building fewer houses at higher densities. Income tax relief on mortgages for shared houses might be one answer. Housing density standards might be reintroduced. General adjustments to mortgage subsidies to owner-occupiers, while not politically palatable, would go a long way to reducing the demand on the private speculative housing market in the outer cities. Levels of household formation will of course be affected by aggregate rates of new housing construction.[60] This brings us back to the scale and distribution of future housing provision in the outer areas; various reforms in the method of formulating housing and land policies are under review, including the specification of housing targets at a regional scale. There is clearly 'an urgent need for a national and regional context for housing assessment since land use policies cannot be prepared in isolation from national economic policies'.[61] For a more effective strategy there would undoubtedly need to be an outer-area dimension. The main impact of recent DoE modifications to structure plan provision has fallen almost entirely on the shire counties without any commensurate guidance on how they might handle development pressures.

The government might strengthen its control over dispersed population growth by preparing guidelines and priorities for new housing construction in different outer areas. This would assist central and local government by permitting the monitoring and review of other public-sector expenditure programmes, notably industry, transport and water services. Better coordination in these spheres of central government activity is essential to the implementation of the other elements of land-use containment, namely the planned growth programmes and countryside restraint policies.

Some observers would like to see a more explicit national dimension to rural land-use policy, either a physical plan or a review of priorities or both.[62] Others favour stronger national commitment to the conservation of rural resources.[36] The criticism of government failure to achieve containment, which is implied by these alternatives, is certainly well made. There is undoubtedly an environmental risk to continued national support for decentralization. Any attempt to promote a more dispersed pattern of low-density housing in the outer areas runs the same risk, especially if the aggregate population and employment are increased. However, it is not clear that a physical plan would be sufficient to contain or redirect growth away from the outer areas or reduce the political tension which might accompany a more *dirigiste* national land-use policy. A more realistic approach would be for central government to strengthen the capacity of local planning authorities to restrict development in the outer areas, and to ensure that they were supported when developers appeal against refusal. Admittedly, there are difficulties created by the absence of specially designated areas of protected landscape in certain outer areas under pressure for expansion. It would therefore probably be sensible to extend the boundaries of the Green Belts into such areas — to create in effect a national Green Belt while retaining the Areas of Outstanding Natural Beauty and National Parks. There would then be a presumption *against* rather than in favour of large-scale development, and it would be left to developers to argue their case for expansion in the context of local rather than national requirements. A national Green Belt would not impair local autonomy since districts would still be free to grant permission for small 'local need' developments. It would indeed strengthen their hand against the large national and regional companies as well as help to bring about a reduction in public spending in the outer areas. Obviously any readjustment of land-use policy would necessitate other parallel approaches to dispersal: modifications in the capital spending programmes of public agencies; guidelines to private-sector interests, especially the principal development companies with a stake in outer-area expansion; and specific encouragement to the small business sector in the industrial and housing sphere. The possible benefits of selective resettlement schemes in the (extended) Green Belt could be examined in the formulation of guidelines to structure plans. The main case for these would be the need to avoid incremental local expansion, and to coordinate small-scale housing, retail, industrial and community development without either peripheral urban expansion or continued expansion of the larger planned growth points. It would certainly be important to control and monitor the overall scale of housing construction in these schemes and to ensure that the private sector contributed to infrastructure costs. The scope for using 'outer city partnerships' as a method of managing settlement change should be examined. If these 'partnerships' included housebuilding, industrial, environmental and government interests, they could prove a practical means of defusing the political tension surrounding so many proposals for urban expansion in the Green Belts.

These suggestions beg many questions. There is little chance of coordinating public-sector programmes when urban policy goals are unclear and when too many agencies are involved. Irrespective of the merits of outer city restraint in favour of inner area renewal, it would be extremely difficult to dismantle those state policies which have favoured dispersal for so long. Only minor shifts in public spending programmes are likely in the short term. The officially disbanded overspill programmes still command substantial investment especially in 'third generation' New Towns, which have gathered a strong economic momentum of their own. Even assuming some consensus on the need for adjustment in public and private-sector programmes, the question of whether central governments are strong-minded enough to tackle for themselves the issue of unplanned dispersal must remain an open one. The problem is that neither political party has a clear view of the relationship between national economic and urban policies. Nor are they eager to jeopardize their fragile relationship with local government. Too little local discretion in urban policy matters would fuel accusations of centralism. Too much — and we are back with dispersal. The weakness of central government has been its reluctance to face this issue squarely.

Strategic planning

The demise of the regional strategies discussed in Chapter 5 and the limitations of structure planning outlined in Chapter 6 suggest we should not expect too much from further developments in regional planning. Yet the strategic regional dimension is missing from current attempts to accommodate development pressures outside the conurbations. The absence of a physical plan for the future of the outer areas is particularly worrying, while compelling demands on land are settled in an *ad hoc* and piecemeal fashion. Indeed, 'there is apparently no appreciation in Whitehall of the need for a wide review of town and country planning for the urban regions and the capital'.[64]

Some kind of strategy for future development in the outer areas would seem sensible. If restraint were encouraged at a national level through an extension of Green Belts, the main purpose of regional strategy would be to formulate and implement a dispersed settlement policy in the outer areas. The large scale of economic planning regions has prompted some commentators to argue that sub-regional rather than regional planning would be advantageous.[65] Within the context of the pressures and problems facing certain local authorities in the outer areas this would seem an appropriate line of argument. However, there are of course many problems in securing effective strategic planning at the sub-regional scale, especially administrative ones. A strong top-down approach would probably be resisted by the lower-tier authorities. Moreover, the failure of the 'growth centre' philosophy accelerates the move away from 'top-down' policies. If sites for growth in strategic plans were more carefully sifted and evaluated, strategic plans might be used to steer and monitor the scale of land released for housing in the outer areas.[66] The requirement upon each district council to find a five year housing supply is unrealistic. Many factors affect the availability of sites.[67] When these factors are accounted for there will be surpluses of housing development in some districts and shortfalls in others. Finally, if strategic planning is to be improved it may need to be less long term and more specific about which locations will come forward for development. Otherwise it risks remaining vague and impractical. To satisfy these apparently simple requirements will not be easy given the present split of planning functions between counties and districts. A way of getting greater collaboration between the planning officers of counties and districts will need to be found if sub-regional strategic plans are to break new ground.

The local level

In its widest sense planning is inseparable from the local political process. In this book containment strategies have been evaluated in terms of the way different agents have perceived and responded to the problems presented by the outer city — a plurality of interests in a complex political process. Will planning within the political process secure the realization of desirable social and environmental goals? There are some grounds for optimism: a closer alliance between environmental lobbies and the interests of professional planners is discernible.[68] The local planning system is being weakened by the present government, yet the environmental and social tensions which have resulted have sparked off an anti-growth outcry among local and national pressure groups. This sometimes reflects a narrow protectionist stand against economic development, but it may provide the beginning of a logical and constructive approach to the formulation of national urban policy. It should be welcomed by planners operating in both the outer and inner areas. Moreover, closer links between planners and politicians may bring about a restatement of planning values. At the local-scale professional planners may find their greatest allies among local councillors disenchanted with growth proposals imposed by central government and the economic agencies without reference to strategic policy. The exposition of containment principles may also be assisted rather than hindered by public participation and local political debate. At national and local levels closer coordination between professional bodies, partnerships between public and private interests, and other means of making agencies more aware of the environmental and social consequences of their decisions, must be important. However, if dispersal is to be managed effectively the major initiatives must come from central rather than local government.

It is certainly true that current political ideology favours greater freedom for market forces and gives greater scope for outer-city dispersal and environmental damage. But the forces of economic and social change can be managed. They do not operate independently of government. Furthermore, the state has usually tried to regulate change more effectively when social conflict threatens its existence — and a rapid lurch towards growth-oriented strategies for the outer city might undermine the social values upon which British society is based. Continued outer-metropolitan growth may prove too high a price to pay for economic recovery. The social costs for the inner cities have only just been counted. Outer area problems are no less acute; possibly they are even more fundamental in the long term. The question is not whether dispersal is good or bad, but whether society, through its political institutions, is prepared to face up to the enormous task of adjusting to urban change.

Notes

1.   E. A. ROSE, Review article, *The Planner*, vol. 69, no. 4, 1983.

2.   S. FOTHERGILL and G. GUDGIN, 'Employment prospects in the Thatcher era', *The Planner*, vol. 69, no. 5, 1983.

3.   A. J. SCOTT, *The Urban Land Nexus and the State*, Pion 1980.

4.   Community Development Project, *The Costs of Industrial Change*, CDP 1977.

5.   R. GLASS, 'Long term destiny of inner cities', *Times*, 6, August 1983.

6.   G. MARTINOTTI, 'Deurbanization and villagization', *International Journal of Urban and Regional Research*, 4, 1980, p. 453.

7.   P. HALL *et al.*, *The Containment of Urban England, Vol. 2* (Allen and Unwin, 1973).

8.   Cambridge Economic Policy Group, Urban and Regional Policy with Provisional Regional Accounts, 1966-78, *Cambridge Economic Policy Review*, vol. 6, no. 2, 1980; *Cambridge Economic Policy Review*, vol. 8, no. 2 (Gower Publishing, 1982).

9.   S. FOTHERGILL and G. GUDGIN, op. cit.

10.   M. FROST and N. SPENCE, 'Urban and regional economic change in Britain', *Geographical Journal*, vol. 147, pt. 3, November 1981; M. FROST and N. SPENCE, 'Unemployment, structural economic change and public policy in British regions', *Progress in Planning*, vol. 16, 1981.

11.   A. TOWNSEND, 'The scope for intra-regional variation in the 1980's, *The Planner*, vol. 69, no. 4, July/August 1983.

12.   Report on New Towns, *Town and Country Planning*, vol. 51, no. 10, 1982.

13.   V. KEEGAN, 'The public spending tale that was the dogma', *Guardian*, 25 August 1983.

14.   Report in *Financial Times*, 19 September 1983.

15.   Consortium Development Ltd. have proposed 12-15 self-contained private 'village' settlements each with 7-8,000 homes (15,000-20,000 population) in the Home Counties around London; 4 or 5 may be on Green Belt land. Their initial plans were discussed in 'Builders get their hooks into the Green Belt', *Planning*, vol. 529, 29 July 1983; 'Still chasing shadows on new villages plan', *Planning*, vol. 533, 26 August 1983.

16.   See for instance Royal Town Planning Institute, *The Planning Response to Social and Economic Change*, First report of a Study Group (RTPI, October 1982).

17.   A. KIRBY, 'The external relations of the local state in Britain; some empirical examples' in K. R. COX and R. J. JOHNSTON, *Conflict, Politics and the Urban Scene* (Longman, 1982).

18.   R. J. JOHNSTON, 'Political geography without politics', *Progress in Human Geography*, vol. 4, 1980.

19.   *Annual Abstract of Statistics*, (HMSO, 1982).

20.   See for instance Industrial floorspace and output tables in Central Statistical Office, *Regional Statistics* (published annually by HMSO).

21.   For a general discussion see J. EASTWELL, *Whatever Happened to Britain?* (BBC and Duckworth, 1982).

22.   R. HUDSON, 'Regional development policies and female employment', *Area*, vol. 12, 1980.

23. P. HALL, 'The geography of the fifth Kondratieff cycle', *New Society*, 26 March 1981.

24. C. BROOK, 'High technology industry and science parks', *The Planner*, vol. 68, no. 6, November/December 1982.

25. H. SIMPSON, 'Planning policies and housing', *The Planner*, February 1983.

26. C. BUCHANAN, *The Stansted Controversy: No Way to the Airport* (Longman, 1981).

27. See for instance P. LAWLESS, *Britain's Inner Cities* (Harper & Row, 1981); S. FOTHERGILL and G. GUDGIN, *Unequal Growth* (Heinemann, 1982); E. OWEN, 'An outward approach to an inner problem', *Surveyor*, 1 April 1982.

28. See for instance the reports 'Barratt backs a winner', *Building*, 11 March 1983; 'Sir Lawrie plays pied piper to the inner city', *Sunday Times*, 6 March 1983.

29. D. POPENHOE, 'Urban Sprawl: some neglected sociological considerations', *Sociology and Social Research*, 63(2), 1979, pp. 255–268.

30. 'Production classes' and 'consumption classes' are discussed in P. HALL, 'Dark prospect', *Town and Country Planning*, vol. 49, no. 1, January 1980.

31. R. OAKESHOTT, 'Valid arguments against the beggar-my-neighbour logic', *Guardian*, 2 July 1981.

32. R. OAKESHOTT, 'Country Towns — the call of the shires', *Economist*, 28 July 1979.

33. J. GERSHUNY and I. MILES, *The new Service economy: the transformation of Employment in Industrial Societies* (Frances Pinter, 1983).

34. C. JENKINS and B. SHERMAN, *The Collapse of Work* (Fakenham Press, 1979).

35. Report on 'share up for tourist trade', *Sunday Telegraph*, 18 September 1983.

36. D. J. EGAN, 'Tourism and employment', *The Planner*, vol. 69, no. 4, July/August 1983.

37. P. HALL, op. cit.

38. I. McCALLUM, 'Employment generation', *The Planner*, vol. , no. , February, 1983.

39. M. TAYLOR and N. BOZEAT, 'Just how constraining is the planning system?', *Planning*, vol. 454, 5 February 1982.

40. G. R. PEARCE and M. J. TRICKER, 'Land availability for residential development' in F. JOYCE (ed.), *Metropolitan Development and Change. The West Midlands: a Policy Review* (Teakfield, 1977).

41. N. HEBBERT, 'The British New Towns: a review of Bracknell, East Kilbride and Washington', *Town Planning Review*, 51(4), 1980.

42. P. SELF, 'New Towns and the urban crisis' (2 parts), *Town and Country Planning*, vol. 48, no. 1, April 1979; vol. 48, no. 2, May 1979.

43. I. M. GILDER, *Rural Planning Policies: An Economic Appraisal. Progress in Planning*, vol. 11, pt. 3 (Pergamon, 1979).

44. D. CRAWFORD, Special Report on Housing, *Guardian*, 18 March 1983.

45. D. KAISERMAN, 'Green Belts — a review of current practice', *The Planner*, vol. , no. , February 1983.

46. G. DARLEY, 'Blueprint for green belt action', *Building Design*, 23 October 1981.

47. A. BLOWERS, 'The twilight of planning, *Town and Country Planning*, vol. 50, no. 3, March 1981.

48. D. EVERSLEY, 'Can planners keep up as the flight from the cities continues to accelerate', Royal Town Planning Institute, Annual Report of Conference, 1982.

49. M. HESELTINE, 'Why we must all make it our business to save the inner cities', *The Times*, 14 April 1982.

50. Association of District Councils, *Rural Recovery: Strategy for Survival* (ADC 1978).

51. R. HATTERSLEY, Paper presented to the British Association, August 1983.

52. P. HARRISON, *Inside the Inner City* (Pelican 1983).

53. Labour Party, *Out of Town, Out of Mind: A Programme for Rural Revival* (1981).

54. Association of Municipal Authorities, *Investment in Recovery* (AMA, July, 1981).

55. D. OWEN, 'Local government has a duty to balance the books, Whitehall does not', *Guardian*, 5 August 1983.

56. Social Democratic Party, *Green Paper on Devolution* (1982).

57. K. J. BUTTON, 'Employment and industrial decline in the inner areas of British Cities — the experience of 1962–1977', *Journal of Industrial Affairs*, vol. 6, no. 1, 1978.

58. D. KEEBLE, 'Industrial decline, regional policy and the urban-rural manufacturing shift in the UK', *Environment and Planning A*, vol. 12, no. 8, 1980.

59. A. TOWNSEND, op. cit.

60. The inter-relationship between housing supply and the calculation of future housing demand is discussed by the Joint Land Requirements Committee. *Is there sufficient housing land for the 1980s?* (Housing Research Foundation, February, 1982).

61. Joint Land Requirements Committee, *Is there Sufficient Housing Land for the 1980s? Paper 11. How many houses have we planned for: is there a problem?* Housing Research Foundation, February, 1983).

62. See for instance G. MOSS, *Britain's Wasting Acres* (Architectural Press, 1981); A. GILG, 'Needed: a new Scott inquiry', *Town Planning Review*, vol. 49, 1978.

62. D. SCOTT, 'Time for another Scott Report: problems of rural land use', *Country Life*, vol, 165, no. 4277, 1979.

63. J. DAVIDSON and A. MAcEWEN, *The Livable City* (UK Programme Committee for World Conservation Strategy, 1982).

64. 'A plan by any other name', *The Times*, 8 August 1983.

65. See for instance R. J. GREEN, 'Planning in the rural sub-regions: a personal view', *Countryside Planning Yearbook*, vol. 1, 1980; G. SMART, 'Strategies in decline?', PTRC Summer School proceedings, 1980.

66. Approaches to monitoring are discussed by J. HERRINGTON, 'Monitoring Household movements to increase policy effectiveness in structure and local plans', PTRC, *Policy Analysis for Urban and Regional Planning*, vol. P174, 1979.

67. 'Using land with responsibility', *Housing Planning Review*, vol. 36, no. 4, Winter 1980.

68. N. HEBBERT, 'The land debate and the planning system', *Town and Country Planning*, vol, 50, no. 1, January 1981.

Glossary

This glossary is intended to help the layperson understand some of the planning descriptions and phrases used in the test. It is selective and not intended to be a definitive list.

Area of Outstanding Natural Beauty An area of attractive countryside (e.g. the Chilterns) where there is a strong presumption that local planning authorities will restrain urban development, although planning controls are the same as in other areas. Proposals for new AONBs are formulated by the Countryside Commission under the Countryside Act 1968 in consultation with local interested groups and individuals.

Assisted Area An Area of Britain where firms can receive special financial assistance (e.g. Regional Development Grants) from the Department of Industry. Three main types of area existed in 1982: Development Areas, Intermediate Areas and Special Development Areas. The Conservative government elected in mid-1979 has made a number of modifications to regional policy which include cutting back the spatial extent of Assisted Areas. As from August 1982 the AAs cover 25 percent of the working population compared to the previous figure of 40 percent.

Circular Publication which gives advice to local authorities and other agencies about how to interpret central government policy.

Development Corporation Government agency established under the New Towns Act 1946 with special powers to acquire land, build factories and develop the infrastructure necessary to develop the New Towns in England, Wales and Scotland. The Conservative government announced that the functions of the DCs were to be transferred to the local authorities. The process of 'winding down' is likely to be complete by the late 1980s in England and Wales but probably not until the late 1990s in Scotland.

Economic Planning Boards and Councils The Boards are a committee of senior central government civil servants based in the Economic Planning Regions (there are eleven in the United Kingdom, including Northern Ireland). The Boards' role is to co-ordinate the policies and programmes of the principal government departments. The Economic Planning Councils, which were abolished in July 1979, included distinguished representatives of local government, the trade unions and universities, who were brought together to formulate regional economic development strategies for the Economic Planning Regions. They were never given executive power to implement the strategies.

Examination-in-Public A statutory public inquiry into certain issues relevant to the policies and proposals contained in a structure plan. The Secretary of State decides which topics will be raised (in the light of objections to the plan and what he considers important) and only those groups or individuals invited by the Secretary of State may attend. A decision on the findings of an EIP is made by the Secretary of State. The costs of an EIP are met by the Department of Environment.

Free-standing city   Often distinguished from the conurbations. Some commentators refer to those cities with more than 250,000 people. Free-standing cities experience population and employment decentralization of the same kind, although not on the same scale, as the conurbations (e.g. Bristol, Leicester).

Green Belt   An area of land defined by local authorities around a conurbation or free-standing city with the intention of preventing the physical spread of urban development. Since 1974 the boundaries of green belts have been determined in Subject Local Plans published by both County and District authorities. The governments Circular 'Land for Housing' published in July 1983 asked local authorities to review the boundaries of Green Belts to ensure their permanency and the adequacy of provision for housing land, especially on the inner boundaries.

Growth Points   Individual settlements or groups of settlement which have been chosen as strategic locations for the allocation and co-ordination of investment with the purpose of either promoting economic and social benefits over a wide area and/or concentrating urban development so as to avoid the dispersal of urban growth (e.g. Growth Area, New and Expanded Town, Key Settlement).

Infill   Site for usually not more than one or two dwellings within the existing built-up area of a village or town. Favoured by local planning authorities as a means of accommodating the expansion of settlements without peripheral growth.

Infrastructure   The provision of facilities necessary to open up an area for any type of development (e.g. especially roads, off-site water supply and sewerage, power supply) and the social infrastructure necessary to support a growth of population (for instance, schools and health-care centres). The costs of infrastructure provision usually fall upon the public sector but some facilities may be privately financed (e.g. following a Section 52 Agreement).

Inner City Partnership   Mechanism established under the Inner Urban Areas Act 1978 for bringing together government with economic agencies and other bodies including the Confederation of British Industry and the trade unions for formulating and implementing policies which can stimulate the economic regeneration of inner-city areas. There are seven Partnership schemes in England. No equivalent mechanism exists for managing growth in the outer cities.

Land Bank   An accumulation of parcels of land acquired by private developers in advance of the expectation that market conditions will allow future development to take place and that planning permission will be forthcoming for such development.

Local Plan   Generic term covering three different types of detailed land use plan usually but not always produced by district councils. The three plans are: District Plans, Action Area Plans and Subject Plans. Which types of Local Plan are to be prepared and in what order is governed by the Development Plans Scheme, a list drawn up jointly by county and district planning officers.

Local Planning Authorities Following the Local Government Act 1972 which came into operation on 1 April 1974, local planning authorities in England are the metropolitan county councils (the conurbations) and the non-metropolitan county councils (sometimes known as 'shire' counties) and the district councils. The counties were given strategic planning functions (e.g. preparation of structure plans) and the districts were given responsibility for the implementation of plans and detailed planning control. Powers vary somewhat between the metropolitan and non-metropolitan councils. Under the Local Government Planning and Land Act 1980 most powers of development control were given to the district councils. A similar two-tier local government system was introduced in Scotland in May 1975 but a distinction was drawn between six regional planning authorities (equivalent to non-metropolitan Counties in England) and three general planning authorities which retained strategic and local planning powers.

New Towns State-financed urban developments following the New Towns Act 1946 (consolidated in the New Towns Act 1965). New Towns have been built around existing settlements and have usually required building on greenfield land. Their purpose has been to provide homes and jobs for people leaving the cities (under the planned overspill schemes) and to stimulate regional development especially in the Assisted Areas (see also Growth Points).

Planning Appeal Commonly an appeal by an applicant against the refusal of planning permission (or any condition of the permission) issued by the local planning authority. The applicant can decide whether to submit a written statement or seek a public inquiry although the decision as to whether to hold a public inquiry is the responsibility of the Secretary of State for the Environment. The purpose of a public inquiry is to examine the issues involved publicly and allow the different sides in an issue to present their case. Many appeals on minor matters are now resolved by inspectors appointed by the Secretary of State.

Planning Gain Where a council imposes an obligation on a developer to make some payment or confer some benefit or right in return for planning permission.

Public Local Inquiry To be distinguished from an Examination in Public by the fact that the final decision on the findings of the inquiry is made by the local planning authority which has prepared the Local Plan (usually the district council, though sometimes the county council). The costs of a PLI are met by the local authority.

Section 52 Agreement The Town and Country Planning Act 1971 allows the local authority to enter into an independent legal agreement with developers to guarantee that certain aspects relating to a planning permission can be carried out. Whereas normal planning conditions may be used to ensure compliance on the land which is the immediate subject of a planning application, a Section 52 Agreement may be used to ensure that off-site works are provided (e.g. roads or sewage disposal works). May be used where more than one developer is involved and where the smooth phasing and integration of development is needed.

Standing Conference A group of local authorities who come together to formulate and review issues which cut across the boundaries of any one authority (e.g. transport provision, housing land availability). The most well-known is the Standing Conference for London and South Eastern Regional Planning (SCLSERP).

Statutory Undertaker The public agencies or nationalised industries who are authorised by statute to provide water, electricity, gas, transport and other services.

Structure Plan A document which sets out the principal physical, social and economic policies and proposals for the development of a county and the steps necessary to implement and finance proposals. A product of the Town and Country Planning Act 1968, Structure Plans are prepared by the 54 English and Welsh county councils and the 12 Scottish regional and island authorities. The structure plan is the framework within which the more detailed Local Plans produced by district councils are drawn up.

Sun-belt The area of small country towns and free-standing cities stretching north east approximately between Somerset through Berkshire to Cambridgeshire (excluding Greater London) which is favoured by high-technology and other types of business enterprise because of its pleasant environment, accessible location, and proximity to high-quality labour.

Select Bibliography

Acton, P. 'Electrification boosts public transport in Hertfordshire', *Transport*, vol. 1(3), July/August 1980.

Adam Smith Institute. *Town and Country Chaos*, London, 1982.

Aldridge, M. *The British New Towns: a Programme without a Policy*, Routledge and Kegan Paul, 1979.

Alesbury, A. 'Planning appeals the other way round: the number of appeals against the Secretary of State seems to be on the increase', *Architect*, vol. 125, no. 12, 1979.

Ambrose, P. *The Quiet Revolution: Social Change in a Sussex Village, 1871-1971*, Chatto and Windus, 1974.

Anderson, M. 'Planning policies and development control in the Sussex Downs AONB', *Town Planning Review*, vol. 52, no. 1, 1981.

Anderson, T. 'Bill aims to boost private housing: Heseltine to sweep away red tape', *Building Design*, no. 452, 1979.

Archer, R.W. 'Prospects for private enterprise new towns', *Official Architecture and Planning*, July 1971.

Armen, G. 'Programming of social provision in new communities — some case studies and conclusions', *Town Planning Review*, vol. 47, no. 3, 1976.

Ash, J. 'Public participation: time to bury Skeffington?' *Planner*, vol. 65, no. 5, 1979.

Ashworth, G.J. 'Planning policies on land for housing', Department of Town Planning, Oxford Polytechnic, MSc Thesis, 1981.

Association of District Councils, *Economic Development by District Councils*, ADC, 1982.

Association of District Councils. *Rural Deprivation*, ADC, September 1979.

Association of District Councils, *Rural Recovery: A Strategy for Survival*, ADC, 1978.

Association of Municipal Authorities, *Investment in Recovery*, AMA, July 1981.

Avon County Council. *County Structure Plan: Situation Report, Employment*, Avon CC, May 1976.

Avon County Council. *County Structure Plan Revised Written Statement*, November, Avon CC, 1981.

Avon County Council. *A Draft Strategy for Economic Development*, Avon CC, October 1982.

Barke, M. 'Some aspects of population and social change in Glasgow, 1961-71', *Professional Geographer*, vol. 30(1), 1978.

Barker, B. 'The sale of council houses: A housing policy and political issue', Department of Town Planning, Oxford Polytechnic, MSc Thesis, 1980.

Baron, T. 'Planning's biggest and least satisfied customer: Housing', *Town and Country Planning Summer School: Report of Proceedings*, RTPI, September 1980.

Barrett, S. and Underwood, J. 'Planning at the crossroads — a review of 1980', *Planner News*, vol. 67, no. 3, 1981.

Bassett, K.A. and Short, J.R. 'Patterns of building society and local authority mortgage lending in the 1970s', *Environment and Planning A*, vol. 12, 1980.

Bassett, K. and Short, J. *Housing and Residential Structure: Alternative Approaches*, Routledge & Kegan Paul, 1980.

Bather, N. 'The speculative residential developer and urban growth', Department of Geography, University of Reading, Geographical Papers, No. 47, 1976.

Bather, N. 'The speculative residential development and urban growth', Department of Geography, University of Reading, Geographical Papers, No. 47, 1976.

Bennett, R. *The Geography of Public Finance: Welfare Under Fiscal Federalism and Local Government Finance*, Methuen 1980.

Berkshire, Hampshire and Surrey County Councils, *The Reading, Wokingham, Aldershot, Basingstoke Study*, Berkshire, Hampshire and Surrey CCs, 1975.

Berry, B.J.L. (ed.) *Urbanization and Counter-Urbanization*, Urban Affairs Annual Review, vol. 11, Beverley Hills, Sage Publications, 1976.

Best, R.H. 'The extent and growth of urban land', *The Planner*, vol. 62, 1976.

Best, R. *Land Use and Living Space*, Methuen, 1981.

Bichard, M. 'Inter-authority collaboration', *Municipal Journal*, vol. 28, June 1974.

Blacksell, M. and Gilg, A. *The Countryside: Planning and Change*, Allen and Unwin, 1981.

Blair, A.M. 'Farming in Metroland', *Countryman*, vol. 85(4), 1980.

Blair, A.M. 'Urban influences on farming in Essex', *Geoforum*, vol. 11(4), 1980.

Bloomfield, S. 'Problems in the pipeline', *Building*, vol. 237, no. 7109, 1979.

Blowers, A. *The Limits of Power: The Politics of Local Planning Policy*, Pergamon, 1980.

Blowers, A. 'The politics of land development', in *Urban change and conflict: an interdisciplinary reader*, Harper & Row, 1981.

Blowers, A. 'The twilight of planning', *Town and Country Planning*, vol. 50, no. 3, March 1981.

Blowers, A. 'Much ado about nothing? A case study of planning and power', Paper for conference on planning theory in the 1980s, Oxford Polytechnic, 1981.

Blowers, A. 'Industry versus the environment in the metropolitan fringe', in Planning and the Quality of Life: proceedings of the 3rd Anglo-German Symposium on Applied Geography, 1982.

Boaden, N. *Public Participation and Planning in Practice*, Pergamon, 1980.

Boaden, N. 'Public participation in planning within a representative local democracy', *Policy and Politics*, vol. 7, 1979.

Bourne, L.S. *Urban Systems: Strategies for Regulation*, Oxford, 1975.

Bracken, I. 'Structure Plans — submissions and alterations', *The Planner*, September 1980.

Brazier, S. and Harris, R.J.P. 'Inter-authority planning: appreciation and resolution of conflict in the new local authority system', *Town Planning Review*, vol. 46, no. 3, July 1975.

Bristow, S.L. 'Local politics after reorganization: the homogenization of local government in England and Wales', *Public Administration Bulletin*, no. 28, December 1978.

British Road Federation, *County Roads Needs in Bedfordshire, Cambridgeshire and Northamptonshire*, BRF, 1978.

Brook, C. 'High technology industry and science parks', *The Planner*, vol. 68, no. 6, November/December 1982.

Brown, A.H. 'Commuter travel trends in London and the South East 1966-1979 and associated factors', *Department of Transport Statistics*, October 1981.

Bruton, M.J. 'The cost of public participation in local planning', *Town and Country Planning*, June 1981.

Bruton, M.J. 'The future of development plans — PAG revisited', *Town Planning Review*, vol. 51, no. 2, 1980.

Bruton, M.J. 'Public participation, local planning and conflict of interest', *Policy and Politics*, vol. 8, no. 4, October 1980.

Bruton, M.J., Crispin, G. and Fidler, P.M. 'Local Plans, public local inquiries'. *Journal of Planning and Environment Law*, June, 1980.

Buchanan, C. *The Stansted Controversy: No Way to the Airport*. Longman, 1981.

Button, K.J. 'The geographical distribution of car ownership in Great Britain — some recent trends', *Annals of Regional Science*, vol. 14, pt. 2, 1980.

Caddy, G.H. 'A Superstore for Oxfordshire', *District Councils Review*, May 1981.

Cambridge Econometrics Ltd. *Policies for recovery*, 1981.

Centre for Agricultural Stategy, *Land for Agriculture*, CAS Report 1, 1976; *Strategy for the UK Forest Industry*, CAS Report, University of Reading, 1980.

Census for England and Wales. *Population Trends*, vol. 25, Autumn 1981.

Champion, A.G. 'Counter-urbanisation and rural rejuvenation in Britain: an evaluation of population trends since 1971', Department of Geography Seminar Paper No. 38, University of Newcastle-upon-Tyne, 1981.

Champion, A.G. 'Population dispersal — a national imperative', *Environment and Planning A*, vol. 14, no. 2, 1982.

Champion, A.G., Clegg, K. and Davies, R.L. *Facts about the New Towns: a Socio-Economic Digest*, Retailing and Planning Associates, 1977.

Checkoway, B. 'Large builders, federal housing programmes and postwar suburbanization', *International Journal of Urban and Regional Research*, vol. 4, no. 1, 1980.

Cherry, G. *The Evolution of British Town Planning*, Leonard Hill, 1974.

Cherry, G. 'Homes for heroes — semis for by-passes: how housing for the masses developed between the two wars', *New Society*, vol. 47, no. 852, 1 February 1979.

Cheshire County Council, *County Structure Plan: Approved Written Statement*, Cheshire CC, 1979.

Cheshire County Council, *County Structure Plan: First Alteration Consultation Report*, Cheshire CC, March 1982.

Cheshire County Council, *Structure Plan: Report of Survey Summary*, Cheshire CC, February 1977.

Chiddick, D. 'Hertfordshire's housing study identifies "need" areas', *Surveyor*, vol. 153, no. 4532, 19 April 1978.

Clayton, K. 'Pulling the plug out of Strathclyde', *Planning*, vol. 402, 23 January 1981.

Cloke, P.J. *Introduction to Rural Settlement Planning*, Methuen, 1983.

Cloke, P.J., Ayton, J. and Gilder, I. *The Planner*, July/August, 1980.

Cloke, P.J. and Shaw, D.P. 'Rural settlement policies in structure planning', *Town Planning Review*, vol. 54, no. 3, July 1983.

Coleman, A. 'The Countryside Endangered', *Country Life*, 2 July 1981.

Coleman, A. 'Is Planning really necessary?' *Geographical Journal*, vol. 142, 1976.

Coleman, A. 'Land use planning: Success or failure?', *Architects Journal*, vol. 165, 1977.

Collins, C.A. 'Consideration of the social background and motivation of councillors', *Policy and Politics*, vol. 6, no. 4, 1978.

Collins, J. and Ross, M. 'Green Belts: now sacrosanct?', *Planning*, vol. 482, 20 August 1982.

Community Development Project, *The Costs of Industrial Change*, CDP, 1977.

Coppock, J.T. (ed.) *Second Homes: Curse or Blessing?* Pergamon, 1977.

Council for the Protection of Rural England, 'Grass roots revolt, dozens of parishes to unite', CPRE, 1 June 1981.

Council for Protection of Rural England, *Planning — Friend or Foe?* CPRE, 1981.

Countryside Commission, *Countryside Issues and Actions*, CCP 151, April 1982.

Countryside Review Committee, *the Countryside — Problems and Policies*, HMSO, 1976.

County Planning Officer's Society, *County Planning and the Local Economy*, March, 1981.

County Planning Officer's Society, *The Development Plans system: the needs of the 1980s*.

Cowan, R. 'Land supply for housing', *Roof*, vol. 6(3), May/June 1981.

Cowan, R. 'Mr Heseltine's Budget', *Town and Country Planning*, vol. 50, no. 4, April 1981.

Cox, K. ed. *Urbanization and conflict in market societies*, Methuen, 1978.

Cox, K.R. and Johnston, R.J. *Conflict, Politics and the Urban Scene*, Longman, 1982.

Darke, R. and Walker, R. *Local Government and the Public*, Leonard Hill, 1974.

Darley, G. 'Blueprint for green belt action', *Building Design*, 23 October 1981.

Davidson, B.R. 'The effects of land speculation on the supply of housing in England and Wales', *Urban Studies*, vol. 12, 1975.

Davidson, J. and MacEwan, A. *The Livable City*, UK Programme Committee for World Conservation Strategy, 1982.

Davies, G., Hickling, D., Wrigley, M. 'Going beyond the problem areas of Strathclyde region', *Planning*, vol. 413, 10 April 1981.

Deakin, N., and Ungerson, C., *Leaving London: Planned mobility and the inner city*, Heinemann, 1977.

Deeble, D. 'De-industrialisation means unemployment', *Geographical Magazine*, vol. LIII, no. 7, April 1981.

Dennis, R. and Clout, H. *A Social Geography of England and Wales*, Pergamon, 1980.

Department of Environment. *British Cities: Urban Population and Employment Trends 1951–71* (Urban change in Britain 1951–71, Final report, part 1), Research report 10, 1976.

Department of Environment, *Circular 10*, HMSO, 1970.

Department of Environment, *Circular 102*, HMSO, 1972.

Department of Environment, *Committee of Inquiry into the system of remuneration of members of local authorities*, HMSO, 1977.

Department of Environment, *Development Control — Policy and Practice* Circular 22/80, HMSO, 1982.

Department of Environment, *Development Plans*, Circular 23/81, HMSO, 1981.

Department of Environment, *Form and Content of Local Plans: Local Plans Note 1/78*, HMSO, 1978.

Department of Environment, *Land Availability: A Study of Land with Residential Planning Permission*, DoE, 1978.

Department of Environment, *Land for Housing*, Draft Circular, July 1983.

Department of Environment, *Local Government and the Industrial Strategy*, HMSO, 1977.

Department of Environment, *Local Plans progress to 31 March, 1982*, HMSO, 1982.

Department of Environment, *Memorandum on Structure and Local Plans*, Circular 55/77, HMSO, 1977.

Department of Environment, *Memorandum on Structure and Local Plans*, Circular 4/79, HMSO, 1979.

Department of Environment, *Non-Statutory Plans*, Circular 58(1), HMSO, 1974.

Department of Environment, *Planning Gain*, Property Advisory Group, HMSO, 1980.

Department of Environment, *Private Sector Land Requirements and Supply*, Circular 44/78, HMSO, 1978.

Department of Environment, Review of Rural Settlement Policies 1945–1980, Martin and Voorhees Associates, October 1980.

Department of Environment, *Strategic Plan for the South East Review — Government Statement*, HMSO, 1978.

Department of Environment, *Structure and Local Plan Regulations*, Circular 22/82, HMSO, 1981.

Department of Environment, *Town and Country Planning Cooperation between authorities*. Circular 74/73, HMSO, 1973.

Department of Environment and Economist Intelligence Unit, *Land Availability — a study of land with residential planning permission*, DoE, 1978.

Department of Transport, *Policy for Roads: England 1980*, Cmnd 7908, HMSO, 1980.

Department of Transport, *Transport Policy*, Cmnd 6836, HMSO, 1977.

Derounian, J. 'The impact of structure plans on rural communities', *The Planner*, vol. 50, no. 1, 1981.

Dix, M.C. and Pollard, H.R.T. 'Company-financed motoring and its effects on household car use', *Traffic Engineering and Control*, vol. 21, no. 11, November 1980.

Dobson, M. 'Green Belts: planners play canute', *Planning*, vol. 482, 20 August 1982.

Donnison, D. and Soto, P. *The Good City: A Study of Urban Development and Policy in Great Britain*, Heinemann, 1980.

Dorset County Council, *South East Dorset Structure Plan: Submitted Written Statement*, Dorset CC, 1978.

Drudy, P.J. (ed.), *Water Planning and the Regions*. Regional Studies Association, Discussion Paper 9, 1977.

Egan, D.J. 'Tourism and employment', *The Planner*, vol. 69, no. 4, July/August 1983.

Elson, M. 'Fringe development', *Local Government News*, October 1982.

Elson, M. 'Perspectives on green belt local plans', Department of Town Planning, Oxford Polytechnic, Working Paper 38, 1979.

Elson, M. 'Research review: land use and management in the urban fringe', *The Planner*, vol, 65, no. 2, 1979.

Elson, M. *The Urban Fringe: Open land policies and programmes in the metropolitan counties*, Report commissioned by Countryside Commission, December 1977.

Evans, S.C. 'Planning for local needs in an area of growth restraint', Department of Town Planning, Oxford Polytechnic, MSc Thesis, 1980.

Eversley, D. 'Can planners keep up as the flight from the cities continues to accelerate?', Royal Town Planning Institute, Annual report of conference, 1982.

Forbes, J. and Robertson, I. 'Patterns of Residential Movement in Greater Glasgow', *Scottish Geographical Magazine*, vol. 97, no. 2, 1981.

Fothergill, S. and Gudgin, G. *Unequal Growth: Urban and Regional Employment*, Heinemann 1982.

Frost, M. and Spence, N. 'Urban and regional economic change in Britain', *Geographical Journal*, vol. 147, pt. 3, November 1981.

Fudge, C. (ed.) *Approaches to Local Planning*, University of Bristol School of Advanced Urban Studies, Working Paper 17, 1981.

Gault, I. 'Green Belt policies in Development Plans', Oxford Polytechnic, Department of Town Planning, Working Paper 41, 1981.

Gee, F.A. *Homes and Jobs for Londoners in New and Expanding Towns*, Office of Population Censuses and Surveys Social Survey Division, HMSO, 1972.

Gershuny, J. and Miles, I. *The New Service Economy: the transformation of Employment in Industrial Societies*, Frances Pinter, 1983.

Gilder, I.M. *Rural Planning Policies: An Economic Appraisal, Progress in Planning*, vol. II, part 3, Pergamon, 1979.

Gilg, A. 'Needed: a new Scott inquiry', *Town Planning Review*, vol. 49, 1978.

Gilg, A.W. (ed.), *Countryside Planning Yearbook*, vol. 1, Geo Books, 1980; and vol. 2, Geo Books, 1981.

Gillon, S. 'Selling rural council houses', *Town and Country Planning*, vol. 50, 1981.

Gloucestershire County Council, *County Structure Plan: Submitted Written Statement*, Gloucestershire CC, 1979.

Gober, P. 'Central Cities and Suburbs as distinct place types: myth or fact?', *Economic Geography*, vol. 58, pt. 4, October 1982.

Goddard, J.B. 'British Cities in Transition', *Geographical Magazine*, vol. 53(8), 1981.

Goddard, J.B. and Smith, I.J. 'Changes in corporate control in the British urban system, 1972–77, *Environment and Planning A*, vol. 10, 1978.

Gordon, I. 'The recruitment of local politicians', *Policy and Politics*, vol. 7, no. 1, 1979.

Green, R.J. *Country Planning: The Future of the Rural Regions*, Manchester University Press, 1971.

Hall, D. 'Assessment of Secretary of State's response to the Strathclyde structure plan', *Town and Country Planning*, vol. 49, no. 11, December 1980.

Hall, P. *et al. The Containment of Urban England*, 2 vols., Allen and Unwin, 1973.

Hall, P. 'Dark prospect', *Town and Country Planning*, vol. 49, no. 1, 1980.

Hall, P. (ed.) *The Inner City in Context*, The final report of the Social Science Research Council Inner Cities Working Party, Heinemann, 1981.

Hall, P. *Urban and Regional Planning*, Penguin, 1974.

Hall, P. 'The life and death of a quasi quango: the South East Planning council', *London Journal*, vol. 6(2), Winter 1980.

Hall, P. 'The geography of the fifth Kondratieff cycle', *New Society*, 26 March 1981.

Hall, P. 'Planning for no growth', *New Society*, vol. 43, no. 808, 1978.

Hall, P. 'The counterurbanization process: urban America since 1970', *Environment and Planning A*, vol. 10, no. 8, 1978.

Hall, P. and Breheny, M. 'Whither regional planning?', *The Planner*, July/August 1983.

Hall, P. and Hay, D. *Growth Centres in the European Urban System*, Heinemann, 1980.

Hamilton, F.E.I. 'Aspects of industrial mobility in the British economy, *Regional Studies*, vol. 12, no. 2, 1978.

Hamnett, C. 'The conditions in England's inner cities on the eve of the 1981 riots', *Area*, vol. 15, no. 1, 1983.

Hamnett, C. 'Owner-occupation in the 1970s: ownership or investment?' *Estates Gazette*, 262, 1982.

Hamnett, C. 'Regional variations in house prices and house price inflation, 1969–81', *Area*, vol. 15, no. 2, 1983.

Hamnett, C. and Randolph, W. 'The Changing population distribution of England and Wales, 1961–81: a clean break or consistent progression?' *Built Environment*, vol. 8, no. 4, 1983.

Hampshire County Council, *Mid-Hampshire Structure Plan: Approved Written Statement*, Hampshire County Council, 1980.

Hampshire County Council, *South West Hampshire Structure Plan: Approved Written Statement*, Hampshire CC, 1980.

Hampshire County Council, *South Hampshire Structure Plan: Approved Written Statement*, Hampshire CC, 1977.

Harloe, M. *Swindon: a Town in Transition*, Heinemann, 1975.

Harrison, P. *Inside the Inner City*, Pelican, 1983.

Harvey, D. *Social Justice and the City*, E.A. & B. Checkoway, 1973.

Haywood, S.W. *The Determinants of Industrial and Office Location: Survey of Estate Agents and Property Development Companies*, Joint Unit for Research on the Urban Environment, Aston University, Research Note 1, 1979.

Healey, P. 'On implementation: some thoughts on the issues raised by planners current interest in implementation', in Minay, C. (ed.) *Implementation, Views from an Ivory Tower*, Department of Town Planning, Oxford Polytechnic, 1979.

Healey, P. 'Regional Policy in the South East: How far can restraint and local needs be reconciled?', *Town and Country Planning*, vol. 49, no. 11, December 1980.

Healey, P. *Statutory Local Plans — their evolution in Legislation — administrative interpretation*, Oxford Papers in Planning, Education and Research, vol. 36, 1979.

Healey, P. *et al. The Implementation of Development Plans*, Report of an exploratory study for the Department of Environment, Department of Town Planning, Oxford Polytechnic, February 1982.

Healey, P. *et al.* 'The implementation of selective restraint policies: approaches to land release for local needs', Working Paper 45, Department of Town Planning, Oxford Polytechnic, 1980.

Hebbert, N. 'The land debate and the planning system', *Town and Country Planning*, vol. 50, no. 1, January 1981.

Hebbert, N. 'The British New Towns: a review of Bracknell, East Kilbride and Washington'. *Town Planning Review*, vol. 51(4), 1980.

Henderson, A. 'Using land with responsibility', *Housing and Planning Review*, Winter 1980.

Herbert, D.T. 'Population mobility and social change in South Wales', *Town Planning Review*, vol. 43, no. 4, 1972.

Herington, J. 'Circular 22/80 — The demise of settlement planning?' *Area*, vol. 14, no. 2, 1982.

Herington, J. 'Monitoring Household movements to increase policy effectiveness in structure and local plans', *PTRC, Policy Analysis for Urban and Regional Planning*, vol. P174, 1979.

Herington, J.M. 'Rural settlement policy and housing mobility: a discussion of research findings', Report for SSRC Department of Geography, Loughborough University, Research Paper No. 6, 1981.

Herington, J. 'The reasons for household movement to rural settlements in outer Leicester', Department of Geography, Loughborough University, Research Paper No. 5, 1980.

Herington, J. and Evans, D. 'The social characteristics of household movement in "key" and "non-key" settlements', Research Paper No. 4, Department of Geography, Loughborough University, 1980.

Herring, Son, and Daw, *Property and Technology — The Needs of Modern Industry*, 1982.

Hertfordshire County Council, *County Structure Plan*, Hertfordshire CC, 1975.

Hertfordshire County Council, *County Structure Plan: Alterations*, Hertfordshire CC, 1980.

Hooper, A. 'Land availability', *Journal of Planning and Environmental Law*, November 1979.

Hooper, A. 'Land for private housebuilding', *Journal of Planning and Environmental Law*, December 1980.

House, J.W. (ed.), *The U.K. Space: Resources, Environment and the Future* (2nd edn.), Weidenfeld and Nicolson, 1977.

House-Builders Federation, *Housing land in the South East: a Joint Report*, Standing Conference for London and South East Regional Planning and House-Builders Federation, November 1981.

Hudson, R. 'Regional development policies and female employment', *Area*, vol. 12, 1980.

Jenkins, C. and Sherman, B. *The Collapse of Work*, Fakenham Press, 1979.

Johnson, J.H. (ed), *Suburban Growth*, Wiley, 1974.

Johnston, R.J. *Geography and the State: an essay in political geography*, Macmillan, 1982.

Johnston, R.J. 'Political geography without politics', *Progress in Human Geography*, vol. 4, 1980.

Joint Land Requirements Committee, *Housing Allocation in Structure and Local Plans*, House-Builders Federation, February 1982.

Joint Land Requirements Committee, *Is there Sufficient Housing Land for the 1980s? Paper 1: How Many Houses Should We Plan For?* Housing Research Foundation, February 1982.

Joint Land Requirements Committee, *Is there Sufficient housing land for the 1980s? Paper II: How many houses have we planned for — is there a problem?* Housing Research Foundation, February 1983.

Joint Monitoring Steering Group, *A Developing Strategy for the West Midlands: Updating and Rolling Forward of the Regional Strategy to 1991*, Birmingham 1979.

Joint Unit for Research into the Urban Environment, *Land Availability and the Residential Land Conversion Process*, University of Aston, 1974.

Jones, C. 'Population decline and home ownership in Glasgow', University of Glasgow, Department of Economic and Social Research, Urban and Regional Studies Discussion Paper, vol. 26, 1978.

Jones, P.M. 'Trading Features of hypermarkets and Superstores', *Urban and Retail Planning Information*, June, 1978.

Joyce, F.E. (ed.) *Metropolitan Development and Change: The West Midlands — A Policy Review*, Teakfield, 1977.

Keeble, D. 'Industrial decline, regional policy, and the urban-rural manufacturing shift in the U.K.', *Environment and Planning A*, vol. 12, no. 8, 1980.

Kent County Council, *County Structure Plan: Approved Written Statement*, Kent CC, 1980.

Kent County Council, *Schedule of Proposed Alternatives to the Written Statement*, Kent CC, April 1981.

King, A.D. 'Historical patterns of reaction to urbanism in the case of Britain, 1880–1939', *International Journal of Urban and Regional Research*, vol. 4, no. 1, 1980.

Kirk, G. *Urban Planning in a Capitalist Society*, Croom Helm, 1980.

Kosinski, L.A. (ed.), *Policies of Population Redistribution*, Geographical Society of Northern Finland for the IGU Commission on Population Geography, Oulu, 1981.

Labour Party, *Out of Town, Out of Mind: A Programme for Rural Revival*, 1981.

Lancashire County Council, *Central and North Lancashire Structure Plan: Submitted Written Statement*, 1980.

Land Decade Educational Council, *Land Use Perspectives*, LDEC, 1979.

Lawless, P. *Britain's Inner Cities*. Harper & Row, 1981.

Leach, S. 'Battle of the two tiers', *Planning*, vol. 487, 24 September 1982.

Leach, S. and Stewart, J. *Approaches in Public Policy*, Institute of Local Government Studies, Allen and Unwin, 1982.

Leicestershire County Council, *County Structure Plan: Approved Written Statement*, 1976.

Lever, W. 'Employment change in urban and regional systems: the U.K. case', Department of Ecology and Social Research, University of Glasgow Urban and Regional Discussion Paper 28, 1978.

Lloyd, P. and Dicken, P. 'Industrial Change: local manufacturing firms in Manchester and Merseyside', *DoE Inner City Programme Number 6*, 1982.

Lock, D. 'Asset stripping the New Towns', *Town and Country Planning*, vol. 48, no. 7, 1979.

Lock, D. 'Land for houses', *Town and Country Planning*, vol. 46(6), 1978.

Lomas, G. 'Marching backwards on regional development'. *Town and Country Planning*, vol. 48, no. 7, October 1979.

Long, T. 'Rag-bag of control advice', *Planning*, vol. 412, 3 April 1981.

Long, T. 'The missing link', *Town and Country Planning*, vol. 52, no. 6, June 1983.

Low, N. 'Farming and the Inner Green Belt', *Town Planning Review*, vol. 44, 1973.

Lowe, P. 'Amenity and equity: a review of local environmental pressure groups in Britain'. *Environment and Planning A*, vol. 9(1), 1977.

Lowe, P. and Goyder, J. 'The land lobby: a political analysis', *Town and Country Planning*, vol. 50, no. 1, 1981.

Lowe, P. *et al.* 'The mass movement of the decade — environmental pressure groups', *Vole*, vol. 3, no. 4, 1980.

Macgregor, M. 'The rural culture, *New Society*, 9 March 1972.

Mackie, J.W. 'Goodbye Rural Berkshire? Development Pressures in Central Berkshire and South East England,' Report for Binfield and Warfield Parish Councils, 1982.

Martin, R.L. 'Job loss and the regional incidence of redundancies in the current recession', *Cambridge Journal of Economics*, vol. 6, 1982.

Martinotti, G. 'Deurbanization and villagization', *International Journal of Urban and Regional Research*, 4, 1980.

Massey, D. *The Anatomy of Job Loss*, Methuen, 1982.

McCallum, I. 'Employment generation'. *The Planner*, February 1983.

McDonald, S. 'How grows the thistle?' *The Planner*, vol. 69, no. 4, July/August 1983.

McDonald, S. 'The Regional Report in Scotland', *Town Planning Review*, vol. 48, no. 3, 1977.

McKay, D.H. (ed.), *Planning and Politics in Western Europe*, Croom Helm, 1982.

McKay, D.H. and Cox, A.W. *The Politics of Urban Change*, Croom Helm, 1979.

McLaughlin, B. 'Rural settlement planning: a new approach', *Town and Country Planning*, vol. 44, no. 3, March 1976.

Melville-Ross, T. 'Down market lending by building societies', *Housing Review*, 30, 1981.

Merseyside County Council, *Merseyside Draft Green Belt subject Plan: Written Statement*, Merseyside CC, 1980.

Miller, C. and Miller, D. 'Local authorities and the local economy', *Town and Country Planning*, vol. 5, no. 6, June 1982.

Moore, N. and Leach, S. 'An interaction approach to county/district relationships', *Policy and Politics*, vol. 7(3), 1979.

Moore, N. and Leach, S. 'County/district relations in Shire and Metropolitan Counties in the field of town and country planning', *Policy and Politics*, vol. 7, no. 2, 1979.

Morrison, B. 'The progress of structure plans in England and Wales', *Built Environment*, vol. 4, no. 4, 1978.

Morton, J. *Local Government News*, 12 June 1981.

Moseley, M. 'Is rural deprivation really rural?' *The Planner*, vol. 66, no. 4, 1980.

Moseley, M. *Power, Planning and People in Rural East Anglia*, Centre for East Anglian Studies, University of East Anglia, 1982.

Moss, G. *Britain's Wasting Acres: Land Use in a Changing Society*, Architectural Press, 1980.

Moss, G. 'Land Council and its Objectives', *Town and Country Planning*, vol. 50, no. 1, January 1981.

Moss, G. Associates, *Rural Services: Report of a Pilot Study of Statutory Provision and Accessibility in Leicestershire*, Graham Moss, 1982.

Munton, R. 'Agricultural land use in the London Green Belt', *Town and Country Planning*, vol. 50, no. 1, January 1981.

Murie, A. and Forest, R. 'Wealth, inheritance and housing policy', *Policy and Politics*, vol. 8, 1980.

Murie, A. *et al. Housing Policy and the Housing System*, Allen and Unwin, 1976.

Nathaniel Lichfield & Partners and Goldstein Leigh Associates, *The Property Market Effects of the M25*, January, 1981.

Newby, H., Bell, C., Saunders, P. and Rose, D. 'Farmers attitudes to conservation', *Countryside Recreation Review*, vol. 2, 1977.

Newby, H. *Green and Pleasant Land? Social Change in Rural England*, Pelican, 1980.

Nottinghamshire Environment Committee, *Draft Green Belt Subject Plan*, Nottinghamshire CC, December 1981.

Nottinghamshire County Council, *County Structure Plan: Approved Written Statement*, Nottinghamshire CC, 1980.

Oakeshott, R. 'Country Towns — the call of the shires', *The Economist*, 28 July 1979.
O'Connor, K. 'The analysis of journey to work patterns in human geography'. *Progress in Human Geography*, vol. 4(4), 1980.
Office of Population Censuses and Surveys (1981) Census 1981, Preliminary Report, England and Wales, HMSO.

Pacione, M. (ed.) *Progress in Rural Geography*, Croom Helm, 1983.
Pahl, R.E. 'Commuting and social change in rural areas', *Official Architecture and Planning*, July/August 1966.
Pahl, R.E. *Urbs in Rure: The Metropolitan Fringe in Hertfordshire*, Geographical Paper no. 2, London School of Economics, 1965.
Pahl, R.E. *Whose city? And further essays on urban society*, Penguin 1975.
Parkinson, C.N. 'Two nations', *Economist*, vol. 222, 25 March 1967.
Parsons, D.J. 'Rural gentrification: the influence of rural settlement planning', Department of Geography, University of Sussex, Research Paper, No. 3, 1980.
Patten, J. 'Villages in Surburban London', *Geographical Magazine*, vol. 48(12), 1976.
Penning-Rowsell, E.C. 'Planning and water services: keeping in step', *Town and Country Planning*, vol. 51, no. 6, June 1982.
Phillips, D. and Williams, A. 'Council house sales and village life', *New Society*, vol. 58, no. 993, 1981.
Planning Advisory Group, *The Future of Development Plans*, HMSO, 1965.
Popenoe, D. 'Urban sprawl: some neglected sociological considerations', *Sociology and Social Research*, vol. 63(2), 1979.
Potter, S. 'The last of the New Towns', *Planner News*, July 1982.
Powell, A.G. 'Strategies for the English Regions: Ten Years of Evolution, *Town Planning Review*, vol. 49, no. 1, January 1978.

Rand, C. 'Rural planning on the block', *Planning*, vol. 221, 5 June 1981.
Report of the Royal Commission on the Distribution of Industrial Population, cmnd. 6153, HMSO, 1940.
Rogers, A.W., (ed.), *Urban Growth, Farmland Losses and Planning*, Rural Geography Study Group, Institute of British Geographers, 1978.
Royal Town Planning Institute, *The Planning Response to Social and Economic Change*. First report of an RTPI Study Group, 1982.

Salt, J. and Flowerdew, R. 'Labour migration from London'. *London Journal*, vol. 6(1), Summer 1980.
Schiller, R. 'Superstore impact', *Planner*, vol. 67, no. 2, 1981.
Scott, A.J. *The Urban Land Nexus and the State*, Pion, 1980.
Scottish Development Department, *National Planning Guidelines*, Circular 19/77, HMSO 1977.
Scottish Development Department, *The New Scottish Local Authorities: Organisation and Management Structures*, HMSO, 1973.
Seeley, I.H. *Planned Expansion of Country Towns*, George Godwin, 1968.
Self, P. *Cities in Flood: the problems of urban growth*, Faber and Faber, 1961.

Self, P. 'New Towns and the urban crisis', *Town and Country Planning*, vol. 48, no. 1, April 1979 and vol. 48, no. 2, May 1979.

Self, P. *Planning the Urban Region: A Comparative Study of Policies and Organisations*, Allen and Unwin, 1982.

Self, P. 'Whatever happened to regional planning?', *Town and Country Planning*, vol. 49, no. 7, July/August 1980.

Sharp, E. 'Super-ministry: the first steps', *Built Environment*, April 1972.

Shaw, J.M. (ed.) *Rural Deprivation and Planning*, Geo Books, 1979.

Shaw, G. and Williams, A. 'The regional structure of Structure Plans', *Planning Outlook*, vol. 23, no. 1, 1980.

Simmie, J. *Power, Property and Corporatism: the Political Sociology of Planning*, Macmillan, 1981.

Simmie, J.M., *Citizens in Conflict: the Sociology of Town Planning*, Hutchinson 1974.

Simpson, H. 'Planning policies and housing', *The Planner*, February 1983.

Smart, G. 'Strategies in decline?', Proceedings of PTRC Summer Meeting, July 1980.

Smith, P. 'Structure Planning: participation and its results', *Town and Country Planning*, vol. 46, no. 1, 1978.

South East Economic Planning Council, *A Strategy for the South East*, HMSO, 1967.

South East Joint Planning Team, *Strategy for the South East: 1976 Review*, HMSO, 1976.

South East Joint Planning Team, *Strategy for the South East Review*, HMSO, 1976.

South West Economic Planning Council, *A Strategic Settlement Pattern for the South West*, HMSO, 1974.

Spring, M. 'What recession? A private new town for 12,000 people is being built near Swindon', *Building*, vol. 239, no. 7153(34), 22 August 1980.

Standing Conference on London and South East Regional Planning, *The Commuting Study*, SCLSERP, SC 1551, July 1981.

Standing Conference on London and South East Regional Planning, *Emerging Issues in the South East Region*. SCLSERP, SC 1640, 23 March 1982.

Standing Conference on London and South East Regional Planning, *Housing Land in South East England*, SCLSERP, November 1981.

Standing Conference on London and South East Regional Planning, *The Impact of the M25*, Report by the Industry and Commerce Working Party of the Regional Monitoring Group, SC1618R, January 1982.

Standing Conference on London and South East Regional Planning, *The Improvement of London's Green Belt*, SCLSERP, SC 620, 21 July 1976.

Standing Conference on London and South East Regional Planning, *Smaller Households*, Report by the Housing Issues Working Party of the Regional Monitoring Group, SCLSERP, SC1617R, January 1982.

Standing Conference on London and South East Regional Planning, *South East Regional Planning: the 1980s*, SC 1500, February 1981.

Steeley, G. Information technology: supply and demand, *Town and Country Planning*, vol. 51, no. 8, September 1982.

Steeley, G. 'Regional planning and regional change in the south east', *The Planner*, vol. 69, no. 4, July/August 1983.

Stephenson, L.K. 'Toward a spatial understanding of environmentally-based voluntary groups', *Geoforum*, vol. 10(2), 1979.

Stevens, T. 'Land for housing', *RIBA Journal*, vol. 88, no. 9, 1981.

Strathclyde Regional Council, *Strathclyde Structure Plan: First Review and Alteration, 1981.*

Suddards, R.W. 'Section 52 agreements: a case for new legislation', *Journal of Planning and Environment Law,* October 1979.

Swann, P. 'Green Belt threat: is it strategic?', *Planning,* vol. 480, 6 August 1982.

Thorns, D.C. 'Suburban values and the urban system', *International Journal of Comparative Sociology,* vol. 16, pt. 1-2, 1975.

Thorns, D.C. *Suburbia,* McGibbon, 1972.

Townsend, A. 'The scope for intra-regional variation in the 1980s', *The Planner,* vol. 69, no. 4, July/August 1983.

Townsend, A. 'Unemployment geography and the new government's regional aid', *Area,* vol. 12, no. 1, 1980.

Turner, E. 'Housing Policy — the need to think small', Unpublished Diploma thesis, Polytechnic of Central London, April 1982.

Turton, R. 'Lessons from the experience of the North West Economic Planning Council', Paper to Regional Studies Association Conference, 14 November 1980.

Treasury, The. *The Government's Expenditure Plan 1982-1983 to 1984-1985. Vol. 1.* Cmnd 8494-1, HMSO, March 1982.

Vining, D. and Kontuly, T. 'Population dispersal from major metropolitan regions: an international comparison', *International Regional Science Review,* vol. 3(1), 1978.

Warwickshire County Council, *Green Belt (Subject) Plan for Warwickshire: Draft Written Statement,* Warwickshire CC, April 1980.

Watts, D. 'Planning: a key to innovation in industry?' *The Planner,* 63(6), 1977.

Watts, P.A. 'The new block grant and controls over local authority capital payments', *Local Government Studies,* vol. 6, 1980.

Waugh, M. 'The changing distribution of professional and managerial manpower in England and Wales 1961-6', *Regional Studies,* vol. 3, 1969.

Weatherhead, P. 'Never a dull moment', *Local Government News,* December/January 1982.

Weatherhead, P. ' "Reasonable" tests for gain circular', *Local Government News,* June 1983.

Webb, G. 'A review of the government's regional machinery 1965-1979', Paper to Regional Studies Association Conference, 14 November 1980.

West Midlands County Council, *Green Belt Subject Plan — Draft Written Statement,* West Midlands CC, 1981.

West Midlands Economic Planning Council, *The West Midlands: Patterns of Growth,* HMSO, 1967.

West Midlands Economic Planning Council, *The West Midlands: An Ecomonic Appraisal,* HMSO, 1971.

West Midlands Forum of County Councils, *The State of Housing in the West Midlands Region,* WMFCC, Birmingham 1982.

White, D. 'Villages of the mind — incoming townspeople reversing depopulation', *New Society,* vol. 53, no. 924, 31 July 1980.

White, P. and Woods, R. (eds.), *The Geographical Impact of Migration,* Longman, 1980.

Whitehead, C. 'Why owner-occupation?', *CES Review,* vol. 6, 1979.

Williams, J. *et al.*'Town Development Act', *Town and Country Planning*, vol. 45, no. 9, 1977.

Williams, J.F.D. *A Review of Science Parks and High Technology Developments*, Driver Jonas, Chartered Surveyors and Planning Consultants, August 1982.

Williams, R. 'Development plans and the definition of Green Belts', *Planning Outlook*, vol. 23(1), 1980.

Woodruffe, B.J. *Rural Settlement Policies and Plans*, Oxford University Press, 1976.

Working Party on Rural Settlement Policies, *A Future for the Village*, HMSO, 1979.

Young, E. 'Call-in of planning applications by regional planning authorities', *Journal of Planning and Environmental Law*, June 1979.

Young, K. and Kramer, J. *Strategy and Conflict in Metropolitan Housing*, Heinemann, 1978.

Index

Abercrombie, 83
Abingdon, 124
agri-business, 152
agricultural land loss, 28, 36, 38, 40, 42, 48, 53, 61, 89, 108, 128, 138, 147, 150, 151, 157, 172
Alsager, 107
Alton, 119
Anglian Water Authority, 72
Area of Outstanding Natural Beauty (AONB), 28, 41, 45, 49, 62, 65-67, 89, 149, 152, 176
Assisted Areas, 29, 71, 102, 103
Association of County Councils (ACC), 98, 139
Association of District Councils (ADC), 159, 167, 173
Association of Metropolitan Authorities (AMA), 66, 133, 139, 174
Atherstone, 119
Avon, 39, 92, 103, 119-120
Aztec West, 38

Banbury, 72, 76, 119, 126
Bar Hill, 22
Barlow report, 61, 82
Basildon, 97
Bedfordshire, 50, 99, 101, 105, 121, 125, 131, 156
Berkshire, 7, 37, 45, 66, 87, 98, 100, 102, 119, 126, 154, 155
  Central, 40, 50, 72, 87, 126, 150, 153, 154, 159, 171
Bicester, 76
Biggleswade, 119
Birchwood Science Park, 119
Birmingham, 3, 14, 28, 49, 61, 76, 121, 124, 136, 157
Blowers, A., 96
Bracknell, 87, 119
Brighton, 14
Bristol, 3, 12, 18, 24, 38, 117, 120
  Bristol/Bath Green Belt, 122
British Railways, 75, 166
Bromsgrove District Council, 121
Brooks, E., 163
Buckinghamshire, 7, 45, 50, 76, 102, 135
Building Research Establishment, 123

Caddy, C., 117
Camberley, 87
Cambridgeshire, 17, 51
car ownership, 18, 47, 75
Cardiff, 24, 28
Central Lancashire New Town, 24, 100
Charnwood District Council, 127, 128
Chandlers Ford, 110, 119
Cheltenham, 103
Cherwell District Council, 83, 85, 100

Cheshire, 14, 37, 43, 44, 45, 83, 85, 100, 103, 104, 106-109, 124, 135, 140
Chester District Council, 122
Chilterns, 72
Circular 7/49, 120
Circular 122/73, 65
Circular 9/80, 128, 129, 137, 138, 141, 151
Circular 22/80, 46, 52, 67, 107, 124, 128, 129, 144, 150
Clifton, 119
Clydeside, 23, 71, 74, 83
Community Land Act, 125
commuting patterns, 7, 14, 16, 17, 25, 44, 45, 50, 75, 87, 91-92, 109, 111-112, 120, 135, 136
commuter villages, 7, 22, 44, 110, 119, 156, 157
Congleton, 74
Cotswolds, 19, 101
Council for Protection of Rural England (CPRE), 66-67, 76, 88, 141, 147-148, 150-151, 154, 159, 160
Council for Small Industries in Rural Areas (CoSIRA), 68, 71
councillors, 48, 98, 120, 129, 152, 159
counter-urbanization, 12, 14-15
Countryside Commission, 62
Country Landowners' Association (CLA), 151, 152
County Planning Officers' Society, 140
Country Parks, 151
Crawley, 119
Crewe, 74
Cumbernauld, 23, 68, 71, 108, 166
Cumbria, 14
Cwmbran, 24

Dacorum district, 102
Daventry, 51
Dawley, 51
Dennis, R. and Clout, H., 8
Department of Economic Affairs, 84
Department of Environment, 13, 46, 52, 61-78, 83, 85-90, 93, 96-100, 106, 108, 118-129, 133, 135-138, 142, 150, 154-156, 159, 172, 175-176
Department of Industry, 61, 62, 71, 82, 83, 85, 86
Department of Transport, 61, 62, 74, 75, 76, 117
Derby, 117
Development Control Agreement, 117
Development Corporations, 23, 51, 68, 70
Directorate of Environmental Protection and Rural Affairs, 68
Donnison, D. and Soto, P., 18
Dorset, 100
Drewett, R., Goddard, J. and Spence, N., 13
Dumbarton, 38, 71
Durham, 38, 43

East Anglia, 14, 19, 26, 151, 161
East Hampshire, 74
East Kilbride, 23, 108
East Midlands, 165
Economic Planning Councils, 82, 84-5
economic processes, 25, 163, 164
economic recession, 3, 19, 20, 24, 36, 40, 42, 53, 54, 104, 120, 140, 148, 154, 164
economic recovery, 53, 62, 64, 66, 67, 74, 77, 85, 99, 101, 106, 113, 163, 165, 167, 173, 175
Ellesmere Port, 43
employment creation, 3-4, 102-105, 108, 109, 165, 168, 169
employment shifts, 2, 18, 25, 27, 30, 42, 53, 72, 104, 109, 113, 164, 166, 168, 175
Employment Transfer Schemes, 71
environmental preferences, 20, 103, 133, 148, 170
Essex, 37, 45, 72, 97, 121
Expanded Towns, 1-5, 7, 14, 19, 20, 26, 28, 45, 46, 50, 61, 65, 68, 70-72, 86, 87, 119, 126, 148, 165
exurbia, 7
Eynsham, 119

Fareham, 110, 119
farming, 151-2
Farringdon, 119, 122
Fothergill, S. and Gudgin, G., 26
fragmented farms, 152
Frimley, 87

Glamorgan, 20, 24, 38, 43, 45
Glasgow, 1, 13, 20, 23, 28, 50, 108
Gloucestershire, 14, 101, 103
Graham, Jack, 133
Greater London, 22, 26, 28, 46, 49, 83, 84, 89
Greater London Council, 87, 126, 154, 166
Greater Manchester, 43, 83, 135, 136, 140, 145
Green Belts, 3, 4, 13, 22, 28, 30, 36-42, 44-50, 62, 65-67, 74-78, 83, 87, 89, 91, 93, 98, 100, 102-104, 108, 109, 112, 113, 118, 120, 121, 122, 124-126, 133-135, 138, 144, 147, 150-154, 155, 158-160, 163, 165, 167, 171, 172, 174, 176, 177
Green Belt Society for Greater London, 153
Groby, 119
growth centres, 4, 14, 22, 24, 48, 50, 67, 70-72, 85-90, 92, 100, 110-112, 125-128, 142, 153, 170-173, 178
growth spiral, 99, 122
Gwent, 24

Hall, P., 41, 82, 85, 170
Hamilton, 71, 110, 119, 126, 127, 128, 156, 157
Hampshire, 7, 17, 37, 152
    mid, 84, 100
    north east, 84, 87
    south, 89, 110
    south west, 100

Harpenden Society, 156
Harrison, P., 174
Hemel Hempstead, 102
Herefordshire, 14, 121
Hertfordshire, 21, 22, 37, 66, 98, 99, 100, 102, 118, 119, 156
Heseltine, M., 50, 64, 159, 160, 173
High Weald, 66
Hooper, A., 133
Horsham, 119
House-Builders Federation, 66, 87, 134, 135, 139, 140, 142, 144, 150
house prices, 20, 22, 44-49, 112, 120, 137, 141, 148, 172
house-building programmes, 1, 45, 47, 53, 62, 111, 133, 136, 139, 141
household formation, 21, 46, 87, 105, 106, 108, 134, 135, 157, 164, 172, 175, 176
housing demand, 134, 135, 140, 142, 148, 157
housing densities, 22, 49, 61, 112, 153, 176
housing environments, 19, 20, 43, 112
Housing Green Paper 1977, 141
Housing Investment Programmes, 159
housing land, 21, 22, 38, 44, 46, 49, 50, 61, 62, 65, 87, 88, 91, 93, 105-107, 109-111, 120, 123, 127, 133-138, 141, 144, 152, 154, 158, 171, 178
housing strategies, 27, 45, 46, 53, 63, 70, 100, 105, 106, 108, 109, 112, 125, 129, 135, 138, 159, 172
Hull, 28, 117
Humber, R., 147
Hyde, 156, 157

industrial floorspace, 38, 39, 53, 126, 168
industry:
    high technology, 3, 38, 64, 74, 102, 103, 164, 168, 170, 174
    manufacturing, 2, 7, 42, 71, 74, 164, 168
    new firms, 2, 26, 27, 100, 167
    retail, 38, 40, 97, 167, 177
    services, 2, 7, 18, 26, 164, 168-170
    small businesses, 101, 102, 134, 135, 169, 172
    tourism, 169-170, 173
    warehousing, 38, 39, 40, 53, 74, 102, 103, 126, 168
Industrial Development Certificates, 29
Industrial Selection Scheme, 28
infrastructure, 50-53, 62, 63, 86, 91, 101-104, 108, 109, 112, 117, 119, 120, 127-129, 134, 138, 142, 165, 168, 171, 172, 177
inner cities:
    decline, 4, 14, 42
    initiatives, 29, 62, 68, 70, 93, 104, 137, 157, 173, 175
    land supply in, 48-49, 135, 136, 148, 151
    regeneration of, 4, 66, 82, 91, 96, 99, 106, 108, 153, 160, 165, 166, 174
Inner City Partnerships, 92

Ipswich, 14
Irvine, 68, 108

Joint Lands Requirement Committee, 140-144

Kent, 37, 45, 101, 103
Kirkby, 24, 71
Knutsford, 107
Kramer, J. and Young, K. 148-149

Labour party, 49, 173-174
Lancashire, 17, 21, 37, 44, 45, 140
land availability, 26, 44, 49, 50, 102, 106, 112,
    128, 134, 135, 136-139, 141-142, 147, 168
land banks, 133, 134
Land Decade Council, 148, 151, 160
landowners, 149, 151-152
land registers, 136
land use plan, 63, 64, 86, 99, 123, 141, 142, 151,
    176
Lapworth District Plan, 157-158
Leeds, 117
Leicester, 7, 13, 24, 28, 119, 128, 148, 156
Leicestershire, 22, 43, 110, 124, 127, 148, 153,
    156-7
    central, 127, 157, 171
Lincolnshire, 17
Little Bramington Farm, 125
Liverpool, 14, 17, 20, 24, 37, 108, 117
Livingston, 68
Lloyd, P. and Dicken, P., 2
local authority physical planning:
    Action Area Plans, 118, 120
    district plans, 118, 120, 144, 152, 157
    local plans, 60, 64, 77, 107, 108, 117-123,
        129, 137-139, 140, 142, 144, 157
    local need policy, 45, 87, 100, 102, 103, 105,
        106, 108, 109, 111, 121, 124, 125, 176
    Section 52 Agreements, 52, 129
    structure plans, 52, 63, 64, 66-8, 72, 77, 84,
        85, 86, 88, 89, 93, 96-101, 109-112,
        117-118, 120-2, 125-6, 129, 135,
        137-139, 142, 144, 149, 153-157, 159,
        165, 167, 172, 176, 177
    subject plans, 118, 119, 120, 121
local authority finance, 62, 93
Local Government Act 1972, 101, 117
Local Government Planning and Land Act 1980,
    4, 64, 96, 117, 124, 128, 142
local government reorganisation, 13, 30, 63, 64,
    77, 96, 97, 98, 101, 109, 117, 121, 126
Lock, D., 96
London, 1, 2, 3, 7, 13, 14, 19, 23, 26, 38, 40, 44,
    45, 49, 61, 66, 72, 74, 76, 82, 84, 85, 97, 125,
    155
Loughborough, 157
Luton Borough Council, 125

Macclesfield, 43, 107, 119
Malmesbury, 119
Malverns, 19
Manchester, 14, 20, 37, 74, 83, 91, 108, 119, 137
Manpower Services Commission, 71
Merseyside, 23, 38, 71, 85, 91, 108
Metropolitan Economic Labour Areas, 12, 13, 25
Midlothian, 38
Milton Keynes, 51, 70, 87, 89, 119, 157, 166
Ministry of Agriculture, Forestry, Fisheries and
    Food, 36, 62, 76, 144, 158
Ministry of Housing and Local Government, 84
Ministry of Transport, 75
Monmouthshire, 38
motorway programmes, 3, 40, 61, 74, 159, 165
    M25, 40, 41, 74, 75, 76, 84, 154
    M40, 76, 149
Mountsorrel, 119

Nantwich, 74
National Exhibition Centre, 124
National Farmers' Union, 142, 151
National Parks, 66
Neston, 107
New Ash Green, 22
Newbury, 119
Newcastle, 117
New Towns Act 1946, 28
New Towns, 1-5, 7, 13, 14, 19, 20, 23, 24-26, 28,
    30, 37, 43, 45, 47, 50, 51, 61, 63-65, 68-71,
    74, 83-87, 106, 108-109, 119, 163, 165,
    166-168, 170, 171, 177
Northampton, 72, 166
Northamptonshire, 37, 45, 51, 135
Northavon, 120
North of England, 13, 29, 85, 100
Norfolk, 17
North Wales, 14
North West, 23, 25, 44, 71, 91, 124, 140
    Economic Planning Council, 85
North West Water Authority, 74
Northwich, 74
Norton-Radstock, 122
Nottinghamshire, 117, 119

Office of Population Census and Surveys, 46
outer cities:
    definition, 6-9, 15, 150
    economies of, 19, 24, 25, 53, 103, 104,
        109, 165, 168
    migration, 13, 14, 16, 24, 26, 42, 43, 44,
        53, 109, 111
    outer Birmingham, 18, 91
    outer Bristol, 103, 121
    outer Glasgow, 25, 175
    outer Leicester, 44, 113, 119
    outer Manchester, 24

outer Merseyside, 24
outer South East, 7, 18, 21, 23, 26, 43, 45,
    75, 91, 99, 102, 138,
    strategies for, 62, 63, 67, 68, 70, 72, 76, 78,
    84, 86, 89, 93, 111, 128-129, 135, 139,
    142, 152, 155, 159, 160, 168, 175-179
owner occupation, 20-22, 24, 45, 46, 63, 125,
    141, 172, 176
Oxford, 3, 74, 76
Oxford Polytechnic, 142
Oxfordshire, 76, 122, 124, 126

Passenger Transport Authorities, 75
Peterborough, 51, 166
Planning Advisory Group, 97
planning appeals, 37, 49, 63, 65, 67, 123, 126,
    129, 136, 138, 140, 143
planning delays, 136-137, 141
planning gain, 119, 120
planning:
    national, 86, 92, 97, 137, 141, 173, 177, 178
    permissions, 49, 50, 52, 65-67, 102, 105, 119,
        123, 124, 129, 133, 134, 141
    political process, 4, 30, 48-67, 89, 98, 100,
        113, 118, 121, 122-129, 147-160, 163,
        166, 173-175, 178-179
    regional, 50, 63, 70, 72, 78, 83-93, 97, 98,
        105, 141, 172, 174
    strategies, 5, 44, 61, 62, 64, 72, 77, 83, 84,
        89, 103, 109, 112, 117, 120, 122, 135,
        139, 141, 148, 163, 173, 178
    sub-regional, 30, 78, 87, 126, 177
    urban-regional, 23, 30, 41, 61, 78, 82, 83,
        109, 121
planned decentralization, 3, 5, 13, 20, 23, 24, 28,
    30, 45, 50, 53, 68, 70, 77, 92, 147, 150, 163,
    164
population:
    census, 1, 14, 28
    mobility, 25, 44, 47, 107, 111, 125, 148
    retirement, 8, 17, 27, 92
    shift, 2, 12, 13, 14, 23, 25, 27, 30, 52, 53, 87,
        113, 135, 137, 164, 165, 171
Portsmouth, 110, 119
post-industrial economy, 18, 19
Poynton, 107
public expenditure, 48, 51, 53, 61, 75, 82, 101,
    104, 119, 127, 128, 137, 138, 163, 165, 166,
    176
public enquiry, 118, 121, 147
public participation, 149, 153-156, 158, 159, 160,
    163
public protest, 119, 121, 126, 127, 140, 144,
    147-160, 178
Public Sector Borrowing Requirement, 168
public sector housing, 23, 24, 30, 43, 44, 45, 49,
    64, 70, 98, 125, 135, 144, 153, 159, 168
public transport, 7, 18, 47, 75

Quorn, 119, 157, 158

Reading, 14, 126
Redditch, 84
regional industrial policy, 4, 26, 29, 71, 82, 83,
    85, 109, 165, 175
Regional Water Authorities, 63, 104
Renfrew, 71
Ringmer, 7
Robinson, K., 141
Rothley, 119
Royal Commission on Local Government in
    England 1969, 30
Royal Town Planning Institute, 140, 142
Ruddington, 119
Runcorn, 43, 71, 106
rural settlement policies, 24, 28, 30, 44, 45, 50,
    67, 71, 87, 100, 108, 110-112, 122, 125, 128,
    135, 142, 153, 155, 159, 170-173, 177

Salford, 74
Sandy, 119
second homes, 8, 16-17, 27, 92
science park, 38, 39, 53
Scott Report, 61
Scottish Office, 70, 86
Scotland, 13, 43, 70, 71, 85, 86, 97, 122, 136,
    147
SDP/Liberal Alliance, 174
Sherburn-in-Elmet, 119
Sheffield, 117
Shropshire, 17
Shore, P., 127
Skeffington Committee, 149
social polarization, 2, 42, 43, 44, 45, 46, 48, 53,
    63, 70, 100, 109, 112, 160, 168, 169, 171, 173
social services, 45-48, 50, 53, 111, 171
socio-spatial mobility, 19, 20, 28, 42, 44, 46, 47,
    70, 87, 108, 111, 112, 120, 148
Solihull, 119, 124
Somerset, 19, 92, 122
Southam, 119
Southampton, 13, 14, 110, 119, 148
South East, 26, 29, 43, 48, 49, 74, 82, 83, 84, 85,
    102, 155, 166
    Economic Planning Council, 85
    Strategic Plan, 87, 90
South Wales, 25
South West, 14, 17, 165
    Economic Planning Council, 92
Staffordshire, 21
Standing Conferences, 85, 86, 135, 140
Standing Metropolitan Labour Areas, 12, 13
Stevenage, 51, 119, 166
Stoke Prior, 122
Strathclyde, 74, 106, 108, 165, 166
Suffolk, 17
Sun-belt, 3, 18, 19, 26, 168

Surrey, 21, 44, 45, 74, 87, 98, 100, 102
Surrey Amenity Council, 153
Sussex, 7, 21
Sussex Downs, 19
Swindon, 38, 68, 72, 119, 126, 128, 148

Tamworth, 119
Telford, 70
Thames Conservancy, 72
Third London Airport, 149
Thorns, D.C., 12
Toton, 110, 119
Town and Country Planning Association, 68, 108, 109, 150
Town and Country Planning Act 1968, 30, 149, 154
Town and Country Planning Act 1971, 129, 149

Town Development Act 1952, 28, 68, 126
Tyne and Wear, 28, 97

urban-rural fringe, 7, 37, 77, 119, 151, 152
Uthwatt Report, 61

Vale of White Horse District Council, 124

Wales, 13, 14, 17, 24, 29, 44, 85, 97, 136, 147
Warrington, 24, 38, 43, 103, 106, 119, 135
Warwickshire, 45, 119, 157, 158
Water Act 1973, 72
Wells, H.G., 1
Wellingborough, 51
Welsh Office, 91
Welsh Development Agency, 91
Westlea Down, 126

Acknowledgements

Figure 1: Bryant et al, *The Countryside*, Longman, (adapted).

Figure 2: reproduced with the permission of the Controller of Her Majesty's Stationery Office. Crown Copyright.

Figure 3: C. Hamnett and W. Randolph, The Changing distribution of population in England and Wales, 1961-1981. *Built Environment*, vol 8, No. 4, 1982.

Figure 5: *Planning*, Issue No. 501.

Figure 6: Standing Conference on London and South East Regional Planning, 'The Impact of the M25' Fig. 11, SC 1618R, January 1982.

Figure 7: The Daily Telegraph.

Figure 8: Standing Conference on London and South East Regional Planning, South East Regional Planning in the 1980s, February 1981, SC1500.

Figure 9: Reproduced with the permission of the Controller of Her Majesty's Stationery Office. Crown Copyright.

Figure 10: Cheshire County Planning Department, County Structure Plan: Altered Key Diagram, p. 137, County Structure Plan First Alteration Report. John Collins, County Planner, March 1982. The map has been simplified.

Cover photograph used with kind permission of Bovis Homes, Bryant Homes, Costain Homes, Laing Homes, McLean Homes, Pelham Homes, PYE and Wimpey Homes Holdings Ltd. Photograph supplied by the CPRE.